how people work

how people work

and how you can help them to give their best

Roderic Gray

FT Prentice Hall
FINANCIAL TIMES

An imprint of Pearson Education
Harlow, England • London • New York • Boston • San Francisco • Toronto • Sydney • Singapore • Hong Kong
Tokyo • Seoul • Taipei • New Delhi • Cape Town • Madrid • Mexico City • Amsterdam • Munich • Paris • Milan

Pearson Education Limited

Edinburgh Gate
Harlow CM20 2JE
Tel: +44 (0) 1279 623623
Fax: +44 (0) 1279 431059
Website: www.pearsoned.co.uk

First published in Great Britain in 2004

ISBN 0 273 69490 1

British Library Cataloguing-in-Publication Data
A catalogue record for this book is available from the British Library

Library of Congress Cataloging-in-Publication Data
A catalog record for this book is available from the Library of Congress

10 9 8 7 6 5 4 3 2 1
08 07 06 05 04

Typeset in Melior 9.5 pt/13.5 pt by 30
Printed and bound in Great Britain by Henry Ling Ltd, Dorset

The publisher's policy is to use paper manufactured from sustainable forests.

contents

acknowledgements

We are grateful to the following for permission to reproduce copyright material:

Figure 3.1 from *Cluster Profiling in Personnel Selection* (Gray, RJ 2000) © RJ Gray; Figure 3.3 from *Organizational Psychology, a Book of Readings*; 2nd edn (Kolb, D *et al.* 1974) © Pearson Education, adapted by permission of Pearson Education Inc.; Figures 3.4 and 3.5 from *On Organizational Learning* (Argyris, C 1999) © Blackwell Publishing; Figure 4.3 from "How to choose a leadership pattern", in *Harvard Business School Review*, May–June, 1973 (Tannenbaum, R & Schmidt, WH 1973) © 1973 Harvard Business School Publishing Corporation; all rights reserved; Figure 6.7 © John Adair; Figure 8.10 from *The Psychology of Fear and Stress* (Gray, JA 1991) © Cambridge University Press; Figure 8.11 from *Managing Pressure for Peak Performance* (Williams, S 1994) © Kogan Page Ltd.

In some instances we have been unable to trace the owners of copyright material and we would appreciate any information that would enable us to do so.

introduction

It seems so obvious as to be hardly worth saying: organizations are made up of people. The first organizations were probably the extended family groups of our remotest ancestors, and their ability to act *socially* – to work together for a common goal, capitalizing on their collective strengths and overcoming their individual weaknesses – is probably a major reason why today homo sapiens is the dominant species on the planet. The twenty-first century workplace may appear very different from the prehistoric African savannah, but at its deepest level the social behaviour "programming" in human psychology is probably much the same now as it was then.

So, the behaviour – and the performance – of organizations are heavily dependent on the social behaviour and cooperative performance of the individuals in them. There's more to it than that, of course, partly because organizations are *systems*, and as such they have characteristics that can't be found among their individual component parts. And there are other influences too, such as markets, competition, technology and regulation which operate at the whole-system level to affect what an organization is capable of doing. All the same, an understanding of the way individuals are likely to behave in a variety of circumstances can be very helpful in clarifying organizational behaviour in two ways: by giving clues as to just why we see certain collective behaviours when people associate together in groups (or organizations) and by providing metaphors or analogies that can serve as simplified models which help to make things more predictable (although caution is needed: models are not the real thing).

survive and thrive If managers are to be able to influence the way their organizations behave – and so exercise some control over organizational performance – it's essential that they first understand the nature of organizations as social units: how they develop, how they are perceived by their members and by outsiders, and how the individuals who are the component parts of organizations are likely to interact to produce the phenomena of organizational behaviour. Organizational research is increasingly showing that variations in the contributions of individuals can have a profound effect on an organization's ability to survive and thrive in the competitive jungle, and managers with a better understanding of what makes people "tick" will find at least one major dimension of their jobs made considerably easier.

In the course of this book we will examine workplace behaviour from the perspectives of nine key checkpoints for excellent performance. Together, these checkpoints form a "catechism of excellence":

- I know what I'm expected to do
- I want to do it
- I have the ability to do it
- Someone (who matters to me) will notice if I do it
- *I* know how well I'm doing it
- Processes help me to do it
- I have the resources to do it
- The environment is right
- I can do it better next time

Some of these checkpoints can be dealt with quite briefly, whilst others will need extensive discussion. Also, whilst it's tempting to see them as falling into a logical sequence in fact they all need to be addressed more

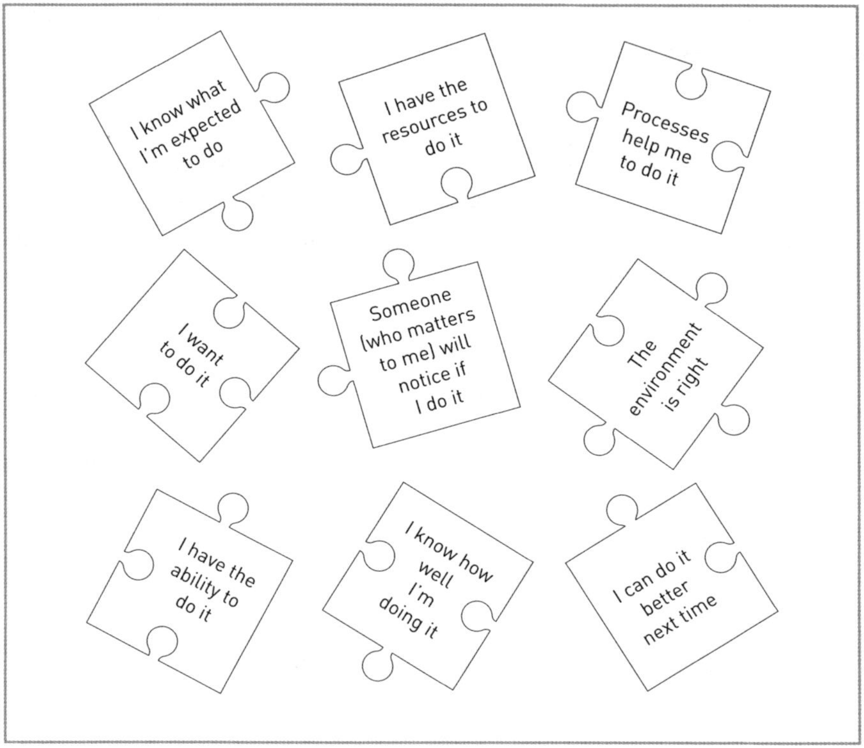

FIG I.1 ● **The excellence jigsaw**

or less concurrently if excellent performance is to be achieved; which is why Figure I.1, above, is a jigsaw rather than a flowchart. Each piece of the jigsaw is covered in one of the chapters, and the completed jigsaw addressed in the final chapter of the book.

making sense

What will, I hope, become clear is that every checkpoint has both individual and organizational implications. Excellent individual performance has to be *facilitated* by the organizational setting, and that means that a vital part of all managers' jobs is to ensure that their people are *allowed* to give their best. In the most general terms this means that people need first to understand what the organization – or at least that part of it that is meaningful to them – is trying to achieve and how they fit in to the overall endeavour. Only then will their own jobs and any personal goals or objectives begin to make sense.

People *want* to do many things. Children may dream of playing for Manchester United, having a hit single, driving a train or getting to Oxbridge. All these dreams represent work, occupation or employment in some form or other, even if children don't always think of it that way. Dreams may change as we grow up, but many dreams (hopefully not all of them) still centre around the world of work. The challenge for organizational management is somehow to match the things they need to get done with things their employees want to do. If jobs are interesting, stimulating and satisfying then people are likely to want to do them; maybe not all the time, but consistently enough to be able to say "I enjoy my work". If on the other hand managers allow jobs to become boring, stultifying and disappointing they close the door on excellence before it has the chance to develop because no-one can put their talents and energy for very long into something they really don't want to do.

Many factors intervene to determine whether dreams ever become reality. Not everyone has the potential to be a sporting hero, and if you're tone-deaf a career in opera may not be for you. Potential is the starting point for any path in life, but almost everyone has potential to do or be *something*. Potential has to be developed and exploited, though, or else it atrophies and is lost. In the workplace, potential needs first to be recognized and then nourished with training, experience and development so that every organization member is enabled to make his or her full contribution.

The way work is organized and the social groupings that cooperate to carry it out can promote or detract from excellent performance. Not all of this is entirely within the control of managers because social units can have their own dynamics and they tend to develop organically. Some things can be managed, though, and there is a wealth of evidence to show that certain characteristics of the work environment are consistently associated with successful outcomes. Many of these characteristics can at least be influenced by managers.

All these issues, and many others, find a place among the pieces of the jigsaw. The final piece is concerned with learning and change at the organizational level; with how the organization – or perhaps just that part of it that concerns the reader – can go about transforming itself into a setting in which individuals are empowered to perform *excellently*.

the Tuesday morning test Because this book is intended primarily to be useful to working managers its content is oriented towards real-world issues: explanations of underlying mechanisms – how and why things work – are set in the context of what to do about it when faced with problems or decisions. For this reason, whilst the book is founded in research and scholarship, I don't dwell too long on theoretical perspectives; the most important or enduring theories get a mention but the focus is on what I think of as the Tuesday morning test: *"that's a fascinating theory but what am I supposed to do with it when I get to work on a cold, wet Tuesday morning?"* Well, most of the book's content has been tested face-to-face with managers and found to be helpful and relevant. Practising managers will find plenty of good advice and guidance in these pages to help them in their interactions with subordinates, peers and superiors, and in a general sense to help make their organization more successful.

one

I know what I'm expected to do (and why it needs to be done)

roles and players There's a well-known "icebreaker" activity in which each member of a group is asked to approach another individual and find out as much as possible about him or her in five minutes. The rules of the game are strict: the only question the "interrogator" is allowed to ask is "who are you?" The question may be repeated as many times as you like, but the "informant" must give a different answer each time, and every answer must be true. When I tried this on a colleague he produced the set represented in Figure 1.1 in just a few seconds, and he was still thinking of additional items later in the day.

Each answer he gave represents a *role* that he plays, at work or elsewhere. Every role carries with it a set of actions or activities, responsibilities and objectives. Sometimes these varying demands fit together quite well, but at other times they may seem to be quite incompatible. The long list of relationships which is defined in this way is called a *role set*. Figure 1.1 depicts the role set of one individual – the "focal person" – or at least, the extremely incomplete definition of his role set that he was able to call to mind on the spur of the moment. In

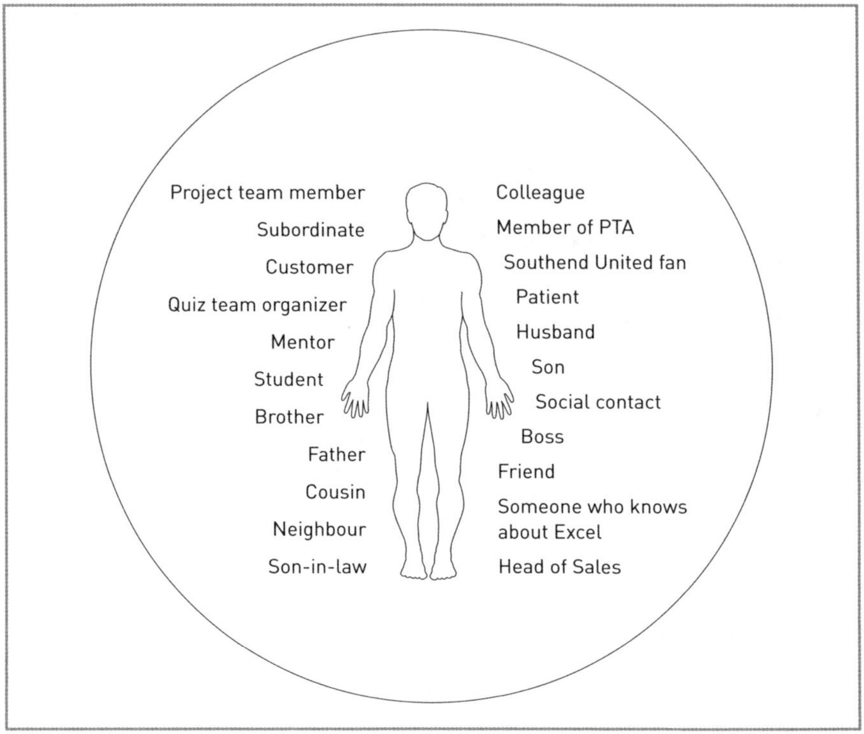

FIG 1.1 ● Who am I?

practice our complete role sets are often too extensive and mixed-up to be very helpful. It's probably more useful to think of multiple role sets: workplace roles, family roles, social roles, etc., although these are likely to overlap to some extent however hard we try to place them tidily in separate "compartments".

what's expected? All the people who, with yourself, go to make up a role set have expectations about what you will do, how you will behave, and how they should behave in their interactions with you. These *role expectations* collectively determine the *role definition* of the particular role under scrutiny. This is a much wider concept than a simple job description, or formal list of tasks and responsibilities; and much harder

set out, what you believe that people expect of you

to pin down. Some of the expectations may well be incompatible. Also, a role definition can sometimes act as a kind of straitjacket; other people's expectations, which may be determined or at least influenced by cultural factors, can make it very hard *not* to behave in certain ways or accept responsibilities that the role imposes on you.

It can be very useful to set out, explicitly, what you believe that people with whom you interact in a specific role expect of you. The form in Figure 1.2 provides a template for this. A word of caution, though: whenever we try to define what other people think, feel or believe we are bound to be wrong. The only question is "how wrong?" The test to apply to this (and all other statements) is "how do I know?" – so the template asks for evidence, which should be as objective and impartial as it's possible to make it.

A comprehensive set of proformas like this will enable you to define each of your roles with quite a high degree of precision, but it only goes

Role:		
People with whom I interact in this role:	Their expectations of me:	Evidence: (how do I know?)

FIG 1.2 ● Role expectations

part of the way because you can only realistically assess (and check) the expectations of people who already interact with you in a particular role. As you act out your role, day by day, you are also likely to find yourself interacting with people who haven't actually met you before. Their role expectations will be determined purely by assumptions about the role itself, and not by any experience of you personally.

giving signals You can exercise some control over these expectations by giving out clear *role signs*; signals that tell other people something about your role. A very obvious role sign is a uniform, which may have additional information such as rank designations which indicate to other people what they should expect from you and what authority, if any, you are entitled to exercise. Most of us don't wear uniforms as such. For us, role signs are displayed in more subtle forms: dress codes, the artefacts of the workplace such as the space someone occupies, the furniture and decor, the technology around a person, a name-plate or job title, whether or not a "gatekeeper" guards access to him or her, and so on. Personal demeanour is actually quite a powerful role sign: if someone behaves with confidence and assurance we tend to assume that he or she has a role that carries authority, which is why career-minded people are often advised to "act up" and conduct themselves as though they are already at the next level in the hierarchy. Of course, if you overdo it people may feel deceived when they find out later that the reality is different, but if you avoid arrogance and don't overstep your authority most people will tend to accept you at your own valuation.

Role signs can be very helpful indicators that allow us to adjust our own behaviour appropriately; so that, for example, we are not unduly familiar when talking to someone important, or unduly deferential when dealing with our peers. This is important enough for the smooth working of society for permanent changes of role to be often marked by some kind of ritual, so that everyone is aware of the change, like a graduation ceremony, or a wedding.[1]

Once you've drawn up a full role definition it's quite likely that you will find that it suffers from one or both of two common problems: *Role ambiguity* and/or *role conflict*.

Role ambiguity – for you – means that you aren't sure what is expected of you in your role, often because the role is defined too rigidly, or not clearly enough,[2] or because you don't know how your performance is being assessed. In this sense role ambiguity isn't always a bad thing, especially if it gives you some latitude to define your role(s) for yourself, but it is known to be a source of stress, which is definitely a bad thing and which we will explore in more detail later.

For other members of your role set *ambiguity* can mean that they don't know what to expect from you. This can cause feelings of insecurity and loss of confidence, not to mention annoyance.

The second kind of role problem – *role conflict* – also takes two forms. Sometimes two or more specific expectations within the same role are incompatible. A common example of this is the requirement to be both a coach/mentor for your people, and at the same time to impose discipline on them. For instance, at appraisal time you may be required to discuss development needs with the people who report to you and also to report on their suitability for promotion, pay increases, etc. It's a well-known drawback of appraisal systems that they tend to handle this conflict rather badly. We'll return to this issue later.

conflicting roles It's also quite likely that different members of the role set have different, and perhaps incompatible, expectations of you.

Potentially even more serious is a role expectation that is incompatible with your personal values. For example, you might be asked by your boss to take an action that you think might infringe health and safety regulations, or financial probity, or employment rights, or shareholder interests, etc., etc. Trying to reconcile your duty to support your boss with your ethical values may cause you serious role problems.

Similar difficulties can arise when one role you have is as a member of a peer group and you find yourself disagreeing with the prevailing views. We will see later that we are strongly psychologically programmed towards compliance with peer group opinions and perspectives and it can be difficult and painful to go against this basic drive. As an example of this kind of conflict, people who disagreed with the unions' policies faced real misery during the UK miners' and firefighters' strikes in the 1980s; caught between their beliefs and peer pressure, often in quite an extreme form.

Role incompatibility doesn't only apply *within* a role. We saw earlier that most of us have several roles which we have to balance out. A much-quoted, but very apt, example of potential incompatibility between the roles played by one individual is the difficulty faced by Pooh-Bah in W.S. Gilbert's libretto for *The Mikado*:

Ko-Ko	Pooh-Bah, it seems that the festivities in connection with my approaching marriage must last a week. I should like to do it handsomely, and I want to consult you about the amount I ought to spend upon them.
Pooh-Bah	Certainly. In which of my capacities? As First Lord of the Treasury, Lord Chamberlain, Attorney-General, Chancellor of the Exchequer, Privy Purse, or Private Secretary?
Ko-Ko	Suppose we say as Private Secretary.
Pooh-Bah	Speaking as your Private Secretary, I should say that as the city will have to pay for it, don't stint yourself, do it well.
Ko-Ko	Exactly, as the city will have to pay for it. That is your advice.
Pooh-Bah	As Private Secretary.
	Of course, as Chancellor of the Exchequer, I am bound to see that due economy is observed.
Ko-Ko	Oh! But you said just now "Don't stint yourself. Do it well".
Pooh-Bah	As Private Secretary.
Ko-Ko	And now you say that due economy must be observed.
Pooh-Bah	As Chancellor of the Exchequer.
Ko-Ko	I see. Come over here, where the Chancellor can't hear us.
	Now, as my solicitor, how do you advise me to deal with this difficulty?

Pooh-Bah	Oh, as your solicitor I should have no hesitation in saying "chance it".
Ko-Ko	Thank you. I will.
Pooh-Bah	If it were not that, as Lord Chief Justice, I am bound to see that the law isn't violated.
Ko-Ko	I see. Come over here where the Chief Justice can't hear us. Now then, as First Lord of the Treasury?
Pooh-Bah	Of course, as First Lord of the Treasury, I could propose a special vote that would cover all expense, if it were not that, as Leader of the Opposition, it would be my duty to resist it, tooth and nail. Or, as Paymaster-General, I could so cook the accounts that as Lord High Auditor, I should never discover the fraud. But then, as Archbishop of Titipu, it would be my duty to denounce my dishonesty and give myself into my own custody as First Commissioner of Police.
Ko-Ko	That's extremely awkward.

Even when the various roles we have to play are not exactly incompatible, we may find that we simply have too many different roles and can't perform all of them properly. This is the other form of role conflict; role *overload*. Role overload will be familiar to anyone who has to juggle family and work responsibilities. It is also increasingly the case that people have more than one distinct job; either within one organization or with different employers. Role overload shouldn't be confused with *work* overload, which simply means having too much to do. Of course, too much work can be a problem in its own right, but it isn't the same problem. Role overload overstretches the individual's tolerance for variety – which is different for each one of us – and makes it likely that some, and quite possibly all, the roles will be performed inadequately.

All of us are likely to suffer to some extent from role ambiguity, role conflict and role overload and it often helps to make these explicit; once they've been identified and described it becomes easier to take effective action to handle them. Also, it's virtually certain that, if you can identify examples of these role-related dysfunctions affecting yourself, then other people in your workplace are also experiencing similar issues. You may well be able to help the people around you by the way you impose your own role expectations on them, and this could have noticeably beneficial effects on their performance as well as improving workplace relationships.

There are a variety of role problems that, if not tackled, can leave both you and other people bewildered about just what you are there *for*, and make it hard to carry out any of the roles as well as you could. Clarifying your role(s) will give you more focus, as well as enabling you to prioritise more effectively. It will also make your interactions with others – peers, subordinates and superiors – much more effective.

The way to do this is first to identify your various roles, then define just what is expected of you in each of them, and by whom. You will then be in a position to make conscious decisions about how you will fulfil each role. You might even find that you can offload some of them.

goals and objectives

For most employees, workplace roles are likely to be rooted in some kind of formal or informal *job description*. This is by no means as straightforward as it might seem. It's tempting to think of individual jobs as following logically from a process of deconstructing an organization's strategy and goals. Once these had been determined, the various functions or departments which would each carry out part of the strategy could be identified. These functions/departments could then be sub-divided further on similar lines, until eventually the contribution required from each individual employee (or group of employees doing similar work) could be defined.

However, because organizations tend to develop "organically" they are seldom quite as neat and tidy as this – except maybe just after the latest restructuring – which is why formal job descriptions are usually no more than partial accounts of the work which is actually performed. Bear in mind, though, that it isn't necessarily always in an organization's best interest to have clear, unambiguous job descriptions. Managers typically look for qualities like intelligence, initiative, experience or decision-making when recruiting staff, and devising a job description that doesn't inhibit employees from putting these qualities to work can be problematic. Job descriptions can easily be stifling and/or bureaucratic; if they are, then either the work suffers or the job description just gets quietly ignored.

Still, having the basic outline of the job set down in writing at least gives us a clue about what's expected in terms of things like hours of work, general job content (tasks, duties, responsibility levels, authority, etc.) and relationship mapping (reporting lines, subordinates, peers, customers, suppliers, etc.).

where do I fit in? Perhaps more valuable is that each employee understands what the organization is trying to achieve and how he or she is expected to contribute to the broader organizational strategy and goals. It would be hard for individual employees to make a contribution towards the overall corporate goals, however much they might want to do so, unless they knew what the organization was trying to achieve.

This has a very real impact on organizational performance because it enables employees to work within their own functions without constantly having to refer upwards for guidance. If staff don't know why they are being asked to do things the most they can contribute is precise execution of instructions, but if they understand the purpose of their work in many cases detailed instructions will be unnecessary; they will bring their own intelligence, skills and creativity to the task, making hundreds of daily low-level choices and decisions sensibly and without

individuals should always be able to see how their work will contribute

people who have identified objectives for themselves tend to perform better

the need for constant close supervision. Individuals should always be able to see how their work will contribute to something bigger.

What helps enormously in this is for everyone to be clear about what they are required to achieve, or to use the common terminology, their current objectives. It may be helpful here to define an objective as *an intention to which resources have been assigned.* Once you start to invest time, energy or money or materials into something it changes from a vague wish or daydream into a genuine goal.

There's a considerable body of research on the effects of defined objectives on performance at work and some of this research may seem confusing, even contradictory at times, but through it all a pattern emerges. It's clear, for example, that if people have a challenging and specific objective they are likely to perform better than if they are just told to "do your best" but only – and this is vitally important – if they *adopt* the objective, i.e., make it their own.[3] If objectives are simply dictated by other people it can actually be a disincentive,[4] although a competent and sincere "selling" effort may be enough to persuade people to adopt the objectives you need to achieve. Wherever possible, though, the surest way is for the affected people to participate in defining the objectives from the outset, and this has other benefits as well. For example, people who have identified objectives for themselves tend to perform better, cooperate more effectively with others and even have better health.[5]

clarity leads to performance There are several reasons why having clear objectives can lead to better performance. First, people are motivated to look for the best ways to achieve the objective, secondly attention and effort are concentrated on objective-relevant activities and away from other things, and thirdly people are led to persist with the task until the objective is achieved.[6]

The first of these mechanisms probably doesn't have too many negative aspects, except where rigid adherence to fixed procedures is essential. The other two, though, have definite risks attached, including the danger that the end may come to justify the means and the development of a sort of tunnel vision which prevents proper attention being given to other needs.[7] This may also lead to inappropriate persistence, when the objective really should have been changed or abandoned.

If having clear objectives generally acts to improve performance, there are some circumstances in which it can have the opposite effect. Sometimes it seems that whilst objective-setting can lead to increased quantity of output this may be balanced by reductions in the quality of what is being done.[8] This can be particularly evident when something complex or novel has to be achieved, when tough objectives can actually impede performance.[9] This is consistent with observations from stress research, which indicate that the more brainpower a task requires the more calm, relaxed and unpressured the conditions need to be for optimum performance.[10]

how smart is SMART?

So, the case for having clear objectives is strong, provided that any special circumstances are taken into account; few things are one hundred per cent certain or unambiguous where human behaviour is concerned. We should now consider how best to go about defining objectives in the workplace. An acronym that is widely quoted as guidance for defining objectives is SMART, which stands for:

Specific,

Measurable,

Agreed,

Realistic, and

Time-related.

This is helpful, but not completely free of issues. The value of objectives being agreed – or we might equally well use the term "adopted" – has already been pointed out, and not many people would argue that objectives ought to be **un**realistic (although that doesn't stop some managers setting unrealistic objectives in practice). It would be useful, though, to look more closely at the other three criteria in the SMART acronym.

It's possible that there could be some *dis*advantages in making objectives too specific. The arguments here are similar to those that apply to job descriptions; it isn't always useful to restrict initiative. This issue can only be resolved by careful consideration of the individual circumstances. The only broad guidance is that objectives should be defined in terms which are *appropriate* for the situation.

Making objectives measurable sounds like good common sense. Actually, from a performance management perspective what we really mean is that we need ways to *assess* performance. Measurement should always be seen as a tool used in the assessment process, rather than an end in itself, and it needs to be used with great care. The two main reasons for investing resources in measurement are first that it provides data and secondly that it (may) change behaviour. There's an old maxim: "what gets measured gets done", which is often put forward as a guiding principle for managers. In fact, I see this as more of a problem statement; remember the ancient wisdom: "be careful what you wish for, your wish might be granted".

distorting behaviour Negative effects of measurement arise mainly from the *distortion of behaviour* that is introduced when individual factors are measured. There is also the awesomely difficult problem of finding measures which truly reflect the *performance* – in meaningful terms – of the organization. If you tried to list *all* the factors that influence performance in your own workplace and then to measure first the strength/level of each factor, individually, and secondly the way(s) the factors impact on each other you would probably find it almost impossible. The complexity of all the factors and their interactions is such that devising genuinely useful measurement schemes is extremely difficult. The temptation is to fall back on measuring factors because they are measurable, rather than because measuring them serves a useful purpose. The risk in this is that behaviour will be distorted in favour of the factor that is measured, and without full knowledge of how this impacts on everything else; the overall effects are likely to be unpredictable. Interestingly, in June 2003 the UK's parliamentary monitor, the Audit Commission, published a report on the National Health Service in which it observed that the policy of setting numerous detailed performance targets for the NHS was having a detrimental effect on patient care. Effort and resources were being focused on meeting targets rather than dealing with the real needs of patients.[11]

A second and perhaps rather tangential issue here is that measurable factors that can act as useful indicators of what's going on may become unreliable when they are used as objectives or targets. This is a phenomenon first described in the field of economics and known as Goodhart's Law, which has been summarized as "when a measure becomes a target, it ceases to be a good measure".[12] I would add two corollaries to this:

1. if they are used to assess people's performance, indicators *always become targets*, and
2. if progress towards an objective is assessed on the basis of specific measures, those measures *replace the original objective.*

Another major problem with measurement regimes is that they can make it difficult to deal with important, possibly urgent, matters which weren't thought of when the measurements were devised. A poignant example of this in action is described by journalist Nick Davies.[13] He describes how a small unit in Avon and Somerset police fought for years to expose and prosecute members of an extensive paedophile ring. Senior officers gave the unit little support, denying it essential resources and sometimes withdrawing the resources it did have. Although several men were successfully prosecuted the team is convinced that many more have escaped and are likely to remain at liberty, due to lack of police resources to continue the investigations. The British Home Office at that time (2000) evaluated police forces against 37 specific criteria, none of which covered child abuse. Perhaps for this kind of reason Michael Rose[14] suggests

by the time we are able to measure the results it's too late

that SMART objectives can sometimes be DUMB:

Defective,

Unrealistic,

Misdirected, and

Bureaucratic.

why, not what If measuring the individual factors involved in good performance is difficult and can lead to unexpected or undesirable effects, it's tempting to measure *outcomes* instead. Unfortunately, this isn't really the answer, although it's a very widespread practice. The main problem here is that outcomes are (or may be) the *effects* of what's being done; looking at results tells you *what* happened but it doesn't tell you *why*. Managers really need to be able to work on causes: by the time we are able to measure the results it's too late. But, as we've already seen, picking on the relatively few causal factors that we can both identify and measure is unsatisfactory in various ways. Any solution to this dilemma is bound to be a compromise, but the best approach seems to be to concentrate on *behaviours*: are individual members of the team doing the "right things", in the "right ways"? If they are, then we should encourage the behaviour(s); *even if on this particular occasion the outcome was less than satisfactory*. If they are not, then use positive approaches to correct them.

As for making objectives *time-related*, once again there are arguments both for and against. Having a deadline to meet can certainly have the effect of concentrating the mind, and resources, on completing the task. In this sense, the deadline is itself an objective, and has the same benefits and dangers as other objectives. It's important that the deadline should be achievable and realistic, and rational: arbitrary tight deadlines damage morale and do nothing to improve effectiveness, but we

flexibility may be the guiding principle for all objective-setting

shouldn't overlook Parkinson's Law, which says that "work expands so as to fill the time available for its completion".[15]

As with other aspects of objective-setting, flexibility is essential; circumstances change and new priorities occur, and it may be quite appropriate to alter deadlines and other targets to meet the needs of the situation. In fact, flexibility may be the guiding principle for all objective-setting. The real world doesn't stand still, and reluctance to adapt to changing needs can spell disaster.

Our understanding of what is expected of us at work operates at three levels: we have to understand the organization's overall purpose, aims and strategy; we need to understand our own general role or function within this framework; and we need to be clear about our immediate and specific objectives, targets and so on.

Understanding is the vital factor here. Just being told what to do can never produce excellent performance; the best possible outcome from this is exact compliance with instructions. If we both understand *why* and have some personal ownership of the objective we can bring intelligence, creativity and commitment to the task. Only then can the results rise above the merely adequate and begin to approach excellence.

"I know what I'm expected to do" checklist

How many different answers could you give to the question "who are you"?

How many different answers if you only count workplace roles?

What are the role expectations each of the people in your role set has of you?

What ambiguities, conflicts and overloads does your main workplace role entail?

If you have people who report to you, can you identify their role ambiguities, conflicts and overloads? What could you do to help?

What factors are measured and used to assess performance in your workplace?

What positive effects and what negative effects does measuring each of these factors produce?

Can you state clearly and explicitly your organization's overall purpose, aims and strategy?

Can you define these factors for your own job?

Can you define them for the job of someone who reports to you? Would his/her version be the same as yours?

notes and references

1 Handy, C (1985) *Understanding Organizations,* 3rd edn, Harmondsworth, Penguin

2 French, JRP, Caplan, RD & van Harrison, R (1982) *The Mechanisms of Job Stress and Strain,* Chichester, John Wiley

3 Locke, EA (1968) "Toward a theory of task motivation and incentives", *Organizational Behavior and Human Performance,* Vol. 3. pp. 157–89

4 Robertson, IT, Smith, M & Cooper, D (1992) *Motivation Strategies, Theory and Practice,* London, IPD

5 Deci, EL (1992) "The history of motivation in psychology and its relevance for management", in VH Vroom &, EL Deci (eds) *Management and Motivation,* London, Penguin

6 Robertson *et al.*, op. cit.

7 Wright, PM (1994) "Goal setting and monetary incentives: motivational tools that can work too well", *Compensation and Benefits Review,* May–June, 41–9

8 ibid.

9 Kanfer, R (1994) "Work motivation: new directions in theory and research", in CL Cooper & IT Robertson (eds) *Key Reviews In Managerial Psychology* Chichester, John Wiley

10 Hockey, GRJ & Hamilton P (1983) "The cognitive patterning of stress states", in GRJ Hockey (ed.) *Stress and Fatigue in Human Performance,* Chichester, John Wiley

11 Audit Commission (2003) Report: *Achieving the NHS Plan,* London, Audit Commission

12 Prof. Marilyn Strathern, quoted in McIntyre, ME (2001) *Goodhart's Law,* available at: www.atm.damtp.cam.ac.uk/people/mem/papers/LHCE/goodhart.html

13 Davies, N (2000) "A terraced street in suburbia that shrouded a guilty secret", *The Guardian,* 25 November

14 Rose, M (2000) "Target practice", *People Management,* 23 November, 44–5

15 Parkinson, CN (1958) *Parkinson's Law,* Penguin (paperback, 1986)

2 two

I want to do it

motivation There are broadly two reasons why people do things; because they want to, or because they have to. If we are doing something because we have no choice, it's likely that we will do no more of it than absolutely necessary, and that we'll stop doing it as soon as we possibly can. I won't say much more here about coercion and threat as management techniques, although most of us will have encountered them in some degree at some time in our careers and I will return to the subject later. For now, I will simply state the following principle: someone who threatens us is, by definition, an enemy; and people don't work willingly and enthusiastically to further an enemy's objectives. Furthermore, many people would positively relish the prospect of getting back at an enemy if the opportunity arises. I really don't recommend this as a basis for working relationships.

there are broadly two reasons why people do things; because they want to, or because they have to

people don't work willingly and enthusiastically to further an enemy's objectives

So, in this context the word *motivation* refers to whether, and how much, a person wants to do something, the amount of effort and care they are prepared to put into it, and how long they are willing to keep on doing it. In management this word is often used as if it refers to something one person or group does *to* another, as in "how can I motivate my team?" We should be very blunt about this: what this question means is "how can I manipulate the minds of my people so that they will (willingly) do what I want?"

Of course, this isn't necessarily a bad thing. Managers do need to get their people to do the things the organization wants done, and the manipulation involved doesn't have to be malicious or harmful (or covert). The use of this terminology, however, does carry an implication that the manager needs to get people to do things they wouldn't otherwise want to do. (Does this explain the use of the word "compensation" as a euphemism for pay?) It's crucial that people *want* to do the things the organization needs because it's the voluntary element in everyday behaviour that can give that added impetus of enthusiasm, engagement and commitment that turns barely adequate performance into good or even excellent performance. Accepting this premise leads us to ask "why *do* people want to do things?" If the answer to this were to be expressed as an equation, it might look something like Figure 2.1.

In other words, an impossible sum to work out, even if we had access to

Reasons for doing things	=	Number of things that might be done	X	Number of people there are	X	Circumstances of each person

FIG 2.1 A motivation equation

all the information it calls for. This makes it all the more surprising that so many people believe there's a simple answer when it comes to "motivating" employees.

work now, reward later?

Many popular conceptions of motivation are based on the premise that we do things because we expect to derive some subsequent benefit from our actions; that behaviour is motivated by the rewards that follow it. This idea has been around for a long time and forms part of the set of management assumptions and attitudes that Douglas McGregor[1] in the 1950s and 60s called *Theory X*; a perspective that also assumes that people have to be controlled, directed and threatened to get them to do the work required of them. McGregor also noted that almost all the management literature around at that time seemed to be firmly based on this theory. These rewards are called *extrinsic* rewards because they are not part of the activity itself. This perspective assumes that the amount of effort people will put into an activity depends on their analysis – conscious or subconscious – of how likely they are to be able to do what is required, how likely it is that doing what is required will lead on to the desired outcome, and how much they really want that outcome anyway.[2]

There is another set of rewards that may be associated with an activity that are termed *intrinsic* rewards, meaning the satisfaction or pleasure that comes from the activity itself. If we apply the concept of motivation to a hobby or pastime – e.g. golf, amateur dramatics, football, hang-gliding, chess, etc. – it might be hard to argue that the motivation to engage in the activity comes mainly from the "rewards" people expect to receive after they have stopped doing it rather than from the activity itself, and yet people still engage in these activities with enthusiasm. People even sometimes engage in activities which they find enjoyable even though the outcomes may actually involve "negative rewards", like drinking too much alcohol, for example. Douglas McGregor saw no real distinction between work and these other, enjoyable activities, and suggested that an alternative management perspective could exist that trusted people to take pride and pleasure in workplace activities and to make workplace decisions for themselves. He called this alternative perspective *Theory Y*.

The distinction between intrinsic and extrinsic rewards and their influence on people's motivation to perform workplace tasks are important principles in managing people. In general, the more attractive, enjoyable, satisfying, etc. the *activity itself* is, the less significant any *subsequent* reward becomes in motivating someone to perform that activity. Many, though certainly not all, incentive schemes ignore this principle and rely on rewards of various kinds linked directly with outcomes or results to "motivate" people to perform well. Research has shown that this approach is often counter-productive, and has very real potential to divert attention and energy away from the work itself and into doing whatever is required to gain the reward – e.g. what is *measured* – instead. Of course, the intention of such schemes is that these two factors should actually be the same thing, but achieving this is very difficult indeed (see the comments about measurement, above). In general, studies of workplace motivation have tended to show either no clear association between financial incentives and performance,[3] or negative effects, arising mainly from the way rewards divert the focus of motivation.[4, 5]

In my own research[6] I have found that incentive payments, which are supposed to motivate people to do more or better than "standard" performance, often come to be regarded as part of the normal pay expectation. The possibility of *not* receiving them comes to be seen as a threat; a kind of punishment for not doing well enough, as illustrated in Figure 2.2. Threats have been strongly associated with poor work outcomes:

In fact, performance-related pay schemes aren't always very popular with line managers either, who sometimes feel that they are being used to implement policies they don't necessarily support, and who may

the more attractive, enjoyable, satisfying, etc. the *activity itself* is, the less significant any *subsequent* reward becomes

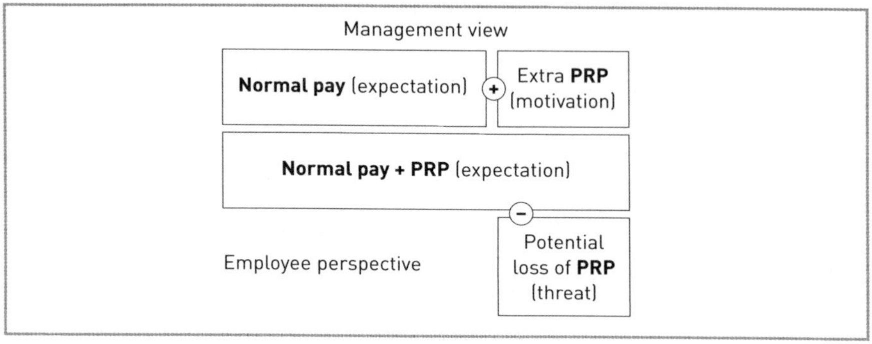

FIG 2.2 ● **PRP – Two perspectives**

have different priorities from the designers of PRP schemes, such as maintaining trust and good working relationships among their people and between people who report to them and themselves.[7]

be fair Another factor creeps in here, which is the need for people to feel that they are being *fairly* rewarded, by comparison with relevant people. There's some research evidence that workers who feel under-rewarded tend to adjust their productivity, in terms of quality or of quantity, downwards to what they consider to be a "fair level".[8, 9] The research suggests that this can sometimes work the other way too: so that people who feel they are being *over*paid tend to raise their productivity to deliver what they consider to be a fair return to their employers.

It's obviously quite hard to achieve a situation where people perceive themselves to be fairly, or even generously, rewarded for the work they do by comparison with others that they consider appropriate benchmarks, not least because people's perceptions of their own worth may be very different from the estimations made by their managers. Still, transparency and an underlying intention to treat people fairly are excellent basic principles on which to build any reward system, even if there are problems to be overcome in putting them into practice.

What all this means is that rewards form just a part, even if it's an important part, of the overall experience of work which influences an individual's motivation. If you rely solely on extrinsic rewards – which won't be available until after the job's completed – to persuade people to do what needs to be done it may actually detract from their performance. Even if the approach seems to be working, don't imagine that people will be primarily interested in the task itself; it will only be a means to an end, and don't expect excellent performance; *adequate* will be quite good enough from the performer's point of view. If, on the other hand, you make a real effort to ensure that the work itself is *intrinsically* satisfying and enjoyable, the significance of the extrinsic rewards is considerably reduced.

what's money got to do with it?

So far, I've focused on money as the form of reward that plays the principal role in the workplace, but this is over-simplistic to the point of being just plain wrong for some people. Money was invented to facilitate exchange: one person had something he was prepared to part with, but wanted something he hadn't got. Before money, he had to find someone whose needs and surpluses exactly complemented his own but money made the whole process much more flexible.

People work for a wide variety of reasons; for money, certainly, but the value of that money is that it can be exchanged for the things we really want. If some of those things are provided directly by the work environment the baleful influence of money as the primary reason for being there is weakened, at least to some extent. If this were not the case nobody would ever "downshift", or stick in a job that they love but which pays less than they could get elsewhere, or enter a profession that they find deeply satisfying but which will never make them rich. In fact, a recent study by the City and Guilds of London Institute[10] found that the group of workers in the UK who were most likely to say they were "very happy" at work were care workers, one of the lowest-paid groups. Accountants, pharmacists, media people and estate agents – all tending to be more highly-paid – were least likely to be "very happy" at work. Non-cash benefits are increasingly being openly discussed and asked for by recruits[11] and seen to be a valuable component of "total reward" packages by both staff and employers.

Abraham Maslow[12] tells us that people's actions are motivated by a set of needs, arranged in a "hierarchy" (illustrated in Figure 2.3). Each need only begins to have a strong effect on behaviour once the previous need has been (largely) dealt with, so for example someone who is starving will be more concerned with meeting the need for food than with safety.

He argued that because the ability to meet these needs is often subject to other people's control, society as a whole has a responsibility to prevent the "sickness" of unmet needs, which he compared to the physical sickness brought on by an unmet need for nutrients such as vitamins. Maslow wasn't thinking primarily about workplace behaviour when he devised his model, but his ideas have been applied to work situations almost from the beginning. Although there's really no convincing evidence from subsequent research to support Maslow's ideas about hierarchy, many people find that his hierarchy of needs has an instinctive feel of "rightness" about it. Even without this concept, though, we are still left with a fairly useful list of common human needs that any work environment should aim to accommodate (not forgetting two additional needs that don't have a specific place in the hierarchy: the need "to know" and the need "to understand").

This has far-reaching implications, because it means perceiving work organizations as environments in which people seek to meet not only their basic needs, for food, shelter and so on (which are usually met indirectly by getting paid), but also "higher-level" needs. Organizations

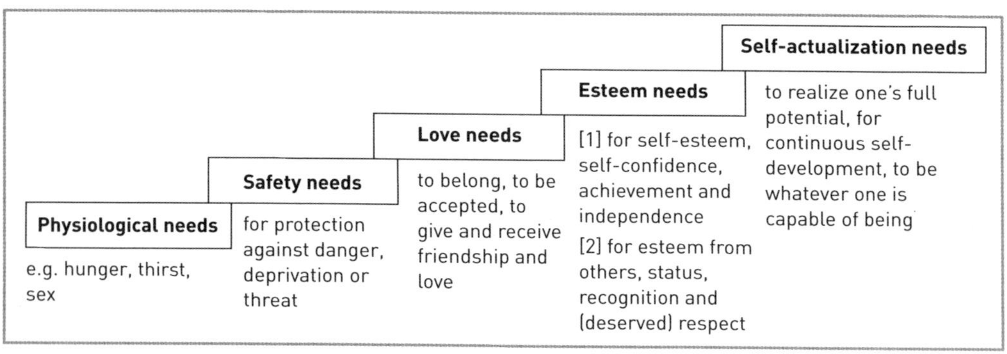

FIG 2.3 Maslow's hierarchy of needs

don't, for example, always see themselves as places of safety and security for their employees. The workplace may provide opportunities to feel accepted, to "belong" and to form friendships, and it may well give some people scope to achieve higher levels of self-esteem and the respect of others. As for self-actualization, I suggest that the world of work would be enormously improved if every organization sought to give its employees opportunities to realize their full potential; to be whatever they are capable of being.

design for fulfilment The actual content and design of people's jobs may have a big impact on their enthusiasm and commitment. Research done in the late 1950s by Frederick Herzberg and colleagues[13] found that there are some factors in an employee's experience of working life that can make him or her feel good, and lead to increased effort, involvement, loyalty and productivity, whilst there are other factors that, if they are missing or unsatisfactory, cause de-motivation, resentment and high staff turnover. If these factors are already satisfactory, however, increasing them or enhancing them doesn't lead to increased motivation. Reasoning that these factors could not produce job satisfaction, but were necessary for the avoidance of *dis*satisfaction, Herzberg called them "Hygiene Factors", on the basis that good hygiene removes health hazards from the environment and so helps to prevent diseases, but even the best hygiene doesn't actually cure anything.

The factors Herzberg and his colleagues identified in each category are as follows (although this list is over-simplified):

Motivators	*Hygiene factors*
Achievement	Company policy and administration
Recognition	Supervision
Responsibility	Working conditions
The work itself	Salary
Advancement	

motivation comes from the satisfaction, interest and enjoyment that the work itself provides

Herzberg's work doesn't enjoy too much academic approval for several very good reasons but some support has come recently from a survey by HR consultants Cubiks, in which only 6% of respondents thought a good pay rise was highly motivating, but an unsatisfactory pay rise emerged as the biggest single cause of employee unhappiness,[14] which is entirely consistent with Herzberg's ideas.

Overall, Herzberg's underlying theme seems fairly robust; that the strongest motivation comes from the satisfaction, interest and enjoyment that the work itself provides, i.e. *intrinsic* motivation. Herzberg's ideas were received enthusiastically by American industry, and he spent much of his subsequent career on consultancy work. His theory involved the idea that if jobs could be made intrinsically more stimulating then improved performance would follow, and that rewards and incentives are not in themselves motivating. Moreover, extrinsic incentives have to be continually reapplied and increased, otherwise they become simply part of the general hygiene of the job and lose their power to motivate. These ideas were understandably popular with top managers (although it's funny how they still don't seem to feel that the principle applies to them, but only to their employees; maybe this is where the two factors really come in).

Herzberg's answer to this was *job enrichment*, which means redesigning jobs to maximise the achievement, recognition, responsibility and interest provided by the work itself. Perhaps the best-known application of Herzberg's job enrichment principle is that developed by Hackman & Oldham[15] who propose five key factors; the higher a job scores on each factor, the more "motivating" it should be:

1. **Skill variety** The job utilizes several different skills/abilities, or involves a number of different tasks.

there's no substitute for matching jobs to people

2. **Task identity** The worker sees a task through from beginning to end, and can see an identifiable product or outcome.
3. **Task significance** Other people are affected by how well the task is done.
4. **Autonomy** The worker can plan his/her own work and choose how to do it.
5. **Feedback** The worker receives clear, direct information about how well he/she is doing.

It's worth repeating here that any "cookbook recipe" for better performance is likely sooner or later to come up against the problem that people are all different. The principles of job enrichment have been shown over time to be very sound, generally, but they may not automatically be helpful for a specific individual in his or her own specific job. There's no substitute for matching jobs to people and there's no short-cut for this. All the same, Hackman & Oldham's five factors continue to provide very useful benchmarks for good job design.

You can use the following "twenty questions" test (Figure 2.4) to check just how conducive your own organization currently is to work-focused motivation. Score each statement 0 to 5 – "completely true without reservation" gets 5 and "completely untrue" gets 0 – and write the score for each statement in the box adjacent to it. The maximum score is, of course, 100, so a perfect organization would get 100% on this test.

Once you've assessed where your organization stands at the moment, you can start to think about specific actions you could take to improve matters. Chapter 9 of this book may help you to decide what to do and how to go about it.

	<True				Untrue>		
People are made aware that their efforts have been noticed and appreciated	5	4	3	2	1	0	☐
Most jobs involve using several kinds of skill or ability	5	4	3	2	1	0	☐
Relations between superiors and subordinates are generally cordial	5	4	3	2	1	0	☐
Most people find their work interesting and stimulating	5	4	3	2	1	0	☐
Pay is not linked directly to people's performance against specific individual objectives	5	4	3	2	1	0	☐
Careful thought is given to job design	5	4	3	2	1	0	☐
People are expected to take responsibility for their own work	5	4	3	2	1	0	☐
People can see what their work achieves	5	4	3	2	1	0	☐
Financial rewards are generally perceived to be fair, by comparison with other similar jobs	5	4	3	2	1	0	☐
There is mutual respect between bosses and subordinates	5	4	3	2	1	0	☐
Promotions are seen to go to people who show the ability to perform well at the higher level	5	4	3	2	1	0	☐
The organization encourages self-development	5	4	3	2	1	0	☐
Overall, working conditions make it easy to concentrate on the work	5	4	3	2	1	0	☐
There is a wide range of non-financial rewards in the organization	5	4	3	2	1	0	☐
There's no job in the organization that could be done badly without affecting someone else	5	4	3	2	1	0	☐
Achievement of specific objectives doesn't determine what bonus, if any, will be paid	5	4	3	2	1	0	☐
People are rewarded in proportion to their overall contribution to the organization	5	4	3	2	1	0	☐
People are challenged to achieve their full potential	5	4	3	2	1	0	☐
People have discretion about how to organize their work	5	4	3	2	1	0	☐
Rules and procedures are fair and reasonable, and applied equitably	5	4	3	2	1	0	☐
						Total score:	☐

FIG 2.4 ● Work-based motivation assessment

Reward policies that are based on simplistic views about human nature, particularly about why people work, are likely to be unsatisfactory in many ways. Understanding something of the complexity of "motivation" may not make a manager feel more comfortable, but it should help him or her to manage people more effectively.

There are many other theories and perspectives relating to workplace motivation, which I discuss in more detail elsewhere.[16] The one message that emerges fairly clearly is that activities that are interesting, stimulating and satisfying in themselves – i.e. are intrinsically motivating – tend to produce better results than activities that are performed solely for an extrinsic reward, i.e. a reward that doesn't have much to do directly with the activity itself and which is probably based on some specified results or outcomes. This means that incentive schemes, if used at all, should focus on *behaviours* rather than outcomes and should recognize individuals' broad contributions to organizational success, rather than specific achievements and successes, which, after all, tend to be quite rewarding anyway.

If a task looks likely to meet these criteria of being interesting, stimulating and satisfying, then it's probable that people will feel that they "want to do it", and if this is the case the outcomes are far more likely to deserve the accolade of excellence.

"I want to do it" checklist

Is your own set of assumptions about people at work best summed up by Theory X or Theory Y?

What about your immediate boss?

Or the top management of your organization?

Does your organization provide every employee with the opportunity to realize their full potential; to be whatever they are capable of being?

If not, what needs to change?

Could you personally make things better? If not, who needs to be made aware of the problems/issues?

What changes would you make to your own job in respect of skill variety, task identity, task significance, autonomy or feedback?

What changes would one of your people make to his/her job, given the chance?

What is your personal experience of PRP, incentives, etc.?

What effect, if any, do they have on your attitude to the work itself?

Do you feel you are rewarded fairly, by comparison with others?

Has there been a time in the past when you felt differently?

Who do you compare yourself with? And how do you make the assessment?

Which aspects of your job, if any, would you want to keep if you no longer needed to work?

notes and references

1 McGregor, D (1960) *The Human Side Of Enterprise,* New York, McGraw-Hill

2 Vroom, VH (1964) *Work And Motivation,* Chichester, John Wiley

3 Guzzo, RA, Jette, RD & Katzell, RA (1985) "The effects of psychologically based intervention programs on worker productivity: a meta-analysis", *Personnel Psychology,* Summer, 7–19

4 Deci, EL (1972) "Intrinsic motivation, extrinsic reinforcement, and inequity", *Journal of Personality and Social Psychology,* **22** (11), 13–120

5 Freedman, JL, Cunningham, JA & Krismer, K (1992) "Inferred values and the reverse-incentive effect in induced compliance", *Journal of Personality and Social Psychology,* March, 357–68

6 Gray, RJ (2000) "Organizational climate and the competitive edge", in L Lloyd-Reason & S Wall (eds) *Dimensions of Competitiveness: Issues and Policies,* Cheltenham, Edward Elgar Publishing

7 Harris, L (2001) "Rewarding employee performance: line managers' values, beliefs and perspectives", *International Journal of Human Resource Management,* **12** (7), 1182–92

8 Adams, JS (1963) "Toward an understanding of inequity", *Journal of Abnormal and Social Psychology,* **67**, 22–436

9 Cubiks (2003) *In Search of the Ideal Manager,* London, Cubiks/PA Group

10 City & Guilds (2004) *Happiness is … being hands on,* The City and Guilds of London Institute, available at www.city-and-guilds.co.uk

11 Carrington, L (2004) "Just desserts" *People Management,* 29 January, 38–40

12 Maslow, AH (1943) "A Theory of Human Motivation", *Psychological Review,* **50**, 370–96

13 Herzberg, F, Mausner, B & Snyderman, BB (1959) *The Motivation to Work,* New York, John Wiley

14 Cubiks, op. cit.

15 Hackman, JR & Oldham, GR (1980) *Work Redesign,* Reading, MA, Addison Wesley

16 Gray, RJ (2001) *Motivation: A Review of the Literature,* available at: www.kumpania.co.uk

3 three

I have the ability to do it

potential Someone's ability to perform a task depends on two "internal" factors: their potential, and the ways in which that potential has been developed through learning or training. There will also be "external" factors, which are considered elsewhere in this book.

In the management context, "potential" usually refers to the qualities, skills, knowledge and experience a person has including, crucially, their ability to learn, *before* they begin to undertake any specific training or development activity. This could mean the attributes that they bring with them when they start a job, or attributes that are not being fully utilized in their current work role(s). Clearly, not all employees have the same aptitudes and personal preferences, which is why when selecting candidates for a job it is normal to consider whether they are "right" for that particular role, and vice versa. Also, not everyone is of equal intelligence (although this is a concept that is much less straightforward than many people assume). And there may be physical requirements that would enable some people to perform well, but not others. These considerations all relate to whether or not someone has the potential to be able to perform well in a specific job.

Because the tendency is for jobs to become more specialized, recruiting someone who can start doing the job adequately from day one is increasingly unlikely. At the very least the new employee will need to adapt to the new environment and learn new procedures and policies, and so on. For these reasons potential is always likely to be an important factor in recruitment decisions. Organizations typically go to some lengths to recruit the "right" people by first defining the job itself (the job description), then defining the attributes of an ideal candidate (the "person specification"), after which a selection process takes place and with luck an applicant whose attributes closely match the specification is identified and offered the job.

Although this is pretty good as a "top level" model of the recruitment process, it does have numerous pitfalls. I've already mentioned some of the issues relating to job descriptions, and drawing-up an adequate job description for recruitment purposes requires a detailed and intimate knowledge of the role(s) and function(s) the new employee will have to fulfil. Determining the list of personal attributes is equally problematic since it calls for many judgements to be made, often on quite inadequate information. When apparently suitable candidates have been attracted to apply for the job, making the assessments of the attributes they actually possess is another highly uncertain and laborious task. Interviews alone are known to be barely more reliable than tossing a coin[1] and a more sophisticated approach to identifying and testing attributes is essential.

adaptable people Using a structured process can make recruiting suitable people less hit and miss. The technique of *Cluster Profiling*[2] uses charts that group similar or related attributes together in clusters and show the level of attainment or expertise of each attribute the job really requires. When candidates are assessed, their personal levels of attainment are marked on their "personal" versions of the chart and compared with the master chart. Although any individual candidate may not have precisely the attributes required, he or she may well have the right *kinds* of attributes, suggesting that they could easily adapt. This shows up clearly when the personal chart and master chart are compared.

In the cluster chart shown in Figure 3.1, the clusters of the candidate's actual attributes (○) in certain areas fall short of the clusters of required attributes (★) and there are three attributes where the candidate doesn't meet the minimum levels defined as "essential" (shown by the straight lines). On this basis it can be seen that the candidate isn't suitable for the job even though he/she exceeds the requirements in some other respects.

Another candidate's chart might show the clusters of the candidate's actual attributes to be more closely matched to the clusters of required attributes. Provided that the minimum levels of all the "essential" attributes are exceeded this would indicate a much more suitable candidate for the job, even if some specific individual attributes were a little below the ideal.

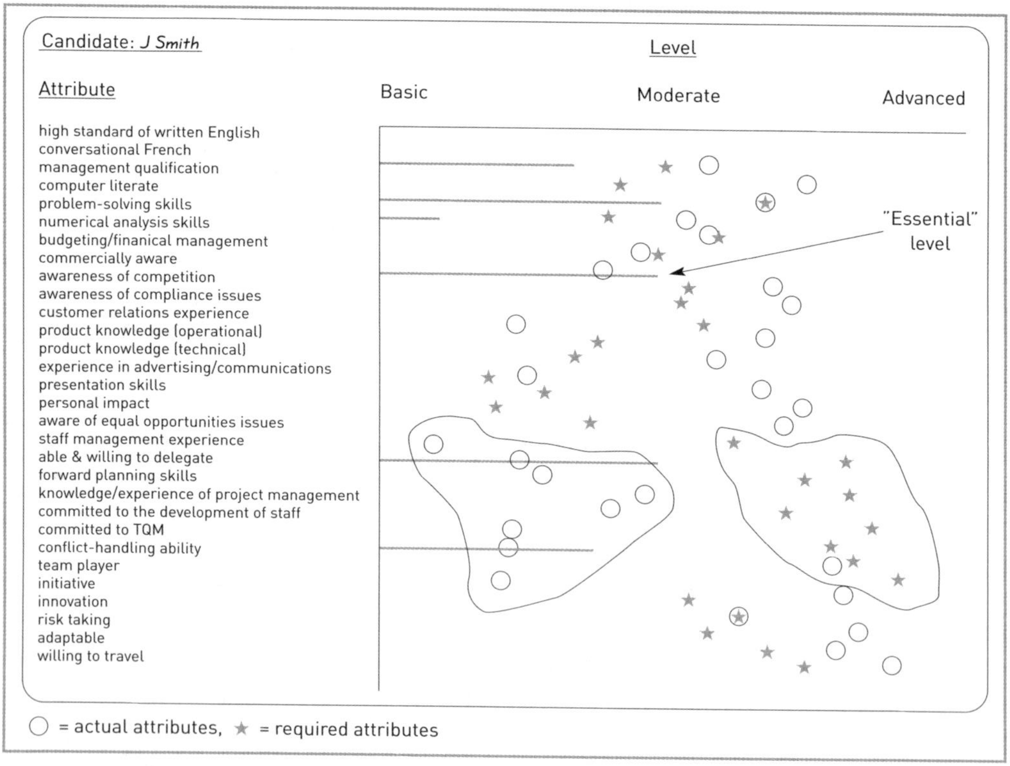

FIG 3.1 ● Cluster profile chart

Source: Gray, RJ (2000) *Cluster Profiling In Personnel Selection* © RJ Gray

Incidentally, recruiting people who significantly exceed the job requirements isn't necessarily a good idea. Over-qualified, or more accurately, under-utilized people are just as susceptible to stress as the over-challenged or overworked, and are very likely to find their work demotivating.[3, 4] Stressed and/or demotivated people tend not to perform very well, no matter how highly qualified they seem to be.

Assessments of potential shouldn't be confined to the process of recruiting people into the organization. It's quite likely that there's a wealth of talent already in the organization that no-one knows about, so it makes good economic sense to make periodic checks – even very informal ones at team or local level – on what individuals could do if only they were given the chance.

learning If we assume that an employee has the potential to do an excellent job, the next step is to ensure that he or she has the necessary skills and knowledge. This usually involves *learning* and applied learning, or *training*. Learning is the key to growth and development, on the personal as well as the professional level, and ability to learn may well be one of the most significant factors in competitive advantage. So it will be worth investing some time and effort into maximizing this attribute, and developing a better understanding of the processes involved could be a good place to start.

Learning has at least two broad dimensions: a behavioural dimension, which people can see in practice as we change what we do and the way we go about things as a result of learning experiences,[5] and a cognitive dimension, which involves changes in the way we understand or "conceptualize" the world around us.[6] Both dimensions focus on change, in behaviour and in understanding, and this is the essence of all learning: people are changed by it.

learning is the key to growth and development

this is the essence of all learning: people are changed by it

We can identify four kinds of learning: learning *facts*, learning *skills*, learning *processes*, and learning *principles*.

fact or fallacy? We learn facts all the time: horses have a blind spot between their eyes; frogs hop faster than toads; light travels at 2.998×10^8 metres per second; the sun goes round the earth once every 24 hours. Except the last one is wrong, of course. This raises a problem with facts – "things certainly known to have occurred or be true"[7] – why do we believe them? How can anything be "certainly known"?

We typically acquire much of our mental database of facts second hand, from teachers, books, newspapers, broadcasting, etc., or just from social contacts. Some of these are deeply flawed as reliable sources.

Facts affecting workplace performance may not always need too much evaluation from this perspective, but they do have to be stored, they usually need to be understood, and they will certainly have to be retrieved when needed. The process of storage and retrieval is what we call *memory*. It appears to operate on two levels, and although there is some dispute about whether there are really two kinds of memory or just different ways in which memory is put to use, the "two process" model is quite a useful way of thinking about it.

Short-term memory, as the name implies, is used for storing relatively small amounts of information for short periods. It's also called working memory. For example, we look up a telephone number in the directory, store the information, and then retrieve it seconds later to dial the number. Shortly afterwards the number is no longer "there" and we would have to look it up again if we needed it. Short-term memory is also easily "wiped clean" by distractions. Most people's short-term memory has been found to have a capacity of roughly seven items but this capacity is effectively increased if the seven items are actually seven groups, each made up of several component items – a process known as "chunking".

Because information is quickly deleted from short-term memory, anything that is going to be needed later has to be transferred into long-term memory. This is perhaps the kind of memory most relevant to the activity of learning. The transfer of information from conscious thought, which is where short-term memory seems to operate, into long-term storage seems usually to involve processing the information in some way. This may be simply by repeating the information to yourself, perhaps many times (called "rehearsal"), by "working on" the raw data until it is thoroughly understood (a process of attaching meaning to the data) or by linking or associating it with sensory stimuli such as images, sounds or smells. The kind of processing that facilitates the passage of information into long-term memory has a profound effect on the ease with which it can be retrieved into conscious thought when it is needed again. This is crucial; when your computer crashes, the manual that tells you how to fix it is of no use whatsoever if it's locked in a drawer to which you don't have a key (or worse, if it's in pdf format on the hard disc that now doesn't work). Similarly, information that has been processed and passed into long-term memory can't be used if it can't be retrieved.

The "keys" that enable retrieval are known as *cues*; these act as "triggers" that open up channels of communication between consciousness and storage. It appears that the more processing that was done at the time of storing the more potential cues will be available for retrieval. So, remembering a particular fact will be easier if when you commit it to storage you ensure that you understand what it means, that you see where it fits into a wider context, and that you make the widest possible range of associations. Then, when you need that fact again, the situation that prompts the need will probably contain at least one and possibly many of the cues that will facilitate access to the stored information.

knowing and doing

Skills might be more accurately described as developed rather than learned. Skill development depends on two vital mechanisms: practice and feedback. This applies both to mental skills,

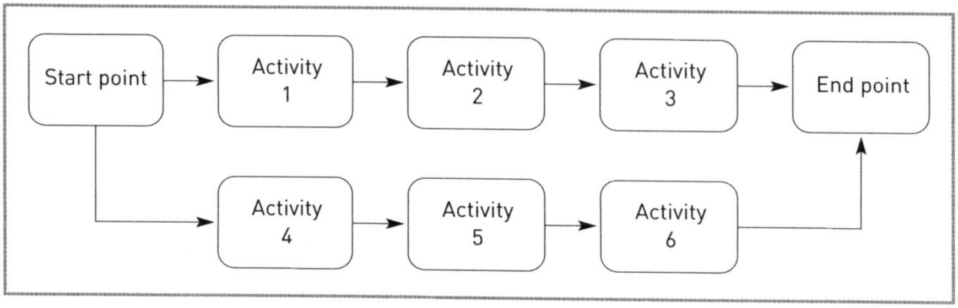

FIG 3.2 ● A process flow

such as negotiating or chairing a discussion, and to physical (or psychomotor) skills like typing, operating a lathe, or reversing an articulated lorry. Practice is fairly self-explanatory, but there will be more about feedback later.

In the context of learning, it's useful to consider *processes* as a separate category from facts or skills, even though it could be argued that skills can involve processes, so the mechanism for learning them is much the same. In this context, processes comprise multiple activities, each of which may involve a variety of skills together with factual knowledge, all linked together in complex or extended packages. There is also some level of understanding involved, and an ability to visualize an outcome, or end-state, that is several steps away from the starting-point, as illustrated in Figure 3.2.

In other words, processes are characterized by complexity, which becomes even more marked when interactions with other people are involved.

Learning *principles* is in some ways the most advanced form of human learning. It is very heavily biased towards understanding, and it provides the key to extending knowledge into new areas. Learning principles involves knowledge of *how* and *why*. This enables existing knowledge and skills to be applied in new situations or to unforeseen problems and opportunities.

how do we learn?

Having looked briefly at the categories or kinds of things that are learned, we should examine some ideas about *how* people learn, which will help us decide on the most effective approaches to learning in various contexts.

A basic principle that underpins most learning has been understood since humans first found out how to tame wild animals: "actions which are rewarded tend to be repeated".[8] The technical term for reward in this context is reinforcement. This principle also tells us that actions, or behaviours, that are not reinforced tend to die out. The effect of this principle on behaviour is called conditioning. As we (or, in fact, virtually all living things, however lowly) get on with our lives, we continually interact with our environment and the things we do have consequences. We discover that certain actions seem to produce results that please us – i.e. are *reinforced* – and so we repeat these actions and before long they get incorporated into our behaviour patterns. Reinforcement can mean almost anything so long as it's perceived as pleasant, so for people in the workplace it could well be signs of approval from someone who matters to us, or of course it could be financial reward.

There are some complications with reinforcement, though. First, we can be misled by apparent connections between events into thinking that one causes the other; mistaking *correlation* for *causation*. For example, if a tribe annually throws a young woman into the local volcano and the volcano hasn't erupted for many years, they may mistakenly believe that it is their action that has produced the beneficial result. A lot of people can get hurt this way.

Secondly, how long *conditioned responses* – or learned behaviours – continue is affected by the consistency of the reinforcement. There are some general guidelines on this: if the reinforcement occurs reliably every time the particular behaviour takes place the behaviour is unlikely to persist for very long if the reinforcement stops. On the other hand, if the reinforcement sometimes occurs but sometimes doesn't, the behaviour may continue for a long time before the message gets through that it isn't being reinforced any more. The general rule is: the less predictable the reinforcement pattern, the longer the conditioned behaviour will take to be "extinguished" after reinforcement ceases.

Thirdly, the reinforcement value of intrinsic rewards, i.e. the pleasure derived from the activity itself, can be quite enough to prompt repetition of a particular behaviour. This happens with animals as well as people.

It is also important that all the reinforcement discussed above has been positive reinforcement, based on reward. Negative reinforcement, perhaps better known as punishment, is much less effective in controlling behaviour and behaviour changes achieved by this means tend to reverse very quickly if the negative reinforcement stops.

Reinforcement can be used to "shape" other people's behaviour. By reinforcing any behaviour that represents a "step in the right direction", patterns are encouraged and developed until they eventually comply with the intended result.

what's most rewarding?

The point of all this is that reinforcement is a powerful driver of behaviour, and can be used as a tool to manipulate other people, but it can be very unpredictable. In the workplace it may be that employees find that they derive more pleasure from circumventing the system than from making it run smoothly, or that the approval of their peers is far more important to them than that of their bosses. Every day is packed with "small actions which have an effect on the environment"[9] and realistically we have to recognize that they are mostly quite random. Much of the behaviour change – or learning – that is based on reinforcement associated with these actions is always likely to be outside anyone's control, but that doesn't mean that managers should ignore the importance of reinforcing appropriate workplace behaviour whenever they see it. In fact, that is the essence of people management at the individual level.

Humans have highly developed *cognitive* (thinking, reasoning) abilities which add an extra dimension to our capacity for learning. Cognitive aspects of learning concentrate on the development of understanding; using intelligence to recognize and define a problem, identify and evaluate possible solutions, then apply and implement the chosen solution. Typical ways of finding solutions to problems would include trial and error, reasoning, and seeking help and information from elsewhere.

for most of us our mistakes have been a valuable source of learning

Trial and error is closely related to reinforcement/conditioning. Of course, there are circumstances in which it would be too risky to be an appropriate problem-solving strategy; some kinds of error can be fatal. Nevertheless, for most of us our mistakes have been a valuable source of learning. We can also learn by observing other people and avoid making mistakes we see them make. Or, more positively, we can copy other people's successful strategies to help us do the right thing. The ability to learn vicariously – by direct observation or, of course, indirectly by reading or other media of communication – vastly multiplies the potential of the trial and error method. It also brings in an element of cognition; an understanding that what happened to (or for) someone else could also apply to me.

Reasoning is a way of making our mistakes in an abstract sphere. It's also a means of applying learning gained in one context to new situations. It would be useful here to distinguish two forms in which this "transferral" process can occur: *Deductive* reasoning observes that something is generally or usually true, and assumes that it will be true about a specific new context. For example, if we observe that cats, in general, seem to like fish, we might reasonably assume that a specific, individual cat will like fish. *Inductive* reasoning goes in the opposite direction. It observes something about a specific case, and assumes that it will be generally or usually true in other contexts. For example, if a manager notes that a particular individual works harder when she shouts at him, inductive reasoning would lead her to suppose that people in general will work harder if they are shouted at. Of course, reasoning can vary in quality – both the conclusions described above could very well be wrong – but rigorous, trained, logical reasoning can produce solutions with a high probability of success. Until they are put into practice, solutions produced by reasoning remain *hypothetical*. In fact, intelligent application of these two methods recognizes that reasoning only produces an *hypothesis*, which needs to be treated with caution until further evidence is available to support or negate it.

everyone has style David Kolb[10] describes a recognizable pattern that human learning follows, which forms a continuous loop. This is illustrated in Figure 3.3.

The "experiential learning cycle" doesn't always have to begin with the "concrete experience"; it could start at the abstract level. Also, whilst all four stages of the cycle apply to everybody, different people seem to derive more learning benefit from one or two of the stages than from the others, possibly as a result of their previous experiences. Observing this, Peter Honey and Alan Mumford[11] say that everyone finds it easiest to learn in one or more of the phases of the Kolb learning cycle and they identify four distinct styles, derived from Kolb's model. They say that most people learn to some extent in all four modes, but will gain more from the style(s) that suit them best. So, Activists get greatest benefit from learning in the Concrete Experience sector, Reflectors gain most from the effort they put into thoughtful consideration of what has

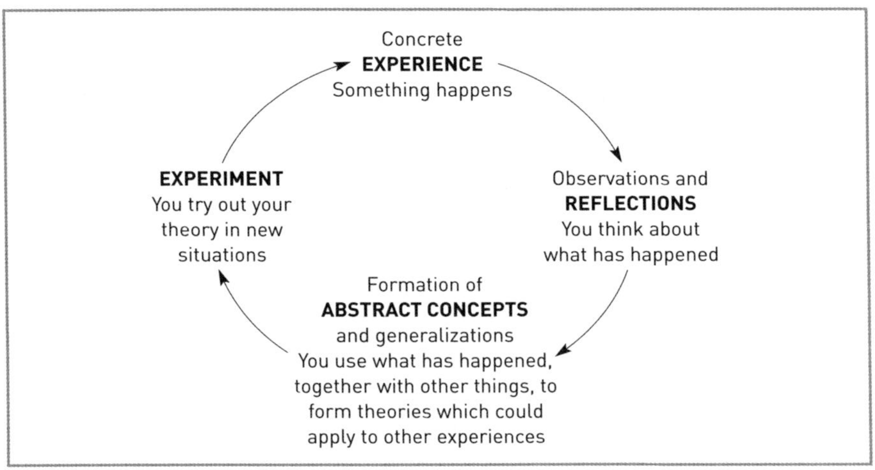

FIG 3.3 ● Kolb's experiential learning cycle

Source: Kolb, D, Rubin, I & McIntyre, J (1974) *Organizational Psychology, a Book of Readings*, 2nd edn, Englewood Cliffs, NJ, Prentice Hall, p. 28.

occurred, Theorists learn most from making sense of underlying meaning, and Pragmatists find applying ideas to new situations most beneficial to their learning progress.

This opens up two possibilities: you can either try to structure your learning so that it fits in with the style(s) you prefer, or you can try to develop your ability to take advantage of learning opportunities that occur in other styles. A prerequisite for taking up either option is to know what your own preferred learning style is, which you can find out by completing a questionnaire.[12]

Both approaches offer potential for enhanced learning, but the general view is that we can't control all the learning opportunities that come our way, so the greatest potential benefit is likely to come from developing our ability to take advantage of them whenever and however they occur. Honey and Mumford provide plenty of practical advice – too much to summarize here – on how to set about extending your learning style repertoire by committing yourself to some actions that will give you practice in using the styles that don't come naturally.

On the whole, learning seems to be most effective, and is retained better, when learners have control over what and how they learn, the learning has some direct relevance to real life and makes good use of the learner's own experience, and involves experience rather than simply theoretical input.[13] The issue of retention is quite an important one here: educational traditionalists sometimes point out that children who have been taught by traditional "chalk and talk" methods often do better in tests than children who have been encouraged to discover things for themselves. The opposite tends to be true, though, if the testing is done long after the learning activity (assuming that the "discovery" learning has been properly structured, of course). In other words, if you want to pass a test but will never need the knowledge again, traditional methods may be best for your purpose (although possibly rather boring). If, on the other hand, the knowledge has real long-term value, then "experiential" approaches may be the better option.

acting it out In the adult and workplace context, this experiential approach to learning forms the basis of a method known as *action learning*. This centres around a real-world project that has genuine significance for a group of participants. As the group works on the project, issues and problems naturally arise and the learners are encouraged to research or devise solutions to the problems. They are helped in this by a skilled facilitator who can provide expert advice and guidance when needed. The theory being put into practice here is that, because the learners themselves have discovered or worked out solutions to genuine real-world needs, the learning experience will be deeper and longer-lasting than if they had simply read or been told the answers.

The effectiveness of action learning for any specific individual depends to some extent on his or her preferred learning style. You would expect it to have more appeal for Activists or Pragmatists than for Theorists. Reflectors can also benefit from this approach (although they might test the patience of the other team members). One disadvantage of action learning that doesn't only affect Theorists is the potential conflict that can arise from having two primary purposes for the whole exercise: to deal with a real-world requirement and to learn something from the experience. In practice, one of these is likely to be dominant to the possible detriment of the other, although this doesn't always happen. Another potential drawback centres around the question of how transferable, or generalizable, the learning is. Earlier I explained that inductive reasoning observes something about a specific case, and assumes that it will be generally or usually true in other contexts. In other words, that truth can be transferred or generalized to other situations, but this is certainly not invariably the case. The value of experience, having "seen it all before", is generally recognized – at job interviews, for example – but maybe "it" isn't really the same this time.

In the real world, this division between theoretical and experiential learning can seem rather artificial. Kolb's cycle tells us that we need to reflect on our experiences in order to learn from them, and we need to put our theoretical concepts into practice to get any benefit from them. Lenin is supposed to have summed this principle up as: "theory without practice is sterile; practice without theory is futile". For this reason most meaningful learning experiences involve a blend of theoretical and practical elements.

Practical concerns may influence our choices about how to handle a specific learning need. Broadly, we could take a "surface approach" which concentrates on completing task requirements, or fulfilling external demands (such as assessment). Although such an approach would not be very satisfactory for long-term learning, there could be circumstances in which task demands override this consideration. On the other hand, we could take a "deep" approach, where the intention is to understand, the focus is on meaning, content is organized holistically into a coherent whole, evidence and argument are carefully weighed up, and previous knowledge and knowledge from other sources are all applied and taken into account.[14] For solid, lasting development a "deep" approach to learning is clearly superior, but it may not be appropriate for the circumstances. Being unclear about the overriding objective can lead to results that are unsatisfactory from all points of view.

in the loop Chris Argyris[15] advocates a model of "double-loop" learning that is applicable both at the individual and the wider organizational levels. He suggests that basic learning models consist of a single loop (shown in Figure 3.4) in which appropriate actions and strategies are learned because they "work", i.e. the consequences of them seem to match with the intentions. Because this is quite rewarding in itself, this is a reinforcement model of learning. If the action doesn't appear to work then something else is tried.

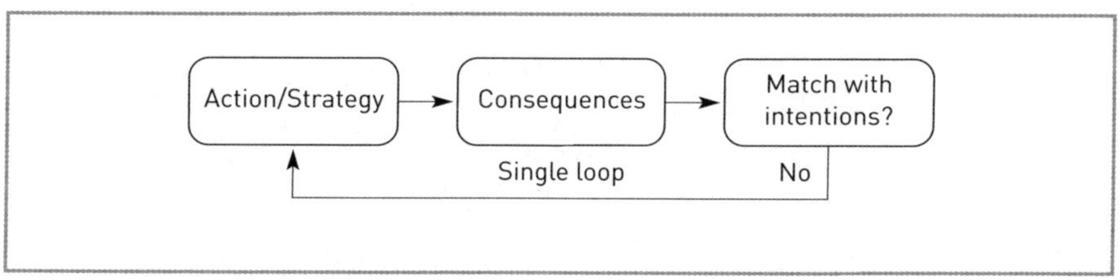

FIG 3.4 ● Single-loop learning

Source: Argyris, C (1999) *On Organizational Learning*, 2nd edn, Oxford, Blackwell. © Blackwell Publishing.

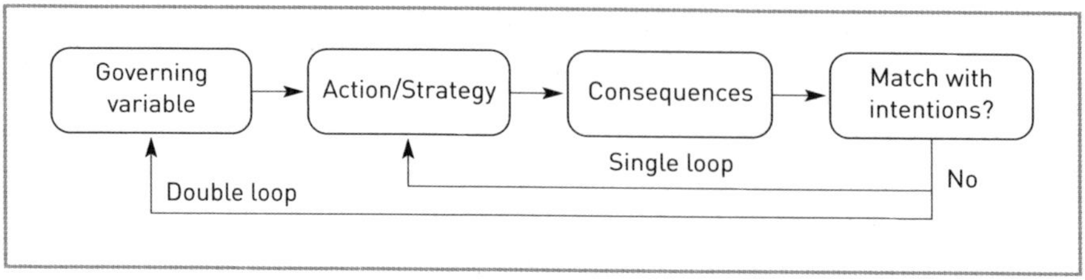

FIG 3.5 ● Double-loop learning

Source: Argyris, C (1999) *On Organizational Learning*, 2nd edn, Oxford, Blackwell. © Blackwell Publishing.

Argyris argues that a particular action or strategy may fail, not because it was simply wrong but because it was based on faulty "governing variables", the underlying bases or principles on which the action or strategy was founded. Governing variables in this model could be assumptions, attitudes, values, the culture, or the theories in use. Double-loop learning (shown in Figure 3.5) involves understanding and re-assessing these governing variables, which makes it a cognitive learning model

Also, I believe it can be very worthwhile to re-examine the governing variables of actions and strategies that *do* work, and ask "why?", because this can provide valuable insights that can be applied elsewhere.

These various models of learning processes are of more than purely academic or theoretical interest. Taken together, they can help to build insight into how we, as individuals, can enhance our capacity to learn and thereby make ourselves more effective, in the workplace and in other dimensions of life. They can also help us to make learning easier for other people for whom we have responsibility.

Learning is a process by which we change our behaviour and/or our understanding of the world around us. Powerful forces, many of which are not obvious to the conscious mind, shape our learning; the most potent of these is reinforcement.

We can exercise some control over our own learning, above all by critically examining things we hear, see or are told and testing assumptions and challenging faulty reasoning. The better we understand something, the easier it is to remember and to apply in new situations. We can also enhance our learning capabilities by understanding our individual learning style and by adopting a variety of approaches to learning, suited to the specific needs of the situation.

training In the context of the workplace, individuals are likely to have their own learning needs and there will be things that employers will need their employees to learn. It would be quite good news if many of the same items appeared in both categories. In fact, it can be beneficial for employers to support learning even where the subject matter doesn't seem to be directly useful in the workplace and most employees would derive at least some personal benefit from learning things their employer needs them to know about, so the commonality between the two lists should usually be quite substantial.

The implementation of learning activity may be called *training* (or education; the precise definitions of these two terms and the differences between them are topics for discussion elsewhere). For our purposes it will be enough to define training loosely as "developing and improving the ability to perform an activity, function or role". This definition allows us to assess what *training needs* there are in an organization. Initially, we will look at this question from the organization's perspective.

When employers consider the things they need their employees to learn it's likely that they have in mind a need for individuals to be *able to do their jobs.* From an organizational perspective we need to begin the process of assessing training needs by considering what is actually meant by "their jobs" and the organizational purposes those jobs are meant to serve.

do the right thing The first indication an organization has that there's a need for training is often when senior managers perceive some difficulty in achieving objectives, or in implementing strategy. There are, or course, many ways in which managers might respond to this kind of perception.

there's little benefit in doing the wrong thing more efficiently

If objectives are not being achieved, or strategy is proving difficult to implement, it might be sensible to begin by checking that the strategy and objectives are right and appropriate; there's little benefit in doing the wrong thing more efficiently! If managers are satisfied that the strategy and objectives are appropriate the next step should be to find out what the barriers are to successful implementation. The possibilities are almost infinite; good, solid information is required. If the investigation shows that a lack of necessary skills, knowledge and/or understanding among employees is a factor, then training may be a solution.

It's useful to split up the organization's training requirements into three levels, according to Tom Boydell.[16] What we have just considered is the first, and broadest, level; the Organizational Level, in which we identify general or organization-wide weaknesses/problems and try to specify training as a means of addressing these issues.

The next level of analysis is the Job or Occupational Level. This involves assessing the skills, knowledge, understanding and attitudes that someone would need in order to do a specific job well. Clearly, this has to begin with a clear idea of what that job entails: its purpose, content, relationships, responsibilities and discretion levels. In other words, a reliable and comprehensive *job description*. The practical difficulties of achieving this have already been discussed but without it further progress will be extremely difficult, so whatever the imperfections this is an essential step in the process.

The third of level of assessment is the Individual Level. This involves forming a clear picture of what skills, knowledge, understanding (and attitudes) each employee actually *has*, then comparing them with what he or she would *need* in order to do the job well (from Level 2).

do we need algebra? Finding out someone's current levels of these qualities may entail a variety of approaches. In some cases a test of some kind may be appropriate and often a test that the individual has already taken can be utilized: a driving test would be evidence that someone can drive, at least to the basic legal level of competence; a professional qualification would be evidence that their competence has been assessed by an appropriate third party; GCSE maths would indicate numeracy, and so on. Note, though, that third-party tests may not precisely match the organization's needs. The GCSE maths assessment, for example, includes geometry and algebra as well as arithmetic, so relying on it might indicate a job-significant deficiency in a quite adequately numerate employee who just couldn't do quadratic equations. Intelligent interpretation is required. For more specialized competencies it might be worthwhile for the organization to devise its own testing procedures. However, this kind of formal assessment can often seem like a "trial by ordeal" to the people being assessed, needs high levels of expertise to devise the tests, and can be expensive. In the vast majority of cases current competence levels should form part of the ongoing performance management environment and beneficial training or development activity should be jointly identified by the individuals concerned and their line managers.

Whatever approach is taken, the outcome should be that the organization can answer the key question: does the individual have the necessary attributes to do an acceptable job?

too good, or good enough If the answer to this is "yes" it would be tempting to say: "Fine! On to the next problem". In fact there can be good reasons to consider using resources on training for employees who are already good at their jobs. One is that if someone is doing a good job now there's every chance that they have the capability to do it even better, although it would be sensible to ask whether it actually needs to be done any better, and if so, how much that would be worth in hard cash. Another reason is that good performers are prime candidates for more demanding or more senior jobs, so training to prepare them for greater responsibility is likely to be a worthwhile investment. There is a potential problem here, identified by Laurence J Peter as "the Peter Principle",[17] which says that "in a hierarchy individuals tend to rise to their levels of incompetence". The implication of the Peter Principle is that good performers tend to get promoted until eventually they end up in a job they do rather badly and that's where they stay. This is usually taken to mean that people are likely to get one more promotion than they really merit, but this is (sometimes) a bit unfair. In fact, it's quite likely that some people get stuck in this way in a job that is unsuitable for their particular talents, whereas they could actually perform very well in the next job up the hierarchy. Unfortunately, no-one will ever find that out.

Some organizations will even consider using resources to support employee training and education that is unrelated to current or envisaged future job functions. One reason for this is that the organization realizes that it can't foresee its future needs with any real certainty so it hedges its bets by investing in training in the hope that employees will thereby be better prepared to cope with the unexpected. You may think that this is rather haphazard. On the other hand it may be just a realistic recognition of the unpredictability of the organizational environment. Another reason why organizations may allocate resources in this way is that they see it as investing in their people. Helping employees to enhance their career potential – or employability – contributes to a favourable "climate" in which people feel valued. It recognizes changing employment patterns that mean lifetime careers with single organizations are no longer the norm but says, in effect: "give us your loyalty now and we'll help you to ensure that you're well-prepared when the time comes for you to move on".

There are disadvantages in people having more skills or knowledge than they need for their current job assignment. A lack of challenge can sap motivation, leading to impaired performance. Worse still, several pieces of research have shown that under-utilization is a significant source of stress and as we will see later stress sometimes kills people as well as having many less extreme ill-effects.

So far we've looked at how organizations might respond if they can answer "yes" to the key question "does the individual have the necessary attributes to do an acceptable/good/excellent job?" If the answer to this question is "no" then a further question has to be asked: "can the situation be improved through training?" If the answer to this further question is also "no" then the issue may be one of performance management, which is covered elsewhere in this book. If it seems likely that training may provide or contribute to a solution, then the organization needs to consider how it should be handled. The full decision process is illustrated in Figure 3.6.

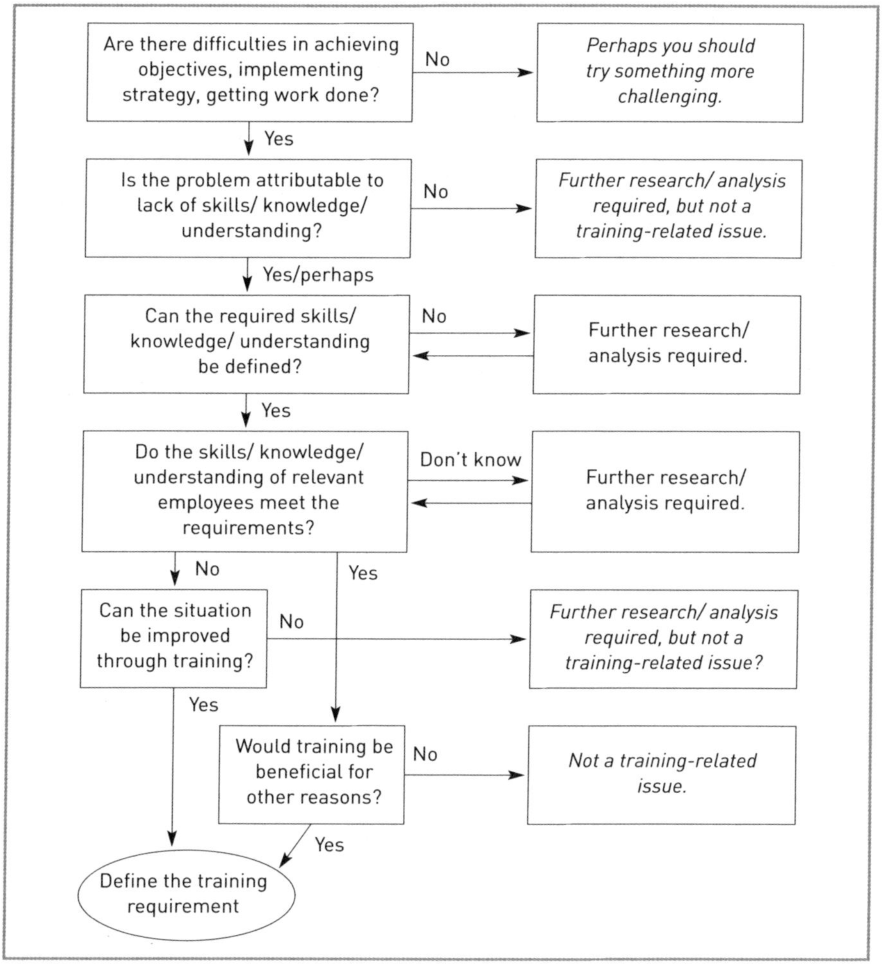

FIG 3.6 ● **The training decision process**

to, or with? In describing the management of training there's a risk of making it seem as though training is something management does *to* employees. It isn't, or if it is then it probably won't be very successful. Rather, training should be seen as a cooperative venture; something employees themselves undertake with the full encouragement and support of management. Having established that principle we can look at a generic training process that can be developed and/or adapted as necessary to meet specific needs.

This process is based on one described by John Kenney and Margaret Reid,[18] but I've added a stage, which I've called *Stage 0*, in front of the four stages they define because I believe it's vital to begin any project – and the implementation of training is a fairly classic form of project – with a clear definition of what it's intended to achieve. The augmented version of the process is shown in Figure 3.7.

In Stage 0 the *purpose* of the training is defined, using terms such as: *Why* is it being done? What is supposed to be *changed* by it? (How will things be different afterwards from the way they are now?) *Who* are the beneficiaries? (Who is it being done *for*?). The *purpose* of the training is a wider concept than the specific objectives, which will be determined next. It would typically refer to organizational objectives, or career aspirations. Knowing *why* is a vital prerequisite for determining *what*.

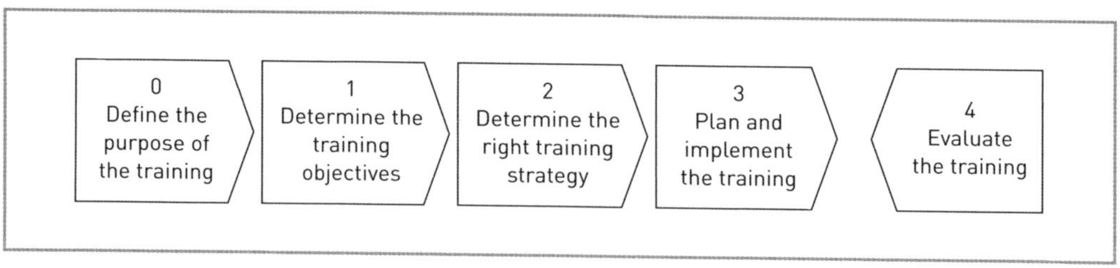

FIG 3.7 ● The training implementation process

training should be seen as a cooperative venture

Once we are clear about what the training initiative is intended to achieve we can enter Stage 1 of the process: *"Determine the training objectives"*. Carefully defined *skills* might well figure in the stated objectives of the training because we would expect that, after undergoing training, employees would be able to *do* something they couldn't do before, or couldn't do so well. We might also expect them to *know* or *understand* something they didn't know before or didn't understand so thoroughly, so defined knowledge might be included among the objectives.

It would be important to be clear about the *standards of achievement* required. This can be difficult to define, but it's important to persevere because loose or sloppy definition can lead to inadequately qualified people struggling with their jobs or, equally, to people with perfectly adequate skills getting rejected. For example, if it's decided that a job requires a "knowledge of" a foreign language, does this mean the sort of "knowledge" that would enable you to find your way to the station in a relevant foreign city, or exchange social pleasantries with callers, or participate fully in a business meeting, or do simultaneous interpretation of sensitive high-level negotiations involving advanced technical jargon? Similarly, "knowing how a car works" would mean quite different things to a new learner driver, a recruit to an evening class on car maintenance, or a graduate engineer applying for a technical job with a major manufacturer. Over-specifying the standard required costs money and causes frustration. So does under-specifying, but for different reasons.

Finally, it would be helpful to know the *context*, or circumstances, in which the new skills or knowledge would be put to use.

Having defined the purpose of the proposed training (Stage 0) and the specific objectives (Stage 1) we can move to Stage 2, which is to determine the best way to realize those objectives. There is a range of common possibilities, including: training on the job, in-house experience, in-house courses, external experience, external courses, computer-based training and distance learning. Sometimes more than one method can be combined or used to complement each other. Selection of the form or method of training should be done on a rational basis, taking several criteria into account.

Wherever comparisons or selections have to be made between two or more "bundles" of factors, it can be a good idea to set out all the elements in a matrix. In this case we might begin by listing all the available options for methods of training, then go on to list all the criteria that need to be considered when making the decision. The blank (unpopulated) matrix in Figure 3.8 provides for the options to be shown on the horizontal axis, and lists on the vertical axis nine criteria that I believe should always be included:

- How well does the option fit the *purpose* of the training?
- How well does it fit the training objectives?
- How likely is it to succeed?
- What are its intrinsic strengths?
- What are its intrinsic weaknesses?
- How readily available are the resources it requires?
- Is it a good use of resources?
- What are the trainee's preferences?

	Option A	Option B	Option C	Option D	Option E	Option F	Option G	Option H
Fit with purpose								
Fit with objectives								
Probability of success								
Intrinsic strengths								
Intrinsic weaknesses								
Availability of resources								
Stewardship								
Trainee preferences								
Other factors (identify)								

FIG 3.8 ● Blank evaluation matrix

Other criteria can (and should) be added to meet particular defined needs.

We will need to look at some of these criteria in more detail.

fit with purpose How well would the option support the purpose of the training? Are there any considerations of strategy or policy which should be taken into account, and is there likely to be any impact (positive or negative) on anything else that's going on or planned for the future?

fit with objectives How well would the option support the defined training objectives? Does it support all of them equally? If not, can we realistically evaluate the overall effect, or should we separate the objectives out and consider each one as a separate criterion?

probability of success How likely is the option to work? (and what exactly does "work" mean in this context? We are probably talking about *transfer of learning* here, meaning how well anything learned in the training environment is remembered and can be effectively applied back in the workplace.)

strengths and weaknesses

The next two criteria, the intrinsic (or possibly generic) *strengths* and *weaknesses* of a particular training method, need to be considered carefully. As an example we might consider the strengths and weaknesses of on-the-job training, often called "sitting with Nellie". The strengths might include: a realistic setting, culture is absorbed along with technical details, there's often high learning transfer and retention, it can seem inexpensive, and some "real" work gets done. The weaknesses could be that: learning tends to be rather hit and miss, learning can be negative if the real job isn't quite the same, the trainee can pick up bad habits, "Nellie" may need training as a coach, training can take longer, and the "real" work is likely to slow down.

Charles Handy, in several of his books, describes how the major oil company he worked for in the 1960s would move employees to different jobs, in locations across the world, each move designed by senior managers as a development experience for the employee. Staff were not expected to question the company's wisdom; refusal to comply could mean losing the job. This kind of planned internal experience used to be highly favoured as a means of developing junior managers in organizations and it's true that regular changes of role and/or location provide breadth of experience. It does carry the risk, though, that the individual employee is never in one place long enough to become really effective in that role. So, in the short term it can be costly in terms of organizational effectiveness, not to mention disrupted lives.

Other forms of planned internal experience might include "loans" to other departments, project work, action learning, and mentoring. A very common example is standing-in for the boss while he or she is away. All of these can be put into operation without completely losing contact with the "base" job and can be monitored and adjusted relatively painlessly as they go along.

Planned external experience might include: secondment to other organizations, visits, for example to customers or suppliers, or even to competitors, trade association or professional institute events, or charitable or community activity.

Secondments can be difficult to organize and should have very specific learning objectives defined in advance. Finding out how other people do things is almost always useful, but the learning doesn't necessarily transfer readily back into the parent organization; context and culture will be different. Where benefits can be gained quite quickly is in finding out how a partner organization, which could be a customer, would *like* your organization to behave. Small adjustments, and simply knowing how the other party operates, can enable the interactions to work much more smoothly. Charitable or community activities may be worthwhile in their own right and may be more helpful to the receiving organization than a simple donation. Learning benefits to the individual secondees or their organizations can be quite dilute, though, so unless a specific learning point can be identified it would be realistic not to expect too much.

Visits serve a similar purpose to secondments, but are much more time-constrained so it's even more important that there should be specific things the visitor wants to learn. Visits have the advantage that they don't usually require the visitors to perform any particular function while they are there, so all the attention can be concentrated on "finding out". Expect to see only what the receiving organization wants to show you.

Organized events often turn out to be little more than several lectures strung together, so are best avoided unless the agenda clearly contains items that look useful. They can be good networking opportunities and it's often possible to learn as much during the coffee breaks as you do in the auditorium.

With all external contacts it's important to remember that learning isn't likely to be entirely one-way. Trainees may be learning useful things about or through another organization, but the people there are probably learning things about your organization too. Often, this is exactly what you want to happen, but the trainees may give away information you would rather they had kept to themselves.

course fishing

Which brings us to training courses of various kinds. In-house courses can be very effective in addressing organization-specific learning needs, especially if subject-matter experts are available, or senior managers can be persuaded to take part to discuss matters of policy or strategy. They can also seem quite cheap because real cash budgets are often low, especially if existing accommodation is used. In fact, resources are being diverted away from business-as-usual to deliver the training, so there are substantial concealed costs. Also, training design and delivery are skilled activities and internal training is often in the hands of people who lack skills in either area, which can severely reduce its effectiveness. Some large organizations have professional trainers on the staff, which slightly blurs the distinction between internal and external provision. This has the advantage of a high level of organizational control over content and quality, but it can allow trainers to become "stale", and over-concerned with staying "on-message", and the training easily becomes insular. The current trend even in major organizations seems to be towards outsourcing training activities, although trends frequently reverse.

External courses, if carefully chosen and quality-checked, can offer a high standard of both design and delivery. Professional trainers should be fully up to date in their subjects and trainees can usually benefit from sharing experiences with people from other organizations. Depending on the nature of the training successful completion may lead to a recognized qualification. On the down side, external training can be expensive, and it may be hard to apply the learning in the parent organization. It can also be extremely frustrating to learn about best practice on a training course only to discover that nobody back in the workplace wants to know. Young, ambitious managers who spend two years on part-time MBAs (often at their employers' expense), learning about advanced strategy and enthusiastically discussing strategic issues with their peers and tutors, often find that no one back at the workplace is likely to be the least bit interested in their views on strategic matters for many years to come. This can lead to significant staff turnover in modern organizations

Computer-based training (CBT) and distance learning (which are increasingly to be found combined in integrated delivery packages, often over the Internet) can be relatively cheap to implement. Their effectiveness is heavily dependent on the learning style preferences, and the self-discipline, of the learner, as well as the quality of the material and the technology. At best they can provide stimulating, multi-sensory input with easy access to tutor support when needed. At worst they may be no more effective than a book from the library, but a lot more irritating.

Having identified the strengths and weaknesses of the various options available in the specific circumstances, there remain three more "core" criteria to list on the evaluation matrix.

availability of resources However attractive a particular option might seem it's essential to be realistic. The various resources of time, budget, skills, personnel, materials and/or equipment must all be available before any decision can be implemented. Can we be sure that they will be? A lack of an essential resource makes any option a non-starter, while degrees of difficulty, inconvenience or side-effects (e.g. having to postpone a product launch because the conference room is in use for training) all act to make an option less desirable.

stewardship Even if it's certain that all the necessary resources will be available, employees of the organization have a responsibility to use those resources to the best effect. This means balancing probable benefits against costs – in whatever terms "costs" are meaningful – and choosing the *optimum* course of action.

trainee preferences Finally, before moving on to special factors additional to this "core" list, the views of the trainee should always be sought and taken into account; if you try to make someone learn against their will, you'll probably fail!

making a choice

So far, the training options available have been identified and the attractiveness of each option has been considered. In order to make comparisons between the options this "attractiveness" must be quantified, at least in relative terms. This can be done by assessing how well each criterion is supported by each option. High, Medium or Low ratings can be used for this, but it will make comparison easier if these assessments are translated into numerical ratings. This also allows extra sophistication, such as negative relationships, but it's important to recognize that the ratings are still only ordinal, or comparative; the numbers are not significant in themselves. Numerical ratings of 1, 3 and 9 can be used to replace Low, Medium and High (this makes the differences clearer than using 1, 2 and 3). If a particular criterion isn't addressed at all by an option then it should be rated 0, or the box can be left blank. In practice it's usually sensible to discard that option unless there are very strong reasons for keeping it in consideration.

Using this schema might produce a completed matrix that looks something like the populated matrix illustrated in Figure 3.9.

The fact that there are two options with the same numerical score means that some fine-tuning will have to be done. Option F seems a better fit with both the purpose and the objectives of the training, but Option H has greater intrinsic strengths and is preferred by the trainee. None of the other options comes close so making a decision shouldn't be too painful; nothing's perfect, after all.

project *train* Once it's been determined what the training is supposed to achieve, why it's necessary or desirable, and how it should be implemented, the next step is to transform intentions into reality. The implementation of a training programme is a project and follows the same criteria of good practice as any other project.

Projects have a natural life cycle, consisting of four basic phases: Definition, Planning, Implementation and Closure. Some of these may be further subdivided if that's necessary or useful. The transition point between one phase and the next is a time for taking stock; checking that everything has been

	Option A	Option B	Option C	Option D	Option E	Option F	Option G	Option H
Fit with purpose	9	3	9	1	3	9	1	3
Fit with objectives	3	1	9	1	3	9	1	3
Probability of success	3	1	9	1	9	9	3	9
Intrinsic strengths	3	3	3	1	9	3	1	9
Intrinsic weaknesses	1	1	3	1	3	3	1	3
Availability of resources	9	3	3	9	3	9	1	9
Stewardship	3	1	9	1	3	9	1	9
Trainee preferences	9	9	1	3	1	3	1	9
Other factors (identify)	1	3	3	9	1	9	1	9
Totals	41	25	49	27	35	63	11	63

FIG 3.9 ● Populated evaluation matrix

done to the required standards, and that everything is ready to proceed with the next phase. This is also the point at which formal authority should be given to continue: each phase means an escalation of cost and if the project no longer seems capable of meeting its objectives it may be better to bring it to a halt, or pause for a radical re-think.

Some of the work for the Definition phase of the training implementation project has already been done. In this phase the objectives are defined, the strategy is confirmed, "in principle" authorization is obtained, and the key participants (the team) are identified.

The next phase – Planning – is where the detailed preparation work takes place. In this phase the team thinks carefully through all the work needed to complete the project and breaks it down into manageable tasks, or work packages. Once all the work packages have been identified they can be arranged in a logical sequence; "once *A* is completed we can begin *B*" and so on. Timetables can be set, and the demand for resources of all kinds can be estimated.

The next phase – Implementation – is easy to describe but, naturally, the most challenging of the project phases to carry out. In effect, implementation is simply doing what you've planned to do. There's a rule of project management that provides a valuable guideline here. It's expressed as an equation:

$$\text{Planning Effort} + \text{Implementation Problems} = \text{A Constant}$$

This means that, if you put the effort into planning, you can reasonably expect to avoid some of the problems during implementation. On the other hand, if you skimp on the planning work you will pay for it in hitches, even disasters, when you come to implement the project. Planning may be more boring than implementation, and doesn't have much visible output, but implementation problems tend to be unexpected, and therefore tend to hurt more.

The final phase – Closure – is the phase where the project is brought neatly and tidily to a conclusion. There is a risk here of confusing this phase of the *project* with the last stage of the training process (Evaluate the Training), but they are different things and need to be dealt with separately. In the closure phase, *project* performance is reviewed. Questions are asked such as: Did the project come in on budget? Could it have been done for less? Was it completed on time? (Were there any scary moments?) Could it have done more or better? Are the "customers" happy? Has the necessary documentation been completed? and Is there anything to be handed over to another person, unit or team? There are also people issues, such as: Has the contribution of everyone on the team been recognized? and even, if it's been a major piece of work, Has everyone got a job to go back to?

how well did it work?

Once the training has been completed Stage 4 in the training process is to evaluate what has been achieved. This takes time and effort, and cost, but without it it will be hard to justify the expenditure, assess the effectiveness of what has been done, or provide feedback to trainers. All of these are necessary as inputs to future training activity.

On this list *justify the expenditure* has been placed first because without a budget allocation everything else becomes irrelevant; there won't be any training. Unfortunately there are many organizations where training is the first thing to go when economies have to be made. This could be among the most short-sighted decisions management ever makes.

Kenny & Reid say that evaluation of training can be done at several levels.[19] These, in ascending order of sophistication, are typically: evaluation of the training experience or event, evaluation of what or how much has been learned, and evaluation of whether and by how much the trainee's performance of the job has changed. These first three levels are mainly concerned with the individual trainee(s).

The fourth level is concerned with the impact of the training on the department where the trainee works, and the fifth level is concerned with the effects on the whole organization. These five levels are in a logical sequence: each one relies on its predecessor to provide information and give focus to subsequent enquiries.

Before considering how evaluation might be carried out at these various levels, it will be helpful to explain two basic concepts that any process for evaluating, testing, or checking anything ought to satisfy: *reliability* and *validity*.

Reliability is a fairly straightforward concept: to be considered reliable the evaluation process should produce similar results under similar conditions whenever it's used.

Validity can be a little more complex. Basically, when we ask if the evaluation process is *valid* we're asking whether it measures the quality or attribute it's supposed to measure. For example, if we wanted to assess the progress of a group of children in English comprehension we might apply a test that consisted of measuring the height of each child and recording it on a chart. Hopefully, you will think this is silly. However, the outcomes could be confusing because there's a fairly strong correlation between height and age, and there's also a correlation between age and language development. Therefore it's likely that a positive correlation might exist between height and language skills and this could be fairly consistent when applied to many groups of children, so it could be reasonably *reliable*, but it could hardly be considered *valid*. If we didn't apply some kind of sanity check, we might be misled into using an invalid test.

We also need to be sure that what we measure is *useful*. Perfectly reliable, and valid, evaluation processes might tell us that employees returning from an "outdoor" training course are now highly skilled at raft-building, but is this what we really need to know?

Common means of evaluation at the first level, that of the training experience or event, include questionnaires (often called "happy sheets"), interviews, group discussions and written reports. Methods like these can provide a lot of information about what the trainee(s) thought about the event content, the methods used, the trainer's performance, and so on, but they have to be treated with some caution. Reactions immediately after the training experience can be influenced by how enjoyable, or not, the trainee found it. Training isn't always fun; it can be hard work and may sometimes involve some robust feedback. It can also be difficult for the trainee to judge how useful the training was until later, by which time memories of the actual experience may have faded.

Evaluation at the next level, that is, of the *learning* that has taken place, will be a familiar concept to anyone who has been through a formal education process. It has a venerable history; candidates for public office in ancient China had to pass rigorous exams. Nowadays, exams are only one of several ways of checking what has been learnt. Other methods include continuous assessment, marked final assignments, observed exercises, mutual assessments in which trainees evaluate each other's performance, project work in which the learning has to be applied to real-life situations, discussion groups, and case studies. Another approach is profiling, in which a record of achievement that covers a range of skills and applications is built up over time.

All these methods present some issues of validity and reliability. Exams, for example, may test a candidate's ability to perform under pressure or remember information, but may not have high validity as a means of predicting performance under other conditions. They may also not be very reliable, as individual candidates' performance may be affected by circumstances on the day of the exam and candidates of similar ability often achieve different results.

Evaluation of the changes in job performance that occur after training presents some difficulties. The problem here is how to tell whether the learning that took place during the training transferred successfully to the workplace. This tends to become more difficult, and demand more effort, as jobs get "broader", more responsible, and involve more individual discretion. For example, evaluation might not seem too hard in the case of an IT support technician who has just received training on installing an organization's standard terminals; after all, either the terminals work when they are installed or they don't. Evaluation could be refined to take account of how long each installation takes, neatness of wiring, etc., and it could be followed up later to check for subsequent problems. The case of a callcentre agent who has recently been trained on handling complaints could involve a more subjective kind of evaluation, and a manager who has been trained in "coaching skills", or "time management", or "finance for non-financial managers" might present some real difficulties in evaluating the training objectively.

When it comes to evaluating training at the departmental level, which involves an assessment of the impact the training has had on the functioning of the department, issues of cause and effect are major concerns. Separating out the influence of training from all the other factors affecting the department's performance, with any real confidence, is going to be very difficult. And when we move out from the department to consider the impact training has had at the level of the whole organization the whole question becomes exponentially more complicated. Rigorous, research-based approaches can provide evidence for the impact of training at either of these advanced levels, but the cost of this can be prohibitive.

cost–benefit All the same, if organizations are to allocate resources for training and development they need to have some assurance that the expenditure will be cost-effective. Perhaps the most satisfactory approach, and consistent with the project model of training activity described above, is to build a business case when the training need is first identified in which the purpose of the training is expressed in terms of tangible benefits at the departmental and organizational level. For example:

> "The enhanced knowledge of spreadsheets resulting from this training will enable an average of 15 man-hours to be saved on the production of monthly budget statements, making the statements available to management one day earlier than at present and saving approximately £4,000 per annum in production costs."

or

> "First-contact complaint closures are estimated to improve from 61% (current figure) to 75% following completion of this training by all customer service staff, saving approximately £18,000 in the first full year and improving customer satisfaction ratings by at least 7%."

It is important to show financial benefits in actual figures that can be (favourably) compared with the costs of the training because cash is the lowest common denominator by which anything in organizational life can be compared with anything else. I also advise showing the potential costs of not going ahead with the training, just to drive the point home.

If this business case approach is taken it becomes relatively straightforward to check whether the specific predictions actually come true. Of course, like most organizational measurement this is extremely simplistic; all kinds of factors could be having an impact and no doubt could be cited in mitigation if the predicted benefits don't quite materialize, but at least training and development have been shown as investments, rather than simply as costs.

Potential, learning and training are essential factors that combine to precede the statement "I have the ability to do it". By careful assessment of potential, and by active facilitation of individual and collective learning and training, managements can help to raise ability levels significantly, with highly beneficial organizational consequences.

Training may be seen as a cost or as an investment. Either view involves spending money but the natural tendency of management is to reduce costs, whereas investment is seen as the conservation and development of assets. The argument for training as an investment in the organization's future is greatly strengthened if training proposals are treated in the same way as other forms of investment, with a costed business case. Some benefits may be difficult to quantify, but estimates can be made and defended, as with other investment proposals.

Individual learning is the foundation of organizational learning, which will be discussed later.

"I have the ability to do it" checklist

What potential do you personally have that isn't being fully utilized or even recognized at work at the moment?

Can you discover at least one talent that you didn't previously know about in each of your colleagues?

How, if at all, do you evaluate "facts" you learn from sources such as teachers, books, newspapers, broadcasting, etc., before accepting them as "true"?

Have you completed a learning styles questionnaire? (If not, you can do one online at **www.peterhoney.com** or in Honey & Mumford's books. Find out about your learning style(s) before undertaking your next learning activity.)

What do you need to do to broaden your learning styles repertoire?

What could you do to facilitate the learning of someone at work?

What would you benefit from learning at this point in your career?

What does your employer need you to learn?

How similar are these two lists?

Can you define, in a few words, your level of ability in a key aspect of your job?

What kind(s) of planned experience – internal and/or external – would enhance your ability to do your job, or your career prospects?

How could you arrange to get that experience in the near future?

Could you arrange such experience for someone who reports to you?

If you apply the evaluation matrix approach to a current training proposal, does it indicate a different decision from the one you would otherwise have made?

Can you construct a business case for a training activity you or one of your people wishes to undertake? If not, what prevents you?

What are the potential costs of *not* going ahead with the training?

notes and references

1 Herriot, P (1989) *Recruitment in the 90s,* Wimbledon, IPM

2 Gray, RJ (2001) *Cluster Profiling in Personnel Selection,* Chelmsford, Earlybrave Publications

3 Fletcher, BC (1988) "The epidemiology of occupational stress", in CL Cooper & R Payne (eds), *Causes, Coping and Consequences Of Stress At Work,* Chichester, John Wiley

4 Cox, T & Griffiths, A (1995) "The nature and measurement of work stress: theory and practice", in JR Wilson & E N Corlett (eds) *Evaluation Of Human Work,* 2nd edn, London, Taylor & Francis

5 Bass, BM & Vaughan, JA (1966) *Training in Industry – The Management of Learning,* London, Tavistock Publications

6 Ramsden, P (1992) *Learning to Teach in Higher Education,* London, Routledge

7 OID (1975) *The Oxford Illustrated Dictionary,* 2nd edn, Oxford, OUP

8 Thorndike, EL (1911) *Animal Intelligence: Experimental Studies,* New York, Macmillan

9 Skinner, BF (1938) *The Behavior of Organisms,* New York, Appleton-Century-Crofts

10 Kolb, D, Rubin, I & McIntyre, J (1974) *Organizational Psychology, a Book of Readings,* 2nd edn, Englewood Cliffs, NJ, Prentice Hall

11 Honey, P & Mumford, A (1982) *A Manual of Learning Styles,* Maidenhead, Peter Honey

12 www.peterhoney.com.

13 Knowles, MS (1980) *The Modern Practice of Adult Education: from Pedagogy to Andragogy,* Englewood Cliffs, NJ, Prentice Hall

14 Ramsden P (1992) *Learning to Teach in Higher Education,* London, Routledge

15 Argyris, C (1999) *On Organizational Learning,* 2nd edn, Oxford, Blackwell

16 Boydell, TH (1983) *A Guide to the Identification of Training Needs,* London, BACIE

17 Peter, LJ & Hull, R (1969) *The Peter Principle,* Souvenir Press (paperback, 1994)

18 Kenny, J & Reid, M (1988) *Training Interventions,* London, IPM

19 ibid.

4 four

someone (who matters to me) will notice if I do it

relationships and feedback If you were to take a moment to map out, literally, on paper, all the relationships you have with people at work and then to rank them in order of how much their opinion of your day-to-day work really affects you it's likely that you would find that the closeness of the working relationship matters more than rank or seniority. Thus, your immediate boss tends to be towards the top of the list, whilst very senior people may not seem anything like as important. Other contacts: superiors, subordinates, peers, customers, etc. tend to appear on the list in direct proportion to their ability to make our lives easier or harder, and this may have very little to do with their formal position in the organization. The reasons *why* the top two or three people on your list matter to you can say a great deal about the nature of your working environment. It can also be revelatory to analyze just what effect(s) their importance to you actually has on your *behaviour* and how this might change if you had no idea whether or not they noticed how good a job you were doing.

If you are responsible for the performance of other people, showing that you are aware of how they are doing reinforces appropriate behaviours and helps to direct their energies. This is very important. A major survey by the Chartered Institute of Personnel and Development in 2003[1] found a correlation between the relationship with front-line managers and employee attitudes. The higher employees rated their front-line manager, the more committed and productive they were.

But just noticing how well your people are doing isn't enough; somehow you have to tell them about it, too. This is called giving feedback. Feedback acts as a powerful positive or negative reinforcer of behaviours and is one of the most valuable tools available to managers. Broadly, feedback may range from specific to general and from positive to negative, as illustrated in Figure 4.1.

The most effective feedback is positive, and tends towards the specific, referring to specific things someone has *done* rather than what (you think) that person *is*. This reinforces the specific behaviours, helping to embed them in the individual's behaviour patterns, so it's the preferred form of intervention in any manager–subordinate workplace relationship. General positive feedback, for example telling someone how much you respect/admire/like them, is usually harmless and can be very beneficial to both parties but it can be rather insipid and, at worst, downright nauseating.

Negative feedback is sometimes unavoidable. When it has to be given it should also be specific and constructive: pointing out specific behaviours or actions that shouldn't be repeated and giving guidance

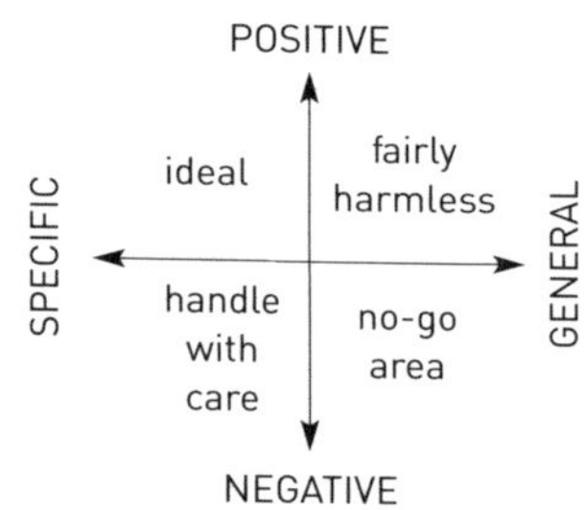

FIG 4.1 ● **Feedback dimensions**

about what should be done instead. It's important to give the recipient time to absorb the feedback, especially if he or she hasn't previously been aware of the shortcomings. Typically, there's an emotional process of response to negative feedback, similar to the process which follows any kind of unwelcome news. This follows the acronym SARA:

Shock or surprise,

Anger or annoyance,

Resistance,

Acceptance.

Unexpected negative feedback is likely to be received initially with a kind of numbness and a lack of understanding. As this wears off it may be followed by feelings of anger, or perhaps more often by disappointment or annoyance. This merges into a resistance phase, where defence mechanisms are deployed, such as aggressive demands for the facts to be substantiated, or outright denial of the facts, shifting the blame and making excuses. These responses may be quite mild, or they may be fierce, which can make giving negative feedback difficult and unpleasant. Some people try to avoid doing it for these reasons, but it is part of a manager's job and shirking it is a dereliction of duty.

The good news is that once these unhelpful phases are out of the way the recipient of the feedback can move into acceptance mode, which is a positive phase where productive questions can be asked for clarification and new forms of behaviour can be thought about and put into practice. The message here is that all four stages are natural. If you are giving negative feedback allow the recipient the space to go through these responses, helping them as much as you can (and don't hold it against them if they say something that isn't very constructive). Then you can build on the acceptance and move on.

If you are the recipient of negative feedback – as we all are from time to time – remember that you are likely to go through this process too. How you handle it can have an impact on your future relationship with the giver of the feedback, especially if he or she doesn't know about SARA.

There is almost never a case for giving negative general feedback. If it isn't believed you will have made an enemy, and if it is believed the damage to the recipient's self-esteem may have serious consequences.

annual event Perhaps the most common way of giving feedback at work is through the mechanism of the appraisal. Although there are many organizations in which appraisals are seldom, if ever, done at all, the norm is probably for them to take place once a year. In fact, the words "annual" and "appraisal" sometimes appear as inseparable as "merry" and "Christmas". Appraisals are often required to serve a variety of purposes such as corrective action, development planning, pay and bonus decisions and promotability assessments, some of which are clearly incompatible. Corrective action to improve performance, and development planning both call for openness and the acknowledgement of weaknesses by the person concerned, whereas most sensible people might prefer to draw attention to their star qualities, rather than their weaknesses, when pay or promotion are at stake. This obvious problem with the single annual appraisal has bothered human resource professionals for as long as that vocation has existed.

The simple solution is to separate the two functions and deal with them at different times. Unfortunately, appraisal is widely perceived as at best a nuisance and often as something of an ordeal by both appraisees and appraisors, so the idea of doing it twice as often tends to be unpopular. This view has some justification. As Charles Handy[2] points out, although the intention of appraisal sessions may be to provide helpful feedback on past performance and suggestions for improvement, they often end up being confrontational and dispiriting. There's a real temptation for appraisees to reject criticism as unjustified or to lower their opinion of the critic so that the criticism doesn't have to be taken seriously. Either response is destructive in that it will block any learning and damage workplace relationships.

appraisal is widely perceived as at best a nuisance

modern approaches to performance management focus on continual feedback

Annual appraisal is also not nearly frequent enough to be of any real value. The feedback being given is so remote from the behaviour being discussed that the mechanisms of reinforcement are unlikely to work.

As well as doubts about the usefulness of the process, its integrity is also open to question. It's very easy for judgements to be made based more on the appraisor's subjective opinions, preferences or style, or on cultural norms, rather than objective criteria.[3]

To address these concerns modern approaches to performance management focus on continual feedback, based on observation of day-to-day behaviours and regular formal or semi-formal dialogues between appraisor and appraisee. The annual appraisal, if it still features in the process, is a summary of progress and formal record of factors which have already been fully explored and are well known to both parties; crucially, it contains no surprises. A typical model might take the form illustrated in Figure 4.2.

At the beginning of the cycle, when the time for formal judgements is still a long way off, a discussion takes place in which objectives are agreed, any questions about the process are resolved, development

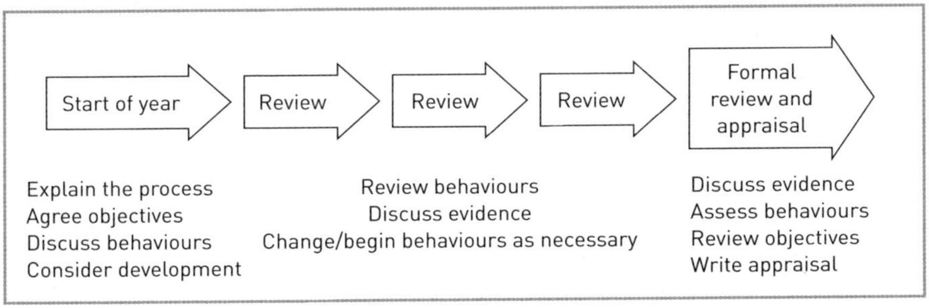

FIG 4.2 ● Performance management model

needs are identified and plans made to address them, and, crucially, the specific *behaviours* that the appraisor will be looking for over the coming year are carefully explained.

At regular intervals during the year dialogues are held during which progress is noted, difficulties are addressed, and the evidence for desirable behaviours is discussed. This gives the appraisee the opportunity to point out things the appraisor may have missed, draw attention to obstacles or difficulties, and make requests. Progress on objectives can be noted and the objectives reviewed as necessary. Above all, if there are any instances of inappropriate behaviours or shortfalls in performance, they can be pointed out and something can be done about them before any formal judgements have to be made. Notes are kept of these dialogues so that when the end of the cycle is reached and the formal appraisal is written it is based on evidence that is, hopefully, agreed or at least is already well known to the appraisee.

competent people The kinds of behaviours that are regarded as appropriate or desirable need to be established by the organization and are necessarily rather subjective. From the early 1980s the term "competencies" has been increasingly used to denote specific applied skills, or in one seminal definition: "those characteristics that differentiate superior performance from average and poor performance".[4]

Characteristics are not, of course, quite the same thing as behaviours but they can be observed as behaviours when they are put into practice. Many organizations base their formal appraisal systems on frameworks of defined competencies, usually based on descriptions of desired behaviours. It can be helpful, although at some risk of being excessively rigid or prescriptive, to specify examples of the kinds of behaviours that would be considered to provide evidence of these competencies. For example, the competency "people management" might be indicated by specific behaviours such as:

- develops cohesive groups/teams
- monitors subordinates' performance
- provides direction in uncertainty

- cultivates a learning environment, which encourages innovation and personal development
- treats others with respect
- encourages people to take responsibility for implementing change.

A study published in 2001[5] listed 41 such behavioural competencies, such as "team orientation", which found a place in the competency frameworks of 78% of the participating organizations, "communication" and "customer focus" (both in 65%), "people management" and "results orientation" (each in 58%) and "problem-solving", which appeared in 55%. Outside this handful of fairly predictable competencies, there was a wide variation in what the hundred organizations that took part in the study seemed to regard as important. It may seem odd, for example, that "interpersonal skills" appeared in only 25% of the frameworks.

Possibly even more surprising, not to say alarming, is that "behaving ethically" and "numeracy" each appeared in only 5% of the frameworks. Does this mean that these behavioural attributes are regarded as unimportant by 95% of UK employers? I would prefer to think that attributes that are taken for granted weren't thought worth mentioning, but personally I believe that a competency framework is incomplete if it leaves out anything that forms part of the "bundle" of attributes on which an individual's contribution will be assessed. If you want employees to behave ethically, make it explicitly part of the assessment, otherwise at least some of them will think you aren't concerned about it.

It's worth pointing out here that competency models like this have been criticised on a number of grounds.[6] It is suggested that, however useful it may be, the competency approach tends to be quite superficial in its application and suffers from several other inherent weaknesses, among which are the tendency to ignore or marginalize cultural and social contexts, the way competency frameworks tend to exaggerate hierarchy, and the dependence of such models on the people involved being highly rational in their decision-making, which is a very dubious assumption indeed, as we will see later.

Whilst the encouragement or reinforcement of appropriate behaviours is an extremely valuable factor in promoting good performance, probably the most significant elements in the whole process are the continual interaction between boss and subordinate and the interest the boss shows in the subordinate's work; "the best fertilizer is the farmer's boot". Care is needed not to let this interest become intrusive; people need space and discretion, as we will see later, but done sensitively and constructively this is a key component of good management practice.

leadership

Managing the performance of others is often characterized as "leadership". Leadership is a very popular topic for management writers, although it is rather noticeable that many writers dealing explicitly with the subject of leadership avoid giving a definition of it. Perhaps the commonest component of definitions found in the literature concerns exercising influence in one way or another. This is quite helpful since it implies, at least, that the exercisers of influence have some ideas of their own about what they want to achieve, or what they want other people to do. In other words, they have vision, and are proactive in trying to turn that vision into reality by involving other people.

In this way we can define leadership in terms of two key constituents: knowing what should be done, and influencing others to cooperate in doing it. Neither of these elements really depends on any formal recognition of authority – although this may well be a factor in how much influence, in practice, a person can exercise over others – both elements seem to be more concerned with the individual.

For a long time organizations have sought to understand what qualities an individual must possess in order to be a good leader; and perhaps even more importantly, how to foster and develop these qualities. Ideas about this have tended to focus on a key question: is leadership a function of what someone *is* or is it a function of what someone *does*? These two opposing views have not been found to provide many useful answers on their own so it has been suggested that the *situation* in which leadership is practised must (sometimes) be taken into account as well. This produces a range of theories, or perspectives, about leadership, which I will briefly review here.

born to lead First, *trait* theories of leadership are based on the idea that leaders are born, not made, which should mean that they can "do" leadership in almost any situation. This used to be a popular viewpoint, the logical conclusion of which is represented by the notion of the divine right of kings to rule over their kingdoms. So popular and prevailing was this view that disagreeing with it could often prove fatal. Researchers working from this orientation have tended to examine the attributes of "great" leaders and attempted to identify common characteristics, or traits. This immediately raises a serious difficulty. If you were asked to list the "great" leaders in history it's quite likely that your list would include a selection of "saints", "heroes" and probably a few "monsters" too. Of course, on closer examination some of the heroes turn out to have been monsters, whilst some of the monsters can be seen as heroes from another perspective and many saints have at least some less-than-saintly characteristics.

The real problem is that few consistent traits have been reliably identified. It's true that intelligence, self-confidence and a desire for power seem to feature quite often[7] but these might be simply qualities that help people achieve positions of influence, rather than useful attributes of leaders in themselves. Some of the leadership "triumphs" of famous historical figures often look more like strokes of luck when rigorously examined, and the same applies to many of the successes listed in the autobiographies of well-known characters from industry.

Acknowledgement of these weaknesses in trait theory led to a modified version, known as *contingency* theory. Contingency perspectives on leadership are still founded in the notion that some people possess inherent qualities that make them more capable than other people of being leaders, but they acknowledge that these special leadership qualities need to be matched to the specific demands of the situation. According to these ideas, people who have leadership qualities possess first a realistic understanding of their own leadership skills. They also have a heightened awareness of context so that they can quickly assess the degree of match or mismatch between themselves and the situation and judge when their particular leadership skill-set will be helpful and when it would be better to step back.[8]

Both these perspectives on leadership are based on the notion that leaders are somehow different from other people, so to ensure an adequate supply of leaders organizations whose bosses hold either of these views would, logically, concentrate on *selecting* the right people rather than relying on development; you can't make a silk purse out of a sow's ear. Believers in trait theory might feel they had done enough once a "leader" had been appointed, but supporters of the contingency approach don't assume that leaders can always lead effectively, regardless of the situation, so they would be likely to see some benefits in the development of natural leaders' capabilities for analyzing situations, and in actions aimed at enhancing potential leaders' self-awareness.

Trait and contingency theories may also have the effect of preserving the status quo; after all, if leadership ability is an attribute people are born with it follows that people who are in positions of power and authority are probably there because they are the *right* people to be there. This leads to a justification of hierarchies – organizational, social and political – on the grounds of "natural selection". It's difficult to evaluate this view because there is no practical way of knowing who else might have done the job just as well, or better.

do the right thing

Increasing dissatisfaction with these explanations led to the development of *situational* theories of leadership, which leave behind the notion that leadership is some kind of inherited talent and focus instead on what leaders *do*. In situational approaches the context is the most important thing; good leadership can be achieved if the context is well-understood and the leader's actions are adjusted to suit the needs of the moment. So, supporters of situational perspectives believe that leadership can be taught and learned.

Variations on the situational approach were explored by a number of researchers and management writers during the 1970s and 80s. Some of the suggestions arising from this work about how managers ought to handle different kinds of situation have been captured in some well-known models that are still taught in management schools today, but they are – in my view at least – rather contaminated by the prevailing assumptions of their era.

Perhaps the most familiar model is the "leadership scale" devised by Tannenbaum & Schmidt.[9] In this model, the leader is advised to choose a leadership style that is appropriate for the particular situation. These styles, or behaviours, can be placed along a continuum ranging from "boss-centered" at one end of the scale to "subordinate-centered" at the other end, as illustrated in Figure 4.3.

Inevitably, the opposite poles of this "continuum" have been labelled Authoritarian (or task-centred), and Democratic (or people-centred) and the inference has been drawn that a concern for getting the job done is at the opposite end of the scale from the people involved. Tannenbaum & Schmidt's article isn't as shallow as that, but, like it or not, the impression is left that the two concerns are somehow incompatible.

Other commentators[10] advised that authoritarian leadership styles would be most effective in situations that were "favourable to the leader" and democratic styles would better suit situations that were "unfavourable to the leader". "Favourable" in this context means that the leader has high formal authority, relations between the leader and

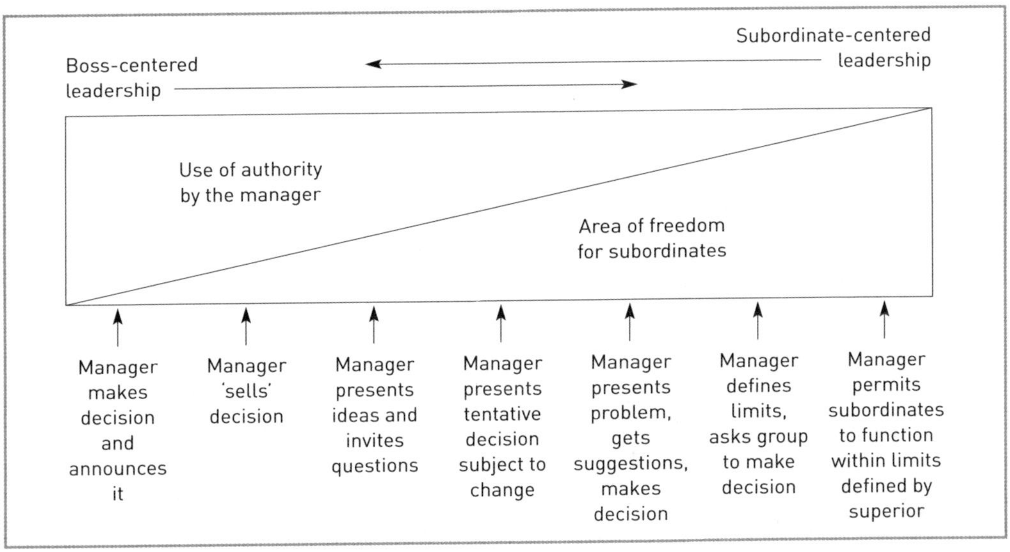

FIG 4.3 ● Tannenbaum & Schmidt's leadership scale

Source: Reprinted by permission of *Harvard Business Review*: Exhibit 1, Continuum of leadership behaviour, from "How to choose a leadership pattern" by R Tannenbaum & WH Schmidt, May–June 1973.

the staff are good, and the task is highly structured. This further reinforces the assumption that democratic styles are for leaders to fall back on when things aren't going entirely their way; they wouldn't want to be democratic if it could be avoided.

My advice here, based on experience and more recent research, is quite the opposite. The democratic styles should be the preferred option, falling back on authoritarian styles only when circumstances require it. For example, when the fire alarm sounds tell everyone to leave the building, don't hold a discussion about the best course of action. Or, when something bad can't be avoided, accept your responsibility as a manager and give instructions clearly and assertively. Otherwise, the benefits of bringing several brains to bear on an issue, and the commitment that democratic approaches tend to foster, usually outweigh the inevitable untidiness of getting everyone involved in decision-making.

Interestingly, research into animal social groups[11] has found that decisions arrived at communally – or "democratically" – are usually more beneficial for the group and its individual members than "despotic" decision-making, and tend to be less extreme. Whether lessons drawn from the observation of animal behaviour can usefully be applied directly to human groups (even in the corporate jungle) depends on how much corroborating evidence there is. You may wish to reserve judgement until you've finished reading this book.

The situational school of thought is still advocated, although in slightly modified forms which take account of the needs "followers" have. One such model[12] positions leadership behaviour against two axes: "task" or "guidance" behaviour and "relationship" or "supportive" behaviour. If followers are confident, willing and able to perform the task, they don't need either much guidance or much support, so the leader can safely delegate. If they are able, but unwilling or lacking in confidence, the leader is advised to encourage "participation" by sharing ideas and facilitating decision-making. If followers are willing and confident but lack ability, the leader should "sell" ideas by explaining and clarifying decisions. If they lack ability, they're unwilling and they lack confidence, then the leader needs to "tell" them what to do by giving clear instructions and monitoring performance closely.

To the extent that this "improved" model treats followers with some respect and acknowledges that people have differing levels of ability, confidence and motivation, I find it more appealing and more consistent with current sociological research than earlier models. You must make your own assessment but a piece of generic advice which applies here is not to try to work in a style which is incompatible with your own personality. Be consistent, treat others with respect, and be yourself.

From the situational perspective leadership skills are based on knowing what to do in various situations, so training and development become paramount in ensuring that everyone who might be required to lead others is equipped with this skill-set, as with the other skills required by managers.

appearance is reality The fourth perspective on leadership that I want to consider here is perhaps the most difficult. From the *"constructivist"* perspective it isn't helpful to dwell either on the attributes possessed by leaders or on factors in the situation, because it's impossible to assess either objectively; everything is "constructed" in the minds of the participants.

From this perspective, what matters is not what the situation or the leader are really like, but rather the processes by which the mental constructs are formed by the people involved. This is highly subjective because what a leader or his or her followers understand about a situation may depend on what information has been provided to them, and what they did with it by way of mental processing when they'd got it. This means that from the constructivist perspective neither choosing nor developing leaders is a meaningful activity. What matters here is to try to maintain some control over how situations are *perceived* by people who matter and to ensure that the appearance of leadership is maintained or enhanced. This is not purely "spin"; from this perspective leadership really *is* – and always was – the *management of perceptions*. This is the way to get things done through other people and to ensure that, as far as possible, people are happy with what's been done and perceive it to have been a "success".

The four perspectives on leadership described above represent a progression of theoretical explanations, illustrated in Figure 4.4.

These begin with the simplistic, but socially convenient, "great man" concepts in which leadership qualities are seen as inherent – or inherited – attributes conferring a right to lead. They are then modified to allow the possibility that a variety of inherent attributes might usefully be matched to specific situations, and perhaps enhanced through appropriate development and training. Next, we see the idea of inherent attributes discarded; leadership is now seen as a function of adopting the "right" style or taking the "right" action for the circumstances. Finally, we move to a constructivist, postmodern perspective in which nothing is objectively "real". Reality is what it's perceived to be by the participants in the situation and leadership consists in managing these perceptions.

All four perspectives are alive and well in modern organizations. Perhaps the "pure" form of *trait* perspective – meaning the belief that someone has the right and the ability to lead simply because they were born that way – is now something of a minority view, but in its modified form as the *contingency* perspective it isn't at all unusual.

Most of today's leadership literature plays down what's disparagingly called the "great man" concept and focuses instead on leadership as more of a facilitation role, the success of which is heavily dependent on organizational context and climate.[13,14] The emphasis is on teamwork,[15] with all participants making their individual contributions and the leadership function working to coordinate and harmonize their efforts. This is what John Adair[16] calls the "orchestra or jazz band model, where you

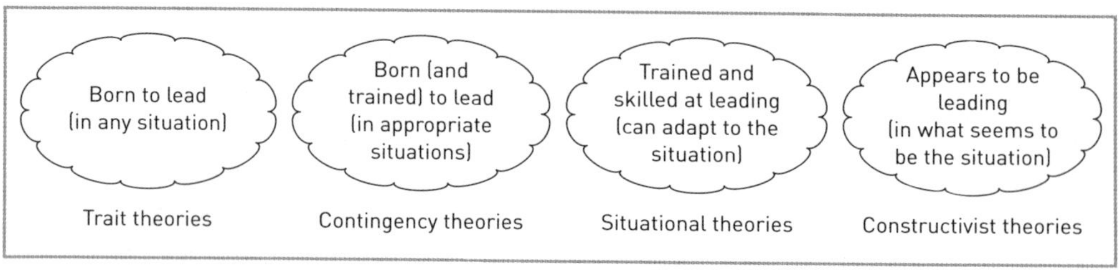

FIG 4.4 Perspectives on leadership

charismatic leaders can be something of a liability

are part of a team but also an outstanding and creative individual". This puts the leader in the role of conductor who "reconciles and harmonizes the individual and the team".

The scepticism shown for the "great man" concept seems to be borne out by research. For example, an extensive survey published in 2001[17] found that, whilst "charismatic" leaders (i.e. those who "strongly articulate an organizational vision, expect high performance from those around them and show determination") tended to produce confidence, respect and even affection in their "followers", charismatic leadership qualities seemed to be unrelated to the performance of the companies studied, except where the business environment was uncertain and volatile, when it did seem to help to a modest extent.

In fact, it seems that charismatic leaders can be something of a liability; their powerful personalities can be damaging to the self-esteem and confidence of those around them[18] and their strength and assertiveness tend to suppress dissent and alternative views. This is dangerous for organizations because access to a range of opinions is a vital ingredient of healthy decision-making. As Keith Grint[19] puts it: "leaders worry about whether they can secure consent, but it may be that securing dissent is the key to long-term success. ... Leaders who think they are infallible tend to surround themselves with yes-men and their arrogance generates a sea of destructive consent – irresponsible followers whose sycophancy imperils the organization". What happens then is that dissenters tend to become marginalized precisely when leaders need independent advice. In time the information flow becomes "sclerotic to the point where only the party line is permitted" and the leader no longer has access to objective information.

leading or managing? All this suggests that trait and contingency perspectives have been effectively dismissed by management thinkers, and *situational* perspectives now predominate. Explicitly, this is probably true but my, admittedly fairly subjective, observation is that *constructivist* ideas implicitly permeate almost all forms of leadership. The management of perceptions is a priority, almost an obsession, in politics, commerce, industry, the media and academia. I surmise that this would not be the case if it wasn't perceived to pay off, so, however cynical it may seem, I incline towards a constructivist viewpoint of leadership. Having admitted that, I'm not sure that it really matters very much. Most of the useful elements of the situational perspective – and I find John Adair's "conductor" and "jazz band" analogies particularly helpful – seem to be concerned with the activity of *managing* rather than with the almost abstract concept of leadership. I tend to agree with Richard Reeves[20] when he suggests that the pressing need today is for fewer leaders and more managers:

> Leaders don't burn the midnight oil poring over the accounts, they spend two days at scenario-planning exercises. They don't make tough decisions about who to hire and fire, they create a climate of creativity. Leadership is a lot more fun. Who wouldn't rather focus on broad-brush strategic issues, rather than getting to the bottom of why the figures for sales leads in the information systems are so erratic? There is a point at which the adoption of a leadership style amounts to the abdication of management responsibility ... Inspiration is nice, but we need some honest perspiration from executives.

power, influence and trust

The notion of leadership is linked in several ways to the concepts of power and influence, and organizations could hardly continue to exist if people within them did not exercise power and influence over other people. Before we can consider these important organizational forces, however, we need to define their meanings. The entry for the word *power* in the *Oxford English Dictionary* fills five and a half densely-printed pages, so it clearly isn't possible simply to assume that it means the same thing to everyone, even when used in similar contexts. For the present purpose I'll make use of a definition of power as "the ability of an individual or group to ensure that another individual or group complies with its wishes".[21] This definition ignores any kinds of power except those concerned with human relationships, but this is what mostly concerns us here. In this definition the wishes of the individuals or groups over whom power is exercised don't really matter very much; they have to comply even if they don't want to. *Influence*, on the other hand, leaves people with some choices; the exercise of influence is to do with conscious or unconscious *persuasion*. Influence cannot ensure compliance, but it can often achieve it by more subtle means.

We should start by looking at the nature of power in a little more depth. A basic truth about the nature of power is that it is essentially perceptual: a construct.[22] In other words, another person's power will have no relevance for us unless we believe in it. If we believe someone has power over us, then they have, even if an objective outside observer would see no basis in "reality" for our belief.

In a workplace, power may take several forms and derive from a variety of sources.

do it or ...

Perhaps the most obvious kind of power is the power to coerce. *Coercion* can take various forms. At its most basic level, it may be raw physical power, which is perhaps not usually found in work organizations but may be seen occasionally in such settings as picket lines or lock-outs, bullying or the physical presence of a dictatorial boss.[23] The more common form in which coercive power is encountered at work is as "the ability to deprive",[24] or the ability and willingness to inflict penalties in quite a broad sense of the word, including such things as: "humiliation and other forms of oral abuse, withdrawal of friendship and emotional support, loss of favours and privileges such as allocation to desirable work, curtailment of promotion opportunities and delayed pay rises".[25]

It is important to reiterate here that coercive power only works if the "victims" believe that the penalty can and will be imposed, and also find the potential penalty sufficiently undesirable to make it worthwhile to change their behaviour. In this respect it has a great deal in common with expectancy theories of human motivation, but in a wholly negative way. The probability of the penalty actually being imposed, rather than merely threatened, is a key factor in the effectiveness of coercive power.

In early eighteenth-century England, picking pockets was a crime punishable by death. Executions were carried out in public, watched by large crowds. Pickpockets routinely operated among these crowds, which suggests that they had low expectations of actually being caught and hanged, and the profits outweighed this low-level risk.

In any case, punishment (negative reinforcement) is known to be much less effective than reward (positive reinforcement) at producing changes in behaviour, especially long-term changes. Earlier, I categorized people who threaten us as enemies, and pointed out that few people would work willingly and enthusiastically to further an enemy's objectives. This, I think, indicates the place of coercive power in the manager's toolkit.

do it and ... *Reward* power, which is also called resource power or remunerative power, is more positive than coercive power. This kind of power arises from the (perceived) control over rewards that the potential recipient desires, such as promotions, pay rises, perks or status. Of course, people may value a range of different things, including approval and recognition, and the ability to manipulate symbols of these less tangible objects of desire, such as public commendations, is a variation of resource power known as "normative power". Again, it is the perceptions of the people over whom the power is exercised that make the difference; if people believe rewards will be forthcoming then the perceived controller of the rewards will have power regardless of whether, in reality, he or she actually possesses that control.[26]

The use of reward power carries some risks; the earlier discussion of the role of reward in motivation should have indicated a need for caution in using rewards simplistically as a management tool. Also, what is intended as reward may be perceived as coercion if people expect to receive it but feel they are being threatened with having the reward withheld.[27]

you *should* do it The third kind of power in organizations is called *position* power, or *legitimate* or sometimes *legal* power. Position power is based on the formal role of the individual within the organization, and so is broadly equivalent to the concept of *authority*. Position power is often signified by organizational symbols like a job title or a job-related personal designation: director, chairman, professor, doctor, matron, captain, which followers see as conferring on the leader the right to give orders.[28] It is this belief that someone has the *right* to give orders, and that others have an obligation to obey them, which is the basis of this kind of power.

Position power is backed up by – perhaps even derived in its entirety from – the power of the organization and to this extent it is, as Charles Handy says,[29] ultimately underwritten by either physical power or resource power. This is quite an important point. If you were to list everyone in your organization who you feel has the right to give you instructions, and then delete from that list all those whom you would obey either because doing so may bring you some form of reward or because not to do so might bring adverse consequences, the remaining list would probably be quite short. Position power also often contains a strong element of resource power, not simply in the control of rewards but also in the access a formal position often gives to networks and information flows.[30] Information is an extremely valuable resource and access to networks – having the right contacts – can be crucial in getting your own way.

For these reasons position power should usually be thought of as a surrogate for other forms of power. At the risk of being thought subversive, I would suggest that a quick analysis of the kind described above can be quite useful in determining just how much power someone else actually has over your freedom of action, but don't forget that their access to networks can be used for you or against you, and they may know things you don't know.

I advise you to do it *Expert* power is the power that someone has because of his or her expertise. It is comparative; anyone is an expert who knows more than anyone else around.[31] Expert power doesn't depend on job title or organizational position but is perhaps best seen as a special kind of resource power, in the sense that the expert has (i.e. controls) skills and/or knowledge that are needed by someone else.

Expert power is one of the few forms of organizational power that can be exercised covertly; someone with specialized skills or knowledge can sometimes apply them to make things happen without anyone else being aware that it's going on.

In some ways *personal* power, or *charisma*, has a lot in common with expert power, but it rests on something rather less tangible than demonstrable skills or knowledge. It depends almost entirely on the attractiveness to others of the individual's personality and the willingness or positive desire of other people to comply with his or her wishes or advice. When the charisma of the holder of personal power is such that other people feel that they want to be like, copy or emulate him or her, this form of power is more precisely defined as *referent* power.

Personal power can be rather ephemeral. It can be "enhanced by position or by expert status, so that a Prime Minister loses some of his charisma when he leaves office, and the sports star fades when dropped from the team. ... It is elusive, is fanned by success and by self-confidence and can evaporate in defeat".[32] On the more mundane level, it may only take one bad mistake, a mean or unkind act, or just an unfortunate combination of circumstances for the charisma to fade. On the other hand, most of us have met people who seem to be able to get away with almost anything.

resistance movement The last kind of power that we will consider here is *negative* power; the power to spoil, block or sabotage. This isn't really a distinct form of organizational power, but rather the negative or illegitimate application of one of the other forms. Negative power may be used as a political instrument: to block the progress of rivals, or to damage competing projects, and so on. Perhaps more insidious, and therefore potentially even more damaging, it may be used as a "resistance weapon" by those who perceive themselves as powerless in the organization. This can take two forms, which Helga Drummond[33] calls "resistance by distance" and "resistance by persistence". The first occurs when employees try to evade management control by "distancing" themselves physically or symbolically, avoiding social contact, maintaining "them and us" attitudes, and doing just the bare minimum of work. "Resistance by persistence" may involve holding management to account, challenging decisions, and demanding greater involvement in the organization.

The need for some control, however minimal, over some aspect of their existence that is felt by people who perceive themselves to be powerless is a well-documented phenomenon in the human experience that has been recorded by several observers of such extreme situations as imprisonment and slavery. Bruno Bettleheim, a psychologist who was interned in Nazi concentration camps in the late 1930s, observed that survival often depended upon retaining some degree of control over decisions, however trivial, which could reassure the inmate that he still functioned as a human being. People who find themselves in a work situation where they feel powerless may try to "win back" some personal control by exercising the negative power that is available to them. For example, "among Roman slaves (and later among Afro-American slaves) the most common form of resistance took the form of guile, lying and indolence. Personal or communal foot-dragging which hindered their owners' economic aims gave slaves a decisive role in their own lives".[34] This can be surprisingly effective. According to one eighteenth-century writer, a slave "without much violence of metaphor, may be compared to a bad pump, the working of which exhausts your strength before you can produce a drop of water".[35]

Of course, modern work organizations have nothing in common with such extreme situations(!), but there may be lessons to be learned. In a Western, twenty-first-century workplace, issues of physical survival are mainly confined to the health and safety context, although this obviously doesn't mean they can be overlooked. But the basics of human nature don't go away simply because they are required to function in a modern workplace. If people perceive themselves to be powerless they

people who feel powerless may try to "win back" personal control

are likely to take whatever steps are available to them to give themselves some feeling of control over their working lives. This may take the forms of "resistance" defined by Helga Drummond, and doing only what is measured, and even that without enthusiasm. It may lead to militancy or support for extremist viewpoints. Or it may go further, including denigrating the organization or senior personalities, or even direct sabotage of procedures, systems or property.

Of course, unless the perpetrator is very careless, the organization will never find out whether or to what extent some of these forms of resistance are being practised. For this reason, even if ethical or humane motives are not enough, it's vital for managements to do their best to ensure that people are not left feeling powerless in their work situation. Individual managers can contribute to this by considering what they can personally do to ensure that people on their teams feel that they have adequate control over their working lives.

gentle persuasion *Influence* works in similar ways to power, in the sense that one person suspends their own judgement and accepts the judgement of another. Unlike power, though, influence works through the voluntary acceptance of suggestions, rather than through any obligation to comply. Some of the kinds of power described over the preceding pages also function as bases of influence; experts, people with senior positions in the organization and people with charisma all find it easier to influence others, even if they lack, or choose not to apply, actual power.

Other factors also tend to increase influence. Researchers[36,37] have found that we are more likely to agree to requests and suggestions of people we know and like, people close to us or with similar tastes and interests to ourselves, and people we find attractive.[38] According to Matt Ridley[39] we are genetically programmed to remember, and evaluate, favours that are done to us and we have a built-in predisposition to repay the "debt" if we can. Stephen Covey[40] calls this our "emotional bank account"; we make "deposits" of favours or kindnesses with another person, and this entitles us to make "withdrawals" when we need them. Of course, the more contact we have with someone the more opportunities there are likely to be to receive and repay favours, building up a strong relationship of reciprocity which may be one of the foundations of social living.

building trust We are much more likely to allow ourselves to be influenced by someone if we *trust* them (assuming that we play an active role in the process of being influenced, which is another – and more complex – issue that I won't try to address here). Trust is an emotive word, which captures many very basic human feelings. Stripped of its emotional content, though, trust comes down to an assessment of the predictability of another person's behaviour; we have expectations, or make predictions, about what other people are going to do, and if we feel confident that our predictions will turn out to be right, we feel trust in those people.[41] This explanation isn't quite satisfactory, because use of the word trust is normally reserved for situations in which we feel we can predict that the other person will act in a way that is beneficial to ourselves. If we feel reasonably confident that the other person will behave in a way that will cause us harm, then the criterion of predictability is fulfilled but we probably wouldn't use the word "trust" to define our feelings.

In assessing the extent to which we feel able to trust people or groups at work, such as an immediate boss, immediate reports, top management, or peers with whom we have everyday work-based contact, it would be quite normal to give qualified answers. For example, you might trust your boss in some circumstances or over certain matters, but in other contexts you might have some doubts. Similarly, you might well trust your people to carry out their usual duties conscientiously and skilfully, but be more cautious about trusting them with something less usual, especially if you could be exposed to some personal risk if they let you down. Generally speaking, trust is a product of past experience; the longer we have known someone and the more dealings we have had with them, the more information we have available on which to base predictions about their future behaviour; i.e. to trust them.

generally speaking, trust is a product of past experience

Most people like to be regarded as "trustworthy", but unfortunately there are no short-cuts to building trust. You have to show consistent patterns of behaviour so that other people begin to feel confident that they know how you will behave in a new situation. As Charles Handy[42] advises, "trust must be given if it is to be received". "Trust is a fragile commodity. Like glass, once shattered, it is never the same again".

In Chapter 4 I've tried to link the ideas of feedback, leadership, power, influence and trust, all of which are important elements of the behavioural dimension that responds to the knowledge that "someone who matters to me will notice if I do it". Feedback shows that what we have done has been noticed by someone else, but this is of little consequence if that person's opinion is not valued, or has no implications for the happiness or wellbeing of the recipient. Leadership – to the extent that it's a meaningful concept – is characterized by the value attached to the leader's opinions, and power, influence and trust all contribute to making one person's opinion of another's performance something that actually matters.

"Active noticing" – being aware of people's performance and making that awareness known to them – is perhaps the most important single factor in promoting excellence at work.

"Someone (who matters to me) will notice if I do it" checklist

In your workplace, whose opinion of you/your work matters most to you?

Why is this?

How are you told about your performance at work?

Is giving feedback valued as a management skill?

What improvements could you personally put in place right now?

Who do you admire as a "leader"? Why?

What is the dominant perspective on leadership in your organization: (a) some people are born with leadership skills, (b) some people have natural leadership skills that need to be matched to different situations, (c) leadership can be learned, (d) situations and perceptions should be managed so that people have confidence in their leaders?

How do you feel about it?

What would be the benefits and drawbacks, for you, if you made your own leadership style a little more "democratic"?

In the workplace context, do you think "leaders" are different from "managers"?

If so, in what way(s)?

What are the main sources of power in your organization, in order of importance?

Who do you think has the right to give you instructions?

Who has personal or referent power in your organization?

How is it used?

Who influences you most at work? Why?

Who is influenced by you? Why?

What is the value to you of being thought trustworthy?

What can you do to make yourself (more) trusted?

notes and references

1 CIPD (2003) "Motivation linked to line managers", *People Management,* 4 December, 10

2 Handy, C (1985) *Understanding Organisations,* Harmondsworth, Penguin.

3 Johnson, P & Gill, J (1993) *Management Control and Organizational Behaviour,* London, Paul Chapman Publishing

4 Boyatzis, R (1982) *The Competent Manager: A Model for Effective Performance,* New York, John Wiley

5 Miller, L, Rankin, N & Neathey, F (2001) *Competency Frameworks in UK Organizations,* London, CIPD

6 Salaman, G & Taylor, S (2002) "Competency's consequences: changing the character of managerial work", Paper presented to the ESRC Critical Management Studies seminar *Managerial Work,* Judge Institute of Management, Cambridge University

7 Bass, BM (1990) *Bass and Stogdill's Handbook of Leadership: Theory, Research and Applications,* New York, Free Press

8 Grint, K (1997) *Leadership,* Oxford, Oxford University Press

9 Tannenbaum, R & Schmidt, WH (1973) "How to choose a leadership pattern", *Harvard Business Review,* May/June, 162–80

10 Fiedler, FE, Chemers, ME & Mahar, L (1978) *The Leadership Match Concept,* Chichester, Wiley

11 Conradt, L & Roper, TJ (2003) "Group decision-making in animals", *Nature,* 421, 155–8

12 Hersey, P & Blanchard, KH (1993) *Management of Organizational Behavior: Utilizing Human Resources,* 6th edn, Englewood Cliffs, NJ, Prentice Hall

13 Maccoby, M (2001) "Making sense of the leadership literature", *Research Technology Management,* September–October, 58–60

14 Useem, M (2001) quoted in Breen B, "Trickle-up Leadership", *Fast Company,* November

15 Bennis, W (2001) "Leading in unnerving times", *Sloan Management Review,* Winter, 97–103

16 Adair, J (2002) Interviewed by Sarah Powell in "Spotlight on John Adair", *Emerald Now*, available at: www.emeraldinsight.com

17 Waldman, DA, Ramirez, G, House, RJ & Puranam, P (2001) "Does leadership matter?", *Academy of Management Journal*, **44** (1), 134–44

18 Binney, G (2003) Interviewed in "Bad luck charm?", *People Management,* 23 October, 10

19 Grint, K (2003) "Leadership lessons from the war", *People Management,* 17 April, 26

20 Reeves, R (2002) "Reality bites", *Management Today,* September, 35

21 Arnold, J, Cooper, CL & Robertson, IT (1998) *Work Psychology,* 3rd edn, Harlow, Financial Times/Prentice Hall

22 Fiol, CM, O'Conner, EJ & Aguinis, H (2001) "All for one and one for all? The development and transfer of power across organizational levels", *Academy of Management Review,* **26** (2), 224–242

23 Handy, *Understanding Organisations*, op. cit.

24 French, JRP & Raven, B (1968) "The bases of social power" in D Cartwright and A Zander (eds) *Group Dynamics,* New York, Harper and Row

25 Huczynski, A & Buchanan, D (1991) *Organizational Behaviour,* 2nd edn, Hemel Hempstead, Prentice Hall International

26 ibid.

27 Gray, RJ (2000) "Organizational Climate and the Competitive Edge", in L Lloyd-Reason & S Wall (eds) *Dimensions of Competitiveness: Issues and Policies,* Cheltenham, Edward Elgar Publishing

28 Huczynski & Buchanan, *Organizational Behaviour,* op. cit.

29 Handy, *Understanding Organisations*, op. cit.

30 ibid.

31 ibid., p.126

32 ibid., p.127

33 Drummond H, (2000), *Introduction to Organizational Behaviour*, Oxford, Oxford University Press

34 Walvin, J (1983) *Slavery and the Slave Trade,* London, Macmillan Press

35 Patterson, O (1967) *The Sociology Of Slavery,* UK, Macgibbon and Kee

36 Cialdini, RB (1984) *Influence: How and Why People Agree to Things,* New York, William Morrow

37 Pfeffer, J (1992) *Managing With Power: Politics and Influence in Organizations,* Boston, MA, Harvard Business School Press

38 Ross, J & Ferris, A (1981) "Interpersonal attraction and organizational outcomes: a field examination", *Administrative Science Quarterly,* 26, 617–32

39 Ridley, M (1996) *The Origins of Virtue,* London, Viking

40 Covey, S (1992) *The Seven Habits of Highly Effective People,* London, Simon & Schuster

41 Clegg, SR & Hardy, C (1996) "Representations", in SR Clegg, C Hardy & WR Nord (eds) *Handbook of Organization Studies,* London, Sage

42 Handy, *Understanding Organisations*, op. cit.

5 five

I know how well I'm doing it

self-evaluation Unless we know what the results of our actions have been, we can't modify them in order to produce the precise behaviour needed.[1] The technical term for this is "knowledge of results", which is a rather clumsy expression so people more commonly talk about "feedback" although strictly speaking "feedback" is a more limited concept. But knowledge of results alone isn't enough to answer the question "how well am I doing?" Any assessment of our own performance is quite a complex process involving both some form of measurement and also a set of criteria against which the meaning of the measurement can be evaluated. Good performance at work depends to some extent on ensuring that there is a high level of commonality between the package of measures and criteria being applied by the individual, and that being applied by his or her boss.

meaningful measures There are a variety of ways in which we can gain information about how well we are doing, or have done, something. They fall into two broad categories: objective measurement systems, and our subjective perceptions of the views other people hold. Perhaps the simplest and most reliable is to have a clear, objective, system of measurement. For example, to assess her performance at running four hundred metres an athlete would use a stopwatch, which would tell her without any "emotional contamination" exactly how long she had taken to run the distance. If she used this objective timing device repeatedly over a number of attempts, she would be able to tell – without the involvement of anyone else – whether her performance was improving, staying roughly the same, or getting worse. This might be all she needs or wants to know. However, if she knew about the basic principle of goal setting – that:

> persons assigned (and adopting) difficult and specific goals outperform persons provided "do your best" (vague and non-specific) goal assignment[2]

– she might also wish to set herself a target, or benchmark. In which case her timings would also tell her just how much more improvement was needed before she could expect to achieve the objective she had set herself. A target like this acts as one of the criteria against which objective performance measuring can be made meaningful.

The athlete's personal evaluation of "how well she was doing" could be a much more complicated assessment than this, though. It would be easy enough to see that she was taking so-many-point-something seconds more than her target time to run the distance, but other factors would have been involved in determining what that target should be. What were her expectations of herself? Should she be aiming at Olympic standards, school sports averages, or something in between? Somehow, before she set the target she would have needed to decide what class of athlete she believed herself to be.

The expectations we have of ourselves can influence the targets we set ourselves and the degree of satisfaction we feel with our performance, as well as affecting our feelings about the fairness, or otherwise, of the judgements other people make. These expectations about what we are capable of achieving are called *self-efficacy beliefs* and they form an important part of our overall self-concept. They help to determine how

the expectations we have of ourselves can influence the targets we set ourselves

we interact with other people and with our environment. [3] People with high self-efficacy beliefs have been found to perform better at a variety of tasks, regardless of their actual (objectively assessed) ability and, importantly, regardless of whether their self-efficacy beliefs were "natural" or had been artificially enhanced by false feedback.[4, 5] One reason that has been suggested for this is that a low self-efficacy belief puts people off trying things; naturally, if you don't try you can't succeed. High self-efficacy, on the other hand, not only leads people to have a go, but also leads them to keep on trying if things don't initially go according to plan, so they overcome problems and often succeed in the end.

Earlier, I suggested that measurement should be seen as just a tool used in the process of *assessment*, rather than as an end in itself. And I warned that it can be something of a blunt instrument, capable of causing problems as well as providing information. Even in the example given above measurements would almost certainly be "processed" by the application of unmeasured factors, such as "that time wasn't bad considering I've got a cold coming on" or "I should have done better with that wind behind me". The greater the range of factors that are taken into account, the more "solid" the assessment of performance feels. Of course, some of these factors can be contradictory: "I'm getting a cold, which would tend to slow me down, but there's a strong following wind, which would tend to help my speed. So how well did I actually do?".

The actual range of factors used to inform the individual's subjective judgement about their workplace performance will be highly context-dependent and personal. From a manager's perspective, though, it's worth putting some effort into ensuring that there are several sources of such "independent" information to supplement the personal feedback that should be part of all performance management systems as described earlier.

chain of persuasion Here, we need to consider feedback from others from the perspective of the recipient. In order to evaluate our performance for ourselves we need to know not only what other people *say* about our performance, but also what they really think, and, crucially, how much reliance we should place on their opinions anyway. This is likely to be influenced by a combination of factors which communications theorists have summarised as the "persuasion chain". This "chain" consists of four links: the communicator, the context, the message, and the audience.

The credibility of the communicator may be affected by their perceived status; we are more likely to believe what people say if we respect them, if we regard them as knowledgeable in the relevant subject area, and if we trust them. We are also very likely to be influenced by our beliefs about their motivation. For example, if a dealer tells us that a used car is in excellent condition we are likely to be sceptical, even if we believe him to be an expert mechanic, simply because we identify an ulterior motive behind the message. On the other hand, if we commission an inspection by a motoring organization we would be likely to believe their favourable report, because we perceive it to be altruistic. Context may be a vital factor, though; if we had just overheard the dealer's opinion of the car being given to his colleague, then we might be more inclined to believe it. On the other hand, if we happened to know the car's previous owner and had frequently heard accounts of it breaking down, then we would lose all confidence in the dealer's honesty and/or expertise and wouldn't be likely to believe anything he said about that or any other vehicle.

The nature of the communication itself can have a profound effect on how believable it is. Messages that are expressed in confident terms have been found to be more persuasive than tentative; uncertain ones[6] and messages expressed in emotive or forceful language can also be more persuasive than those couched in bland or neutral terms.[7]

we need to know not only what people *say* but also what they really think

Messages that go too far may be counter-productive, as some official bodies have found when they have produced advertising intended to frighten people into complying with advice.[8] The research evidence on this is a little contradictory. A study back in 1953[9] found that horrific images of advanced gum disease were less effective than much milder advisory images in persuading people to take better care of their teeth. On the other hand, when similar tactics were tried on smokers[10] in 1967 it was found that high-fear messages about lung cancer had more effect on behaviour than milder messages. In other contexts it has been found that as "arousal" – which can be induced by fear – increases so does our ability to handle problems, but only up to a point. After the optimum level of arousal is reached, ability to cope declines, so it could be that a message that induces too much anxiety takes us beyond what's called our *latitude of acceptance* and gets blocked out by the protective subconscious. This may well be connected with our perception of how much control we can exercise and how credible we perceive the message to be; many people now accept that smoking causes lung cancer and that cancer kills people, but the message that poor oral hygiene might lead to terrible diseases of the mouth might be less credible, even if it's true.

Messages that are contrary to previously held beliefs and attitudes can be harder to accept than ones that are consistent with our existing view of the world and how it works. People tend to find confirming evidence, i.e. facts that seem to support the views they already hold, much more convincing than disconfirming evidence, meaning facts that might lead them to change their minds. Because of this, people with opposing views can often each find support for those views in the same body of evidence.[11] This helps to explain the otherwise quite extraordinary phenomenon of apparently quite intelligent people perversely coming to the wrong conclusions (i.e. conclusions that are different from our own).

audience participation

The final link in the persuasion chain is the "audience", or the recipient of the message. Several studies have found that better educated people are more likely to be influenced if they are presented with both sides of a case, with well-reasoned arguments to show why one view is stronger than the other, while less well-educated people are more likely to be influenced by a more overtly one-sided presentation of the argument. One-sided arguments have also been found to be more persuasive when they are broadly consistent with views that the recipient already holds, whereas ideas that are contrary to what they already believe are best supported by more balanced, or two-sided, arguments.[12, 13]

Another factor is the level of personal involvement the recipient feels in regard to the message. If the content of the communication has a great deal of personal significance for the recipient, he or she is likely to be more resistant to changing established ideas and attitudes.[14]

Perhaps surprisingly, there seems to be little evidence to support the idea that some people are naturally more "persuadable" than others, in other words, that personality factors are involved. Any apparent individual differences may be explainable in terms of the factors already mentioned above, such as education and personal involvement, rather than by intrinsic personality differences.[15]

All this suggests that in the workplace people need something a little more solid than simple feedback from the boss in order to assess for themselves how well they are doing. At best, such direct feedback may only tell the recipient how satisfied the boss is with their performance, and even that message may be evaluated against a confidence scale of some kind. As Douglas McGregor puts it: "the expressed desire to know where he stands may mean, 'I know I am doing a relatively poor job in some respects, but I hope the boss is not aware of it. I would like to be sure this is the case'. Still another meaning might be, 'I know I am doing an outstanding job, and I would like more recognition for it from the boss. He doesn't seem to be aware of how good I am' ".[16]

people need more than simple feedback from the boss

Feedback from a variety of sources, especially if it is consistent, increases the probability that the message(s) will be perceived as objective information. If this variety of feedback complements objective measures that are readily accessible to the person concerned, then a body of evidence is built up which is highly convincing and can be used to make reasoned assessments of performance, leading to behaviour change if that's appropriate, or to increased satisfaction and self-esteem.

Managers should try to ensure that their people have access to a variety of sources of information about their performance, so that when direct feedback is provided it is supported by a body of confirming information. In this way, a recipient is better prepared for the need to make changes in his or her behaviour and is more likely to address these in a positive frame of mind.

"*I* know how well I'm doing it" checklist

If your boss praises you for a piece of work, how do you know that the praise is justified?

If you didn't think you'd done the work particularly well, what effect would the boss's praise have on your opinion of him/her?

What tools, systems or processes could you put in place to ensure that you know how well you are performing?

What could you do to help people who report to you know for themselves how well they are doing?

notes and references

1 Hayes, N (1994) *Foundations Of Psychology,* London, Routledge

2 Locke, EA (1968) "Toward a theory of task motivation and incentives", *Organizational Behavior and Human Performance,* **3**, 157–89

3 Bandura, A (1989) "Perceived self-efficacy in the exercise of personal agency", *Psychologist,* **2** (10), 411–24

4 Collins, JL (1982) "Self-efficacy and ability in achievement behavior", cited in A Bandura "Perceived self-efficacy in the exercise of personal agency", *Psychologist,* op. cit.

5 Weinberg, RS, Gould, D & Jackson, A (1979) "Expectations and performance: an empirical test of Bandura's self-efficacy theory", *Journal of Sport Psychology,* No. 1, 320–31

6 Maslow, C, Yoselson, K & London, M (1971) "Persuasiveness of confidence expressed via language and body language", *British Journal of Social and Clinical Psychology,* No. 10, 234–40

7 Eiser, JR & Ross, M (1977) "Partisan language, immediacy and attitude change", *European Journal of Social Psychology,* No. 7, 477–89

8 Hogg, MA & Vaughan, GM (1995) *Social Psychology,* Hemel Hempstead, Prentice Hall/Harvester Wheatsheaf

9 Janis, IL & Feshbach, S (1953) "Effects of fear-arousing communications", *Journal of Abnormal and Social Psychology,* No. 48, 78–92

10 Levanthal, H, Watts, JC & Pagano, R (1967) "Effects of fear and instructions on how to cope with danger", *Journal of Personality and Social Psychology,* No. 6, 313–21

11 Lord, CG, Ross, L & Lepper, MR (1979) "Biased assimilation and attitude polarization: The effects of prior theories on subsequently considered evidence", *Journal of Personality and Social Psychology,* **37** (11), 2098–109

12 Hovland, CI, Lumsdaine, AA, & Sheffield, FD (1949) *Experiments In Mass Communication,* Princeton, MA, Princeton University Press

13 Kelvin, P (1969) *The Bases of Social Behaviour,* New York, Holt, Rinehart and Winston

14 Himmelfarb, S & Eagly, A (1974) *Readings in Attitude Change,* New York, John Wiley

15 Ajzen, I (1988) *Attitudes, Personality and Behaviour,* Milton Keynes, Open University Press

16 McGregor, D (1960) *The Human Side Of Enterprise,* New York, McGraw-Hill

6 six

processes help me to do it

managing processes

In a long-running BBC TV series senior managers go "back to the floor" to try to do one of the basic jobs in their organizations. They often find it surprisingly difficult. Over and over again they come up against barriers – rules, procedures, custom and practice, lack of authority, lack of response, and so on – which can prevent even keen, motivated and intelligent people from performing as well as they want to.

Most of us find that there are aspects of "the system" that we personally find limiting or obstructive in the performance of our jobs, and if this is true for us as individuals, it's certain to be equally true for our subordinates, peers and colleagues. We would be quite unusual not to feel

if only we had a completely free hand there would be things that we would change

sometimes that if only we had a completely free hand there would be things that we would change in order to make work easier or more efficient for ourselves and our people.

activities aren't isolated The concept of a "process" came up in the earlier discussion of learning where I defined it in terms of multiple activities linked together. Here the definition needs to be made a little more focused on the organizational implications, so I'll make use of a definition that stresses this aspect: "a series of interrelated activities that cut across functional boundaries in the delivery of an output".[1] This definition describes what is usually termed a "horizontal" process, because it goes across the organization, whereas a "vertical" process is one that is confined to a single department or business unit. Both are important but vertical processes tend to be easier to manage, if only because of the established authority structures that commonly exist within such units. According to W. Edwards Deming,[2] who was among the first and perhaps the most eminent advocates of Total Quality Management (TQM), "every activity, every job is a part of a process". In fact, every activity is likely to be part of one or more vertical *and* horizontal processes.

Each activity has three distinct parts, as illustrated in Figure 6.1. *Inputs*, which can include raw materials, complete components, energy, skills, and so on, are followed by *transformation* in which something is done to those inputs to change them in some way. This may involve radically changing their physical character, as when input materials such as calcium oxide, sodium carbonate and silicon dioxide are subjected to heat and converted – or *transformed* – into glass. Or it may mean simply joining them together, as when input materials collected in a flat pack

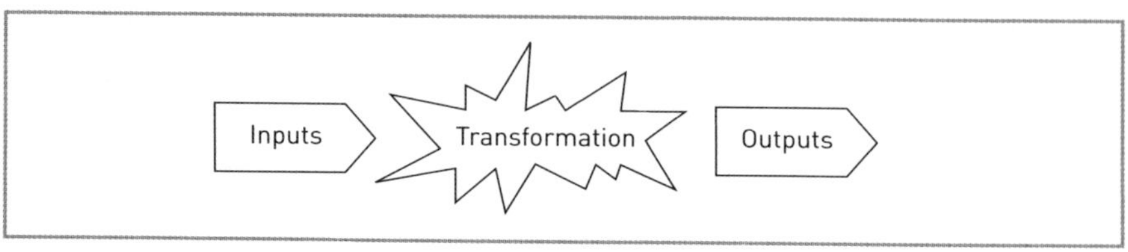

FIG 6.1 ● Activity structure

are transformed into a wardrobe. The third part of the activity is its *outputs*: the results of transformation made available for use or further development. Normally, the outputs would be expected to be worth more in some way than the inputs. In other words, each activity is expected to add value.

Many, perhaps most, organizations are structured along functional lines; people who do certain kinds of work are grouped together, and work that is appropriate for their skills and expertise is channelled to them. In a complex organization not much is done entirely within the jurisdiction of a single department. Rather, work "flows" horizontally through the organization, crossing departmental boundaries (as illustrated in Figure 6.2).

who's responsible? As the work passes through their hands, either literally or figuratively, the various functional experts add to or modify the object of their attention, much as a physical product grows and takes shape as it travels along a production line. For this to work effectively someone needs to be in overall charge of the work flow, specifying and coordinating the inputs required from each of the functional departments. This can be a problematic, or at least a politically sensitive responsibility and many organizations fail to define and support the role adequately.

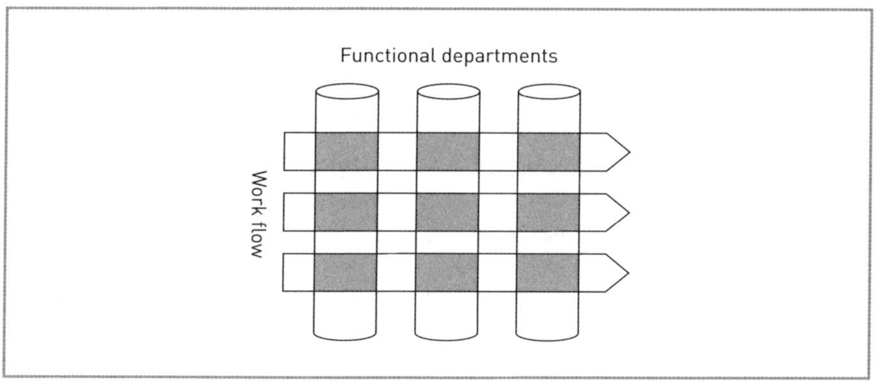

FIG 6.2 Work-flow model

Where the work to be done is unusual or unique this role can be fulfilled by a project manager, charged with seeing the job through to completion and authorised to "contract" with the functional departments for their inputs at agreed costs and to agreed timetables. Where the work is repetitive, though, it's likely to be more economical to define a "process" that will then apply to all similar jobs. In this sense a process is effectively a project plan that is repeatedly recycled.

In ideal circumstances, the best possible process can be worked out just as a project plan would be, starting from nothing and building up the detail step by step until a complete, implementable "route-map" has been constructed. If you're dealing with something that is completely new this would be a sensible way to approach it, and advocates of business process re-engineering (BPR) do, in fact, suggest that this is what organizations should do with established activities in order to maximize efficiency. A less radical approach, though, is to track what actually happens now, document it and identify barriers and inefficiencies so that action can be taken to improve things. A later section of this book will be devoted to change in organizations, so for the moment we will only look at the activity of process mapping.

where do we start?

For example, one process map might track everything that happens to a customer's order from the time the sales clerk answers the phone right through to receipt of payment. You should note here that two apparently arbitrary decisions have already been made. The first was to perceive the process as starting at the point where the sales clerk answers the telephone. Clearly, that activity has *antecedents*, i.e. activities that preceded that phone call, such as product/service design, pricing, marketing, advertising, and technical and policy documentation, maybe even hands-on training so that the clerk knows enough about the product to be able to discuss it sensibly with the customer.

The second decision was to fix the end of the process at the point where the customer's money is safely in our hands. This "activity" probably has *successors*; if we want to keep our customers happy we will need to offer after-sales services like technical advice, repair and maintenance facilities, complaint handling, perhaps upgrade information, and so on. It might have been decided that these were all part of one extended process, or the view could have been taken that they form the activities of a separate process.

These decisions really shouldn't be arbitrary at all; they should reflect some careful thought about how to ensure that things work as well as possible. We may define (and follow) a really effective process to sell our products which ends when we get paid, and we may have another great process to provide first-class after-sales services, but if there's no linkage between these processes the after-sales people won't know that a product has been sold, so the customer will never get to benefit from their expertise. This doesn't mean that it's wrong to define separate processes, only that the "end" of any process always entails a "where do we go from here?" question that has to be explicitly answered.

If we begin to trace our sales process through we can ask the people who actually do the job to provide the information we need to build up a comprehensive picture of "their" activity. We might, for example, ask the sales clerks what they actually do when the phone rings: do they pick up a handset, press a button, touch a screen, or just listen? What do they say? How do they get the information they need to answer the customer's questions? Who keeps them updated? What's hard about the activity? (not "what's hard about the job?" – our horizons here are more limited than that). What usually goes well and what sometimes/often goes wrong? And what happens after the customer rings off? From this information we can describe the components of the activity; the *transformation* that lies at its core, the inputs to the activity, and who provides those inputs, and the outputs, which will lead us to the next link(s) in the chain; who to go and talk to next.

In our example the next step might be the Despatch department, who learn (how?) about the order from Sales and prepare to send it on its way to the customer. In order to do this they need to have the item in stock, and we hear that they get their stock from the Central Depot. Noting that we need to talk to Central Depot we also find out from Despatch that they need other inputs in order to do their job properly, like packing materials, handling machinery and stock management software. Despatch don't deliver the goods themselves, but employ a contractor, who is also one of the next links in the chain, along with Billing who are responsible for preparing an invoice and sending it to the customer. After delivery the contractor returns paperwork to Customer Service, who initiate the After Sales process, and Billing inform Accounts who check that the money is received when it should be. If it isn't, Accounts not only chase up the overdue payment but also inform Customer Service so that the customer doesn't continue to receive facilities that haven't been paid for. The basic process map begins to look something like the illustration in Figure 6.3 (although each of the boxes in the figure summarizes the detail of several activities).

The next step is to make this draft process map available for comment to everyone who might conceivably have anything to do with the process. A good way to do this is cover a wall of a conference room with a large-scale drawing and invite people to drop by and add their comments on

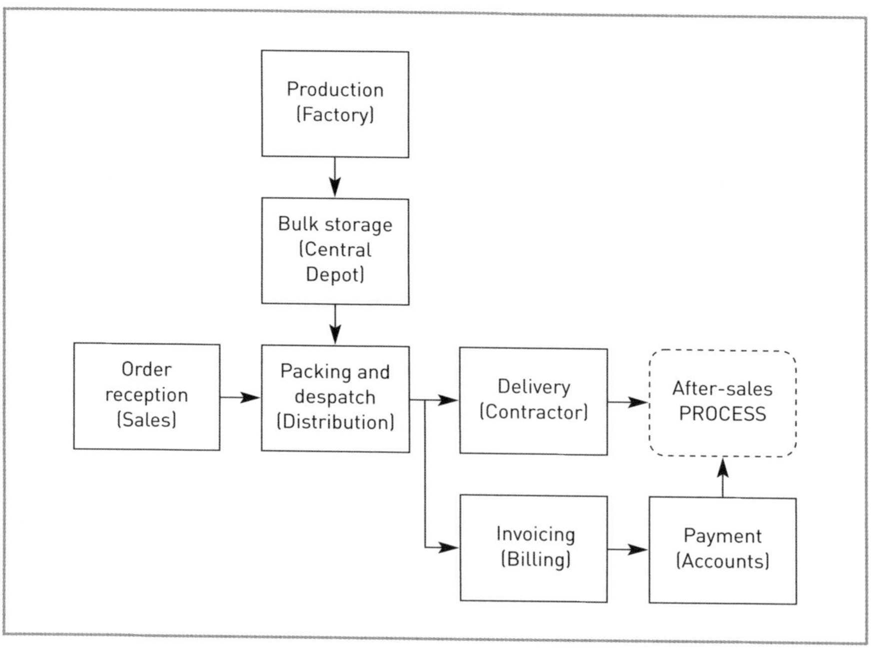

FIG 6.3 ● **A basic process map**

individual departments can develop into personal fiefdoms or baronies

sticky notes. This can uncover all kinds of unexpected detours: individuals or departments that top management had no idea would be involved, but whose contribution is vital to somebody along the route. It would also be an unusual process map that didn't show some unnecessary activity ("what do we do that for?") or uncover some problem that nearly always occurs but no-one has got round to fixing.

Once the horizontal process map has been refined and publicized it has to be put into practice. This means entering into the dangerous territory of organizational politics.

The coalescence of similar activities into functional departments is usually an efficient approach to organizing work, but it brings with it the very real danger that the individual departments can lose touch with each other, developing their own cultures, styles and procedures; this is why you find terms like "silo", "stovepipe" and "chimney-stack" in the literature on organizational structure (see Figure 6.4). Under certain kinds of departmental management they can develop into personal fiefdoms or baronies, engaged in unproductive rivalries.

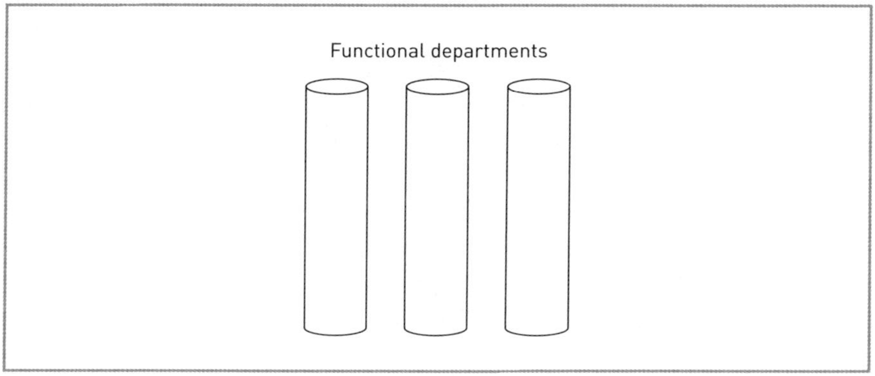

FIG 6.4 ● Functional departments as "stovepipes"

This can lead to serious difficulties at the interfaces between horizontal and vertical processes and makes it essential that every horizontal process has an "owner" with the organizational status, authority and will to find practical solutions to the problems and if necessary enforce those solutions. This carries with it the attendant risk of conflict between the "owner" of the workflow and the managers of the various functional departments, or, even worse, of putting the people who actually perform the work in the dilemma of having two bosses with differing priorities. Enforcement may in any case cause genuine difficulties in departments that have been used to functioning more or less independently and may have requirements that are incompatible with the new process – different kinds of documentation, different engineering standards, different information technology, and so on.

politics and processes These factors of politics, inertia and (genuine) incompatible requirements can combine to make an effective horizontal process hard to implement. An example of this occurred in a major technology company which, in the early 1990s, invested heavily in a new specialist division to manage the development and launch of all its new products and services. The new division developed a horizontal process for this activity that was widely regarded as world class. However, virtually all new products and services needed input and cooperation from the company's engineering division, whose people continued to insist that anything that came to them should accord with their existing vertical processes. Since the new horizontal process differed in several ways at crucial points this wasn't usually possible, but product managers found that unless they complied with engineering division's requirements effectively nothing happened. The process owner, although a senior director of the company, lacked the organizational status to influence the director of engineering to pull his people into line, and the director of engineering couldn't see what the fuss was about. Eventually the product management division was disbanded and the process, externally recognized as excellent, fell into disuse.

How much freedom the individual departments have to do their work their own way depends on several factors, which fall into two broad categories. First, there may be good reasons why a department is likely to make a stronger contribution to organizational objectives if it is allowed to work out its own solutions, identify and seize opportunities and, inevitably, make its own mistakes. On the other hand, it may be more effective to require departments to follow standardized procedures and implement only centrally determined strategies. The more similarities there are between what the different departments actually do, the more likely it is that the latter model will be applied (this is simply a statement of fact, not a value-judgement about whether this is necessarily a good thing or not).

As an illustration of this in practice we might take a (hypothetical) retail chain with 35 shops, all of which operate as "functional departments" but all do very similar, if not identical, things. All have a local management structure but these have very little freedom to modify centrally imposed procedures. Every shop looks virtually the same as all the others, all sell exactly the same products at the same prices, and an employee could easily transfer from the Aberdeen branch to the one in Redruth without needing any retraining on any aspect of the work. However, the procedures and practices of the Accounts, Marketing, Buying and Legal departments are quite different from each other. These departments do very different things and have devised their own ways of doing them, with the full approval and support of top management.

Changing circumstances may prompt a revision of central controls. When a European clothing retailer decided to wind up its UK operation it gave its local managers carte blanche to buy and sell anything they liked for the last few months of trading. Profits soared almost everywhere and some analysts wondered whether the company might not have been able to continue its earlier successes in the UK if only it had been more willing to allow its local managers greater freedom to address local needs.

The first determinant of departmental "empowerment" is therefore, in principle anyway, a reasoned decision about what will lead to optimum effectiveness. The second determinant is much more pragmatic: does the organization have the power, and the will, to insist that departmental managers comply with centrally determined procedures? For example, if the manager of the Portsmouth branch of our hypothetical retail chain decided, for well-considered reasons, to change the shop floor layout, buy in some "special lines" and sub-contract part of the second floor to a caterer to run a coffee shop, would the central management instruct her to return to company guidelines, or would they let her "get away with it"? Would their decision be influenced by changes, for better or worse, in the branch's profit profile? What if they told her to return everything to the company norms and she failed to comply, or, more likely, only partially complied? Direct defiance might, perhaps, bring swift retribution, but what if the Buying department pointed out that purchasing was their prerogative and the Portsmouth branch was infringing company rules by procuring special lines locally. That begins to look like a dispute between departments; will central management support Buying or turn a blind eye?

tragedy The exercise of control, or *regulation*, over the activities of independent or quasi-independent operators is vital for the overall health of the organization. It may be fine (it may not be) for people to be entrepreneurial, to show initiative, energy and autonomy, but unregulated activity can have serious consequences. These may take the form of exposing the organization to harm from "external" agencies, for example, by breaking the law, taking financial risks or damaging the organization's reputation in some way. More insidious, and harder to control, is a destructive, inwardly focused competition for resources and dominance. This may take the form of a phenomenon known as the "tragedy of the commons", using the word "tragedy" here in its dramatic sense of a remorseless progress towards an inevitable conclusion.

The concept is basically simple. Imagine that several herdsmen have the right to graze cattle on a piece of common land. The land has finite resources and will sustain a certain number of cattle, but no more. Collectively, it is in the herdsmen's common interest to keep the total number of cattle grazing the land within this maximum. Individually, though, each herdsman will benefit if he can add more cattle to his own herd, because the grazing is free. If they all do this the land will be overgrazed and will no longer sustain any of their cattle. Garrett Hardin,[3] who first proposed the concept, suggests that without regulation this will inevitably happen when quasi-independent users draw on a common pool of resources.

It's worth noting that an example of this in real life occurred in the fishing grounds off the coast of Canada in the early 1990s: cod (the "commons" in this case) were overfished until commercial returns were no longer obtainable. When fishing ceased, however, stocks did not recover. It was later discovered that crustaceans were breeding in the area at unprecedented rates now that there were insufficient cod to feed on them and keep their numbers down. The crustaceans, whilst providing food for adult cod, were themselves predators of cod eggs and fry. This made little impact on the enormous numbers of eggs produced by the normal cod population, so a dynamic balance of mutual dependency was maintained between the species until overfishing destroyed that balance, with disastrous and probably permanent results.

On the other hand, regulation can protect the common resource. From time immemorial the small farms around Valencia have shared scarce water resources under the authority of a regulatory body, *el tribunal de las aguas*, which meets weekly outside Valencia cathedral. The tribunal's function is to ensure that everyone takes only their fair share of water, at predetermined times, and that the irrigation systems are properly maintained, so that everyone's crops can thrive and no-one can prosper at the expense of their neighbours. The system has worked perfectly for at least eight centuries, probably much longer, and in modern times has been given official legal status.[4] (Blasco Ibáñez's *"La Barraca"*,[5] first published in 1898, gives a fascinating picture of the workings of the tribunal in the context of the novel's plot).

liberty or licence

The point of all this is that too much independence on the part of the organization's "components" can lead to excessive, selfish demands on the common resources which, if unchecked, can overstretch those resources to the point where none of the components can function properly. The way to avoid this is to exercise an appropriate degree of central regulatory control because, as Lenin is supposed to have said, "liberty is precious – so precious that it must be rationed". How much regulation is "appropriate" and where best to apply it are delicate judgements for senior management.

> The best examples of "best" practice in process management focus on the interfaces between departments so that people retain the maximum possible freedom to do their own jobs their own way, but no-one is allowed to grab an unfair share of the corporate resources and working together is made easy because the "contact points" are coordinated. Some level of standardization does occur; the coordination and oversight that process management provides helps to disseminate the research, development, bright ideas, and so on of other people, but the tendency is to keep procedures lean and interfere as little as possible: don't steal people's decisions. It's quite noticeable to a consultant that the more experience an organization has of applying these concepts, the slimmer their manuals of procedures tend to be, and the smaller the bookcase that's needed to hold them.

working in teams

Teams are fashionable. Working in teams is a kind of process model that is increasingly being adopted as an answer to the complexity of many organizational activities, which demands co-operative input from people with a variety of specialist skills and knowledge, as well as support staff. Teams can be an effective way of achieving this.

Extravagant claims are made for the benefits of teams in business and other organizations. Effective teamworking has been suggested as a prime crucial factor in business success.[6] Among the more general benefits claimed for it are: increased productivity, enhanced quality, reduced costs, improved quality of working life, lower staff turnover and absenteeism, less conflict, increased innovation, and better organizational adaptability and flexibility,[7] and that "teams outperform individuals acting alone or in larger organizational groupings, especially when performance requires multiple skills, judgements, and experiences".[8] The evidence for these claims is mainly anecdotal, but a recent study[9] did show that there were significant increases in both service quality and sales figures in self-managed teams (i.e. ones that controlled their own work).

what is a team? Before we can look at the effectiveness of teams we need to establish a working definition of what a team actually *is.* I will be prescriptive here and state categorically that by far the most vital element in turning a group of people into a team is that they should have a *common goal* or purpose. Certainly, the fact that they all happen to report to the same boss won't do it. Everything that has been said earlier about objective-setting applies here, with the added need for everyone in the team to be quite clear about goals, and to be involved in defining them. This needs checking and re-checking regularly; it's quite possible for teams within organizations to have worked together for several years without ever having tested their individual assumptions about the team's purpose.[10]

In examining the motivational factors involved in individual performance I emphasized the fact that *intrinsic* rewards, i.e. the satisfactions that arise from the work itself, tend to be more effective motivators than rewards that follow after the job is done. Teams can derive collective intrinsic satisfactions, which we will return to later. As far as team goals are concerned, I'll quote the advice of Jon Katzenbach and Douglas Smith, who say that: "the hunger for performance is far more important to team success than team-building exercises, special incentives, or team leaders with ideal profiles. In fact, teams often form around such challenges without any help or support from management. Conversely, potential teams without such challenges usually fail to become teams".[11]

the most vital element in a team is that they should have a *common goal* or purpose

This leads us to the second defining characteristic of teams: that they have their own *identity* and the members have a sense of belonging to something special, or at least different and distinctive. A sense of belonging is a fundamental human need that is both a strength and a potential danger. We will look at both aspects in the course of this discussion.

One of the basic reasons why teams are needed at all is that individuals working alone don't have all the skills and knowledge required to get the job done. Therefore, if the team is to achieve its shared objective its members *depend on one another* to contribute their various specialized abilities. The recognition of this mutual dependency is one of the factors which help to strengthen a sense of team identity, and the feeling that one's contribution is needed and appreciated is an important source of intrinsic satisfaction for a team member.

doing the right thing In order to work together the team develops norms, or ground rules of behaviour. These norms are often not consciously recognized by team members but they still exert a powerful influence over behaviour. The "right" thing to do or say, things that should not be done or said, duties, responsibilities and roles within the team can all be established by a process of social learning. It can be helpful to try to make these behavioural norms explicit and this is often an essential starting point if norms need to be changed.

So, to understand a particular team and identify the source of any difficulties it may be having, a useful first step is to run through the checklist of team characteristics. A template for this is provided in Figure 6.5. However, it can be very hard to carry out this kind of analysis on your own team. It often takes an outsider – or *stranger* – to see things that are so deeply ingrained in the everyday life of the team that the team members themselves aren't aware of them. This is one reason why organizations hire consultants, what Charles Handy[12] calls "the ritual form of stranger" in organizational life. If you look at other people's teams you may gain a few insights that you can take back to your own work situation.

Team name/description
Team members:
The common task these people are trying to accomplish:
In what ways do they depend on each other? (What does each member contribute, and what would be the consequence if they failed to make their contribution?):
What distinguishes this team from other teams or groups?
What behavioural norms (ground rules) do they apply?
What development phase is the group now in?:

FIG 6.5 ● Team characteristics

The last box in the template refers to the maturity of the team. The way that teams form, develop and perform was studied by several researchers in the 1960s and 1970s, and there's a consistency in these studies that may explain why a model dating from that time is still regarded as the definitive description of the team development processes. It's also a model for which I can vouch from personal experience of working with teams, although I must add the usual caveat, that nothing in human behaviour is inevitable or invariable.

Bruce Tuckman's model[13] says that groups typically go through five stages: *forming, storming, norming, performing* and finally what he calls *adjourning*, which is usually changed to *mourning* in the UK, presumably because this rhymes better with the other phase-names when said in an English accent. These stages are sequential and developmental, which means that each stage must be satisfactorily completed if the team is to progress successfully to the next one. The model is represented diagrammatically in Figure 6.6.

In the first stage – *forming* – group members are likely to feel some insecurity and a need to be accepted. They may tend to rely on "safe" behaviour, taking refuge in formality. Controversy tends to be avoided and people try to gather information and impressions about the group, the task, and other group members. Feelings tend not to be mentioned and serious topics are not addressed.

The second stage is *storming*. The dominant characteristics of this phase are competition and conflict in inter-personal relations but increasing organization concerning the task, and a need for structure and clarity.

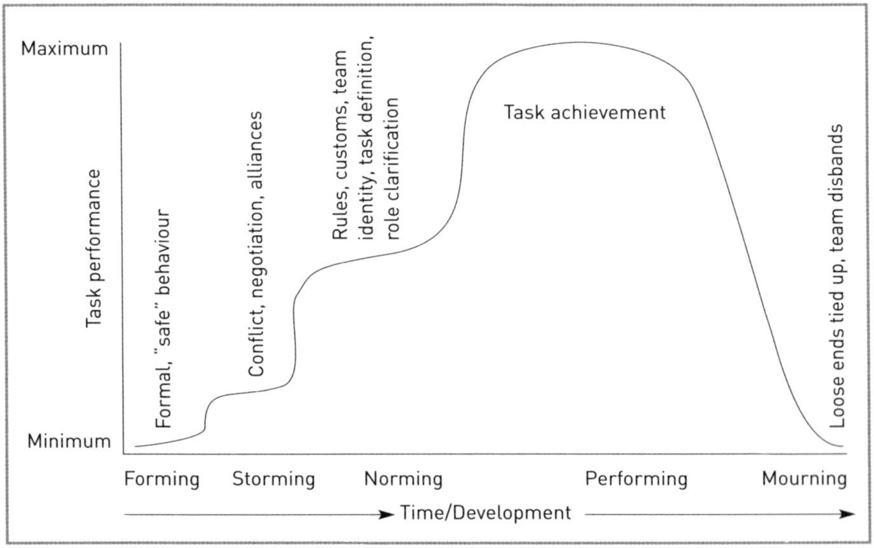

FIG 6.6 ● Five stages of group development

Some members will probably be anxious not to make mistakes, or to reveal their weaknesses or uncertainties, whilst others will see opportunities to impose their own ideas or to dominate the group. Some members may appear not to be participating very much. During this phase alliances may form, break up and re-form. On the positive side, duties get allocated, the nature of the task is defined and the way it is to be tackled is determined. Questions about evaluation, rewards and "terms and conditions" are raised and, hopefully, answered.

walk through the storm Although the conflicts and uncertainties of the storming phase can be uncomfortable, they are necessary; it's through this process that necessary questions get resolved. Groups that try to suppress storming often find that problems occur later, when they may be more serious. When facilitating groups I've found that it pays to get uncertainties, and even grievances, out into the open and to encourage group members to negotiate for the things that are important to them. Paradoxically, this often makes people more willing to grant concessions to other group members, which benefits the group as a whole as well as the individuals.

During the next phase, *norming*, the identity of the group is established. This should be a very positive stage where group members come to appreciate and acknowledge each other's strengths and contributions. A key characteristic of this phase is the free flow of information, ideas and feedback. Members learn from each other. Often, people are willing to change previously held ideas and views. Leadership of the group may well be shared, depending on the needs of the moment. Trust builds up, and a feeling of belonging develops. This is the phase where the "rules" of behaviour – the norms – are established. These can be very powerful; once a group norm is established it can often survive the replacement of *all* the original group members by newcomers[14] (but not all at once!).

it pays to get uncertainties, and even grievances, out into the open

Knowing and complying with the group norms is an important element in membership or belonging.

The fourth phase is *performing*. During this phase the group, having previously built solid foundations, is able to get on with the task in hand and deliver results. The performing phase is characterized by the members' interdependence. Individuals tend to feel more confident, not needing constant reassurance or approval. Morale is likely to be high, and there's a strong sense of belonging to a team with its own identity. Members show concern both for the task and for their colleagues. Problem-solving is cooperative and there is strong motivation to find the best solutions. Unfortunately, not all groups achieve a successful performing phase, and this can often be attributed to unsatisfactory completion, or suppression, of one or more of the earlier phases.

is that it? Bruce Tuckman called the last phase *adjourning*. In fact, I think that the alternative English name *mourning* is a better description because the end of a group that has achieved a strong identity can feel similar to bereavement for some of its members. This phase, naturally enough, is usually reached when the task has been completed, but it isn't always obvious that this has happened. The strong sense of belonging can make group members reluctant to accept that the need for the team is over, which can lead to the persistence of projects that should have been wound up, or to teams searching for new tasks to justify their continued existence. Ideally, completion of the task should be marked by some kind of ceremony or event, by recognition for the participants and by the chance to close off relationships sensitively.

Clearly, the maturity of the team is a factor in its effectiveness; not much is delivered during the forming and storming stages, but results begin to be seen during norming; and performing speaks for itself.

There are some other factors that contribute to effective team working, which will be described next.

membership Groucho Marx once said that he wouldn't want to join any club that would accept him as a member. Having and keeping the "right" people in the group is such a fundamental part of human social behaviour that it's bound to figure in the behaviour of teams in the workplace.

If you were responsible for some task that needed to be handled by a team you might well turn your mind to choosing the ideal people to be team members. You would probably think in terms of the skills and knowledge team members would need to "bring to the party". You might also think about the political aspects; for example: "we'd better have someone from Marketing on board or they won't cooperate", or, at least, you might think of people with useful "connections". Maybe you would consider personal qualities and compatibility as well. I've mentioned these last, but our subconscious drives give them high, probably top, priority in determining who's most suitable to join our teams.

In general, small groups, and larger organizations too, tend to manage their membership by three processes: *selection*, *adaptation* and *attrition*. The primary function of these processes – it would be misleading to say *purpose* because they may not be applied consciously – is to ensure the compatibility of members, the survival and cohesion of the group as a unit, and conformity to group norms. So, groups tend to be careful about who is allowed to join them. There is a snag here, though: in practice there often isn't much choice about who you get on your team at work. Even if you have decided what skills, knowledge and connections you would like to see in one individual team member, it's likely that there won't be all that many people who fit your specification *and* are actually available to join the team. You would be an unusual, and lucky, manager if you could identify two or more people to choose from for each vacancy, so control over *selection* can be problematic in a modern workplace organization. Fortunately, people can be flexible in the way they work and behave in teams and, as mentioned earlier, the establishment of norms means that people *adapt* their behaviour to fit the context in which they find themselves.

shape up or ship out Those who can't, or won't, adapt to the group's requirements are often isolated, "managed out" or persuaded to leave. This is what's meant by *attrition* in this context. Again, this may not be the result of conscious or deliberate action by the team members. The need to maintain group coherence and comfort is very deeply embedded in our species and behaviours that tend to promote these effects may seem perfectly natural, and so pass unnoticed.

The question "how many people make a team?" doesn't have a single, sensible answer; it depends to some extent on the task to be performed and the roles or functions of the individual team members. In general terms, small groups of between five and nine people function socially better than larger ones, perhaps because individuals are better able to participate fully. On the other hand, larger groups are more likely to have the range and diversity of skills, knowledge and talents that will contribute to successful task completion. There's some evidence that as groups approach fifteen or so people, i.e. about double the ideal "social" number, they tend to sub-divide, or produce factions within the overall group structure. Often, this is practical and conscious, as when sub-committees are formed for specific purposes, but it's also seen in the formation of cliques, elites and cabals, which can have negative effects. There's also a tendency for individuals to relax a little when the work is being shared among a group. This phenomenon, which is called *social loafing*, or the Ringlemann effect,[15,16] is more pronounced (but of course less *noticeable*; it only becomes clear when measured) in larger groups.

There are some other factors which have been found to influence a team's effectiveness. A study in the 1960s[17] showed that teams with very distinctive identities found it harder to cooperate with other organizational units. In other respects, however, it seems to be something of an advantage for teams to have a distinctive character or identity of their own, provided that it's broadly compatible with the wider organizational culture.[18]

Rapid and/or frequent changes in team membership can be disruptive, and for individuals joining a new team can be a stressful experience; it takes time to settle in. Teams tend not to function well in climates of insecurity, threat, organizational change, conflict, etc. Disputes among senior people, especially if they relate directly to the team's work, can have a detrimental effect on performance, but positive interest by senior people tends to be helpful. Perhaps surprisingly, teams where ideas and decisions are freely exchanged, debated and questioned, even if they're the leader's ideas, tend to be more successful.[19]

playing the part

In a series of experiments based on business games, Meredith Belbin[20, 21] found that teams were consistently more successful if the team members, between them, made sure that each of eight *roles* or functions was covered by one or more members. These roles relate to the social interaction of the team. Teams where all the roles were covered were consistently more successful than teams composed of the "cleverest", or most highly skilled or knowledgeable people; which as a manager you may find encouraging! Belbin recognized that people will have different preferences about which roles they can take on. It's important to note, though, that most people can perform more than one of the roles successfully. In fact, in smaller teams it's quite usual for one person to take care of two or more roles at the same time. The following are outline descriptions of the eight team roles but don't always use Belbin's own terminology; the precise definitions of the roles and the titles they are given have been refined over the years by Belbin himself and by others.

Each of the roles has an "allowable weakness"; showing these weaknesses won't detract from a person's ability to play their role(s) but it does mean that people have to be tolerant of their team colleagues, and have a right to expect tolerance in return.

The first role we'll look at here is called the *Chairman*. This doesn't refer to the boss, but rather describes a coordinator role. Chairmen like organizing people, coordinating their strengths and using them effectively. Chairmen tend to be good at gaining consensus and buy-in, even among people with differing interests. They often command respect and inspire enthusiasm. They are disciplined, focused and balanced, good talkers and listeners, and have a good sense of timing. Their allowable weaknesses are that they don't have to be the brightest, most intelligent members of the team, or the most creative.

The *Shaper* is a task-leader who likes to influence group decisions and have an impact on meetings. Shapers are extrovert and forceful with plenty of drive and self-confidence and will risk making themselves unpopular to get their ideas across. They focus on prioritization and objective-setting. Their allowable weaknesses are that they can have rather low tolerance for vagueness and lack of precision, in ideas and people. The Shaper is the exception to the rule that you need all the roles in a successful team. You can get by without a Shaper if you've got a good Chairman; if you have both they may clash.

Resource Investigators are relaxed, sociable and extrovert. They look outside the immediate task to bring in fresh ideas, new developments and new techniques. They often have extensive networks of contacts and can locate specialist help when it's needed. Their allowable weaknesses are over-enthusiasm, getting things out of proportion and not following up what they've started.

The *Plant* or *Ideas Man/Woman* is the most imaginative and original member of the team. Natural innovators, Plants like to bring new ideas and strategies to bear on old problems. They enjoy puzzles and problem-solving and see patterns in situations and events. Their allowable weaknesses are that they can be rather introverted, impractical and careless with details. They can be impatient, independent, and not always very good at communicating with team members who don't share their personality characteristics.

The *Monitor-Evaluator* contributes to the team's success by analyzing problems and evaluating other people's ideas and suggestions. Monitor-Evaluators put objective judgement before feelings. They can save expensive mistakes by finding the flaws in unsound proposals at an early stage. Their allowable weaknesses are that they can be over-critical and stifle the creativity of others. They aren't exciting and are often slow (but are usually right, which can be quite annoying).

The *Company Worker* is systematic and reliable. Given clear objectives and procedures to follow, Company Workers help the team to convert ideas and concepts into implementable plans that they will carry out methodically to meet targets and deadlines. They are self-controlled, realistic and full of common sense, and they can be superb administrators. Their allowable weakness is that they can be inflexible, wanting to see new ideas proved before they take them on.

The *Team Worker* (or *Team Builder*) holds the team together, supporting and enhancing the strengths of others and helping to compensate for their weaknesses. Team Workers like people and are liked in return. They can work with others effectively even when they don't agree with them. They are good listeners and help to get communication working. They are flexible and not self-important. Their allowable weaknesses are a tendency to be indecisive, and a dislike for anything that might disturb the team's equilibrium, such as competition and friction within the team. They can be more concerned with process than with the actual task (a pre-Belbin term was "guardian of the process"). They aren't usually very tough.

Finally, the *Completer-Finisher* is the checker of details who can be relied on to find mistakes and omissions. Completer-Finishers are self-controlled with strength of character and a sense of order and purpose. They act as the team's "conscience", keep track of things that need special attention and help to maintain momentum and a sense of urgency. They will go looking for problems if there aren't any readily to hand. Their allowable weaknesses are impatience and intolerance towards team members who don't share their characteristics. They can be unpopular, but this may not bother them too much.

Belbin advises that balance is important; if too many people take the same role they can get in each other's way. Equally, if roles are left uncovered some tasks won't get done. In practice, though, stable teams can often get away with the odd "vacancy".

Awareness is crucial in making use of Belbin's ideas; some roles will probably get covered naturally, but you can't depend on it. Belbin provides a questionnaire – which can be found in various forms in many of Belbin's books and articles, or online at www.Belbin.com – to help identify your preferred team roles so that team leaders can try to ensure that each role is covered by one of the team members.

people make teams make progress Another extremely helpful idea is provided by John Adair,[22] whose focus is mainly on leadership issues. This very simple model shows three overlapping circles, representing task issues, team issues and individual issues, illustrated in Figure 6.7.

Adair says that team leaders need to maintain their priorities in balance if their teams are to be successful. Clearly, the task is important; if there was no task to be performed the team wouldn't exist. In the present context, however, tasks are performed by teams, so it's vital that the team's well-being should be maintained, otherwise the task won't get done. But of course, teams are no more than groups of individuals, organized and interacting in particular ways. So the team will never perform well unless the needs of its individual members are treated with the importance they deserve. Therefore, says Adair, team leaders must pay equal attention to all three factors if their teams are to be successful in what they undertake.

them and us Before concluding this discussion of teams we must consider some of the problems that can affect groups of people working together. I've said that the feeling of belonging can be very rewarding, and that a sense of identity is a feature of many successful teams (although it's also possible for it to act as a barrier to inter-unit cooperation[23]). The need to belong is deeply rooted in our psychology and it has proba-

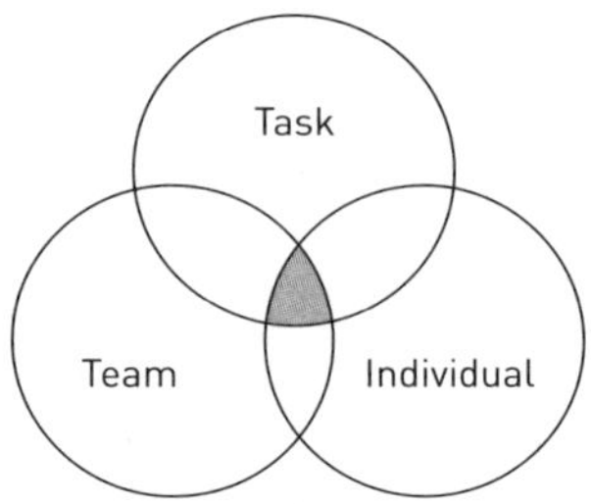

FIG 6.7 ● **Three-circle model**
© John Adair

bly been a factor in the success of our species, but it does have a dark side. Human beings have a tendency to define their belonging, or *inclusion*, in terms of hostility towards those who are *excluded*; "us against the rest". This hostility is very evident on the wider social scale: differences of race, religion, language, class, political views or sexual orientation are familiar sources of conflict. Commenting on differences of English accent and dialect in 1916, George Bernard Shaw wrote in *Pygmalion*: "it is impossible for an Englishman to open his mouth, without making another Englishman despise him". If none of these obvious sources of difference are present, human beings seem actively to look for other ways of differentiating *us* from *them*. The hostility between supporters of different sporting teams is not a new phenomenon; wholesale massacres arising from this cause are reported in ancient Rome, and experiments have shown that groups formed by completely arbitrary selection soon develop inter-group rivalries and hostility.[24]

The tendency to develop a strong group identity, with its implications of collective defence against a hostile world, was thought to be the underlying cause of two phenomena which can affect the decisions made by groups. The first of these is called *risky shift*. As it was first described, in the 1960s,[25] risky shift is the tendency for a group to arrive at collective decisions that are more risky or dangerous than the decisions that individuals, working alone, would have made. This was surprising, because most social psychology theory would predict that groups would be more cautious than individuals in their decisions (which is what was found in the study of animal groups that I mentioned in the discussion of leadership). Subsequent research, however, has suggested that the tendency is towards *polarization* rather than simply towards risk, i.e. a group is likely to make a decision that is more extreme than the "average" of the individual group members' views, either towards risk or towards caution.

The other problematic tendency in the group decision-making process is known as *groupthink*.[26] Groupthink seems to arise when certain characteristics are present together:

- a strong sense of group "identity", or high group cohesiveness;
- very similar beliefs, values, etc., among group members;

- isolation from external influences, information, ideas etc.;
- high stress, arising from external threat or from task complexity.

It shows itself in several ways: an unquestioned assumption that the group must be right; a feeling that the group is united and invulnerable; rejection or discrediting of any information that doesn't support the group's views or policy; intolerance of dissent within the group and negative stereotyping of anyone outside the group.[27]

The effects of groupthink are that the need for unanimity – to avoid any damage to the integrity of the group – becomes paramount. So decisions may be made that are based more on the group's internal processes than on the "real world" factors that the group is supposed to be addressing. Coupled with a belief in the rightness, superiority and moral goodness of the group – and the wrongness, inferiority and wickedness of everyone else – this can lead to bad, even disastrous decisions. An example of apparent groupthink that is frequently quoted is the US-supported invasion of Cuba at the Bay of Pigs, about which President Kennedy is supposed to have asked "how could we have been so stupid?"

The early research in this field, which focused in particular on US foreign policy decisions, has been re-examined by later researchers who have suggested that the factor of excessive cohesiveness is less important than had been thought. Other, more individual, factors concerned with how people cope with stress when making decisions may be more influential. However, the basic model still seems to be fairly sound: groups need to be careful when making decisions and to maintain their openness to ideas, perspectives and information from outside. Feeling superior to everyone else is what the Greeks called *hubris*, and it always leads to trouble.

The characteristics of teams, the processes by which they develop, and the environments in which they thrive can be summarized as follows:

- effective teams have worked through a process of development to arrive at a stage of maturity that enables them to function well;

- they have a clear common goal, which all team members understand and to which all are committed;
- the team has a distinctive identity, which is nevertheless compatible with the wider organizational culture;
- team members are mutually dependent. They have norms (ground rules) that guide their behaviour and relationships. Free speech and mutual respect are prominent among these norms;
- they work in an environment of relative security, changes in team membership are kept to a minimum, and they enjoy the support of the wider organization.

making decisions Managers make decisions all the time, as, of course, does everyone else. Making decisions isn't a special activity but it is a vital one and one that is vulnerable to a number of human frailties. Risky shift and groupthink, which I have just described, are two phenomena that can adversely affect people's decision-making capabilities, and there are others. Fortunately, being aware of the hazards can enable us to avoid some of them and help to take some of the risk out of our decisions.

There is a theory, called the "theory of reasoned action",[28] that human behaviour is controlled by thoughtful analysis. Decisions to do or not do something follow careful consideration of the implications, and behaviour is a product of a person's intentions, which are influenced by attitudes and subjective norms, which are in turn influenced by beliefs. When we considered how to determine which form of training would be most appropriate in a particular set of circumstances we quite explicitly applied this approach, making use of a decision tool based on a two-dimensional matrix through which several options were identified and individually evaluated against a previously defined set of criteria. The results were then compared so that the "best" option(s) became apparent, making it relatively easy to make a decision about which one to adopt (see Figures 3.8 and 3.9).

This is an example of a logical, or sequential, process for making decisions, which might be represented as a flowchart like the one in Figure 6.8.

Unfortunately, research has shown that the theory of reasoned action is very wide of the mark in suggesting that people make their decisions like this in the real world. In fact, as Jeffrey Edwards says,[29] people often "systematically violate the principles of rational decision-making" and do not "consciously generate a comprehensive set of alternatives, evaluate the potential consequences of each alternative, and select the strategy which maximizes well-being". This may seem rather odd, since a logical/sequential process for making decisions would clearly be the sensible way to do things. It raises the obvious question: why would people, and managers in particular, *not* follow such a process?

nobody's perfect

Many managers, if they were put on the spot with this question, might plead lack of time. They might also point out that having *all* the facts available is a luxury that managers very seldom enjoy; which may, of course, be linked with not having enough time to collect the facts. Instead, they typically identify a few options and choose one that they think *could* work. This has been called "satisficing".[30] Working with insufficient data is a normal part of a manager's job.[31, 32] It should also be acknowledged that managers are, after all, people, and therefore subject to the same imperfections as the rest of us.

A key factor affecting the so-called rational model of decision-making is that personality or cultural factors can restrict the options we perceive to be available; if we're not aware of an option in the first place we clearly can't include it in any evaluation process. Even if an option succeeds in battling its way through the filter of personality and culture to

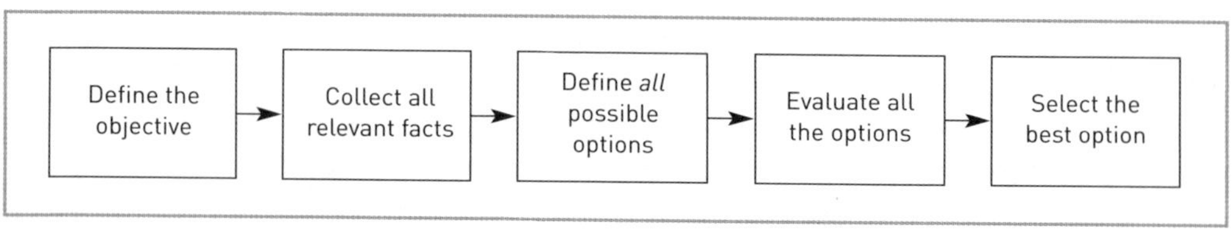

FIG 6.8 Sequential decision-making

enter our conscious thoughts, its relative attractiveness as a course of action is also highly subjective, influenced by the same factors. Opening up our thinking to a wider range of options and improving the objectivity of evaluation are vital for optimal decision-making.

We have already considered groupthink and risky shift, which are prime examples of negative characteristics in decision-making behaviour. There are some other phenomena that can affect the way we make decisions that I will briefly review now. In practice, human decision-making is characterized by the application of *heuristics*, a term that means rules-of-thumb – or theories-in-use – which seem to work fairly well, most times, in most situations. The principles of conditioning would suggest that a theory-in-use that provided positive reinforcement (by working fairly well) quite often would be likely to become firmly established in behaviour.

Heuristics seem to work by providing familiar patterns; if at least some of the characteristics of a new situation seem to match those of a "pattern" or model stored in our mind from earlier experiences then we tend to assume that the new situation is quite *like* the earlier ones, and we act accordingly. Clearly, this process does provide opportunities for things to go wrong; if we assume that a model built up from previous experience tells us all we need to know about a new situation but in fact the new situation is different in some significant way, then the action we take may be inappropriate and possibly even dangerous. Research into heuristics has tended to concentrate on why things go wrong, which is probably the most practical approach, so I will concentrate on some of the more vulnerable processes in decision-making here, but it would be wrong to be too gloomy; heuristics are useful devices that have served us well for countless millennia.

Much of our knowledge about how heuristics work comes from research in the 1970s and 80s[33] that investigated how people estimate *probability*, and then go on to make decisions or take action based on those probability estimates. This research identified a number of ways in which our judgement can be misled.

see one, you've seen them all *Representativeness* is a common heuristic. It concerns our judgement that a specific example is typical, or representative, of a group. This concept is linked with the processes of inductive and deductive reasoning, which I described earlier. Two kinds of information are needed to make an estimate of representativeness, even in quite ordinary situations. These are *likelihood* and *base-rate*. Likelihood is usually a subjective judgement, often based on stereotypes. For example, if a specific person displayed characteristics that we, subjectively, associate with lawyers we might think it likely that he/she is a lawyer. Base-rate, on the other hand, is factual, statistical information about the larger group (technically, the "population") from which the example is taken.

If we were told that the person whose profession we were trying to guess was a member of a group of one hundred people, of whom ten were lawyers and the rest engineers, we ought to take this base-rate information into account; the odds are nine-to-one *against* that individual being a lawyer. In fact, researchers found that people consistently ignored base-rate information in making their judgements. They did this even when the information they were given didn't mention any characteristics that might give a clue about the person's profession. In these cases the subjects often seemed to assume equal (i.e. fifty-fifty) probability of lawyer <> engineer, instead of the statistically much higher probability that the person was an engineer.

Subsequent research has suggested that people may take more account of base-rate information if they are continually reminded of it, rather than being told just once. On the whole, though, it does seem as though we are much too ready to assume that a particular example is *representative*, or typical, of the population it comes from. This is particularly dangerous when it acts to reinforce prejudices. For example, if someone already has a negative attitude towards a particular group or category of people, then any example of a member of that group doing something reprehensible is likely to be seen as representative of the group as a whole, making the prejudice even stronger.

The *availability* of information also influences judgements: "some items of information come more readily to mind than others, and so they are more likely to influence our decisions".[34] This is subject not only to pure chance but also to manipulation. If certain kinds of information, or propaganda, are made readily available we are quite likely to take them to be "true". As an example of this, the 2000 British Crime Survey[35] showed that in the UK overall crime, and most individual categories of crime, were steadily falling, and the chances of becoming a victim of crime in the UK were at their lowest level since 1983, but people continued to overestimate the problem of crime, sometimes wildly. A third of householders believed the national crime rate had increased "a lot" between 1997 and 1999. Crime, of course, makes stories in newspapers – which often have a political agenda – and on TV and radio but the absence of crime, understandably, doesn't. The ready availability of stories about crime influences public perceptions towards an exaggerated assessment of the risks.

Preconceptions, arising from any source, can not only distort our own judgements but also affect the behaviour of others. This may take the form of self-fulfilling prophesies, like Douglas McGregor's Theory X and Theory Y.[36] McGregor's premise was that the attitudes and beliefs that managers held about people would, by influencing the way the managers behaved, bring about a reactive effect in the behaviour of their people. Just how powerful this process can be was shown in some studies, known as the "Pygmalion experiments".[37] These found, initially, that identical groups of rats produced different levels of performance in experiments depending on what the experimenters had been told about them. This is remarkable enough in itself (although fans of Terry Pratchett's books may think they can explain it). The research was extended to school children, randomly choosing one child in five and informing teachers that the selected children were "academic spurters". The selected children were found after a year to have added 22 points to their IQs, a considerably greater, and statistically significant, increase than their peers. The implication of this is that the teachers treated the children differently depending on what they had been told about them, and that these differences in treatment resulted in different rates of progress.

Self-fulfilling prophesies of this kind can have a tremendous impact on people in the workplace. For example, as Margaret Wheatley puts it: "if a manager is told that a new trainee is particularly gifted, that manager will see genius emerging from the trainee's mouth even in obscure statements. But if the manager is told that his or her new hire is a bit slow on the uptake, the manager will interpret a brilliant idea as a sure sign of sloppy thinking or obfuscation".[38] This tendency isn't restricted to the organizational setting, of course. In the wider social setting it may take the form of prejudice against (or, perhaps less commonly, in favour of) groups or categories of "others".

Vividness is a potent cause of distorted judgements; strong images of individual examples make a much bigger impression on us (they are recalled more readily and so are more "available") than statistical information, and examples that are close to home in some way can seem more significant than those that are less directly connected to our own interests and concerns.

very fishy

In discussing leadership I was, perhaps, rather disparaging about the validity or reliability – or indeed the usefulness – of things to be learnt from the autobiographies of famous people in commerce and industry. This is because they are often affected by one or more of the heuristics described above. For example, at an airport bookshop you might spot a copy of *How I Saved the Global Dried Fish Industry* by Joe Crustacio, the well-known former CEO of troubled multinational American Bloater Inc. You hope to pick up some tips on leadership, but as you read Joe's account your judgement could well be influenced by *availability*; you will have the book, and probably not much else to do, for at least the duration of your flight. *Vividness* could also have an impact; with luck the book will have been written (perhaps by a ghost writer) in an exciting and possibly even inspiring style. And you will be woefully short of *base-rate information*; you won't know how many failures Joe had, what disasters he caused, how much better the successes could have been, or, indeed, how much of what happened was actually down to Joe in any sense at all. You will only be told about his triumphs, and only his version!

Applying similar criteria to reports in a newspaper might lead you to question how satisfied you should be that you really know what happened. Or that your opinions about it are genuinely your own. It would certainly be fair to ask yourself what the newspaper journalist, editor and/or proprietor *want* you to think. If you have ever read an account in a newspaper concerning something about which you have direct, personal knowledge you may well have been struck by inaccuracies and misleading implications in the report. If so, inductive reasoning should suggest something about the reliability of other reports in newspapers concerning matters about which you don't have that special knowledge.

Another common heuristic device is the use of *scripts*; we imagine or envisage a plausible situation, making use of what we know of options and possibilities. For example, if someone believes that becoming an airline pilot is a possibility, then he or she may construct a "script" in which she or he mentally plays out the role, imagines gaining the necessary educational requirements, applying to an airline, undergoing the training, qualifying and, finally, doing the job. If it turns out to be hard to imagine achieving all the demands at the various stages in the script, then the option may be discarded. Of course, this may make the script self-fulfilling, for good or for bad; if someone has already mentally discounted an option they are unlikely to take the actions which would be necessary to realize that particular future for them. Similarly, if someone has a clear script for a potential development path they may be more ready to seize opportunities to realize that future as and when they arise.

It's a basic human characteristic to look for causes, reasons or explanations of why things happen.[39] This is generally a positive tendency; it is after all the basis of most advances in knowledge, but it does have a negative side as well. We see what people do and the consequences of their actions; an observer often has no other information to go on, although we may know something about the situational demands, social pressures, etc,. that someone is under. From the rather flimsy evidence of what we can actually see we tend to infer (i.e. make assumptions about) their intentions. We may then go even further and use our inferences about people's intentions to make assumptions about their "dispositions", i.e. about their characters and what they are actually *like*. If the inference is mistaken, which is called "fundamental attribution error", social relationships can be adversely affected.[40]

It's very hard *not* to make these attributions; a number of psychological experiments have demonstrated the strength of our need to do so. For example, audiences listening to political speeches tended to "feel" that the views expressed were actually the speaker's own opinions, even though they had been told that he or she was only reading a prepared script.[41] Similarly, people watching a quiz game tended to assume that the questioners were more knowledgeable than the "contestants", even though they knew that the roles had been assigned completely randomly.[42] This is essentially why actors get sacks of mail addressed to the characters they play, mail that can get quite abusive, even threatening, if the character is a villain. Attributions of this kind are even applied to inanimate objects; in one experiment people watching blobs of coloured light moving around a screen consistently used terms like "aggressive", "timid", "chase" and "hide" when asked to describe what they saw.[43]

good intentions The psychologist of child development, Jean Piaget, observed that very small children tend to judge how "naughty" an action is on its consequences, even if those consequences were quite unintentional.[44] Adults (and the tabloid press) sometimes display similar tendencies, for example by demanding harsh punishment of drivers whose unintended actions lead to fatal road accidents even though the same papers often agitate against the "persecution" of other drivers who act in just the same way, but without tragic consequences. The application of even the most rudimentary thinking skills would show that it's impossible to deter someone from something he or she never intended to do in the first place, so increased penalties associated with these tragic *outcomes* could not possibly have the effect of reducing accidents, although consistently tackling the behaviours that just occasionally lead to such outcomes might do so.

There are many more implications of the attribution process that I won't go into here. The general lesson to take back to the workplace is that we

we may have less control over our decisions than we thought

may have less control over our decisions than we thought, and that assumptions about people are always risky.

Other heuristics that can have unfortunate consequences include *illusory correlation*, in which completely unrelated things are seen as influencing each other in some way. We may also attribute *causation* when in fact there is only *correlation,* i.e. we assume that, because two things tend to go together, one must be *causing* the other. In fact, both may be responding to a third, unidentified, factor. We may be misled by *anchoring*; asked to estimate something, e.g. the percentage of colleagues who are vegetarians, we are very likely to be influenced by a figure previously mentioned to us, even if it's totally baseless or has nothing to do with the question. And we may be subject to *entrapment*, where we have "invested" so much in a situation that we feel bound to continue in it, even after it has ceased to be beneficial to us.

All these heuristics can lead to real problems, but it's important to remember that I've been emphasizing their negative side in order to draw attention to the risks involved. The positive aspects of heuristics are that they help us to tackle day-to-day events very rapidly and, on the whole, quite effectively. Being aware of the possible hazards will probably be quite enough to make a significant improvement in the quality of your own decision-making, and the collective decisions in which you take part.

In this chapter I've tried to show how the way work is organized – the *processes* that are involved in carrying it out – can have a profound impact on effectiveness, and on the quality of working life. I've extended this basic concept to include the social organization of work, specifically the grouping of workers into teams that can achieve collectively things that could never be accomplished by individuals working in isolation. Finally, I've examined a particular kind of process that affects everyone, every day of our lives: the process of making decisions. This is, on the whole, something we are quite good at in practical terms, but in which we have a number of weaknesses and vulnerabilities.

Becoming consciously aware of processes can be a powerful step towards improved effectiveness and the elimination, or at least the drastic reduction, of expensive errors. It's virtually certain that a much better job will be done by someone who can truthfully say "processes help me to do it".

"Processes help me to do it" checklist

What aspects of "the system" do you personally find limit or obstruct you in doing your job well?

What aspects cause difficulties for your people? How do you know?

If you had a completely free hand, what would you change in order to make work easier or more efficient for you and your people?

What are the inputs to the processes in your department's everyday work?

Who provides them?

What are the outputs?

Who uses these outputs as the inputs to their processes?

How rigorously are the "rules" enforced in your organization?

What effects does this have?

If you work in a team, to what extent do you think it has:

- a common purpose?
- a distinctive identity?
- mutual dependency?
- behavioural norms? Can you tell what these are?

What phase is the team currently in?

Did it work through earlier phases thoroughly?

Can you identify any interpersonal issues that impede its performance?

If a group in which you are involved has recently made a decision, did you agree with that decision?

Did you change your mind, or "shift your ground" at all during the decision-making process? If so, why?

Are decisions usually made in your organization by following a logical, sequential process?

Can you see any examples of groupthink in your organization?

Can you think of a recent decision or decision-making process that seems to have been influenced by any of the heuristics described in this chapter?

How would you guard against heuristic-based weaknesses in the future?

notes and references

1 Thomas, M (1994) "What you need to know about business process re-engineering", *Personnel Management,* January, 28–31

2 Deming, WE (1986) *Out of the Crisis,* Cambridge, MA, MIT CAES

3 Hardin, G (1968) "The tragedy of the commons", *Science,* No. 168, 1243–8

4 Revistaiberica (2003) *El Tribunal De Las Aguas Valenciano,* available at: www.revistaiberica.com/Grandes_Reportajes/valencia.htm

5 Blasco Ibáñez, V (1898) *La Barraca,* English edn, published by Harrap, London, 1964

6 Margerison, C & McCann, D (1990) *Team Management,* London, Mercury Books

7 Manz, CC & Sims, HP (1995) *Business Without Bosses,* Chichester, John Wiley

8 Katzenbach, JR & Smith, DK (1993) *The Wisdom Of Teams,* Boston, MA, Harvard Business School Press

9 Batt, R (1999) "Work organization, technology and performance in customer service and sales", *Industrial and Labor Relations Review,* **52**, (July), 539–63

10 Moxon, P (1993) *Building A Better Team,* Aldershot, Gower

11 Katzenbach *et al.*, *The Wisdom of Teams,* op. cit.

12 Handy, C (1985) *Understanding Organizations,* 3rd edn, Harmondsworth, Penguin

13 Tuckman, BW & Jensen, MAC (1977) "Stages of small-group development revisited", *Group and Organizational Studies,* December, 419–27

14 Jacobs, R & Campbell, DT (1961) "The perpetuation of an arbitrary tradition through several generations of a laboratory microculture", *Journal of Abnormal and Social Psychology,* No. 62, 649–58

15 Ringlemann, M (1913) "Recherche sur les moteurs animés: travail de l'homme", *Annales de l'Institut National Agronomique,* **2** (12) 1–40

16 Latané, B, Williams, KD & Harkins, SG (1979) "Many hands make light the work: the causes and consequences of social loafing", *Journal of Personality and Social Psychology,* No. 37, 822–832

17 Lawrence, PR & Lorsch, JW (1967) "Differentiation and integration in complex organizations", *Administrative Science Quarterly,* **12**, part 1, 1–47

18 Gray, RJ (2000) "Organizational climate and the competitive edge", in L Lloyd-Reason & S Wall (eds) *Dimensions of Competitiveness: Issues and Policies,* Cheltenham, Edward Elgar Publishing

19 Gray, RJ (2001) "Organizational climate and project success", *International Journal of Project Management,* **19** (2), 103–9

20 Belbin, M (1981) *Management Teams,* London, Heinemann

21 Belbin, M (1993) *Team Roles at Work,* Oxford, Butterworth Heinemann

22 Adair, J (1983) *Effective Leadership,* Aldershot, Gower

23 Lawrence & Lorsch, "Differentiation and integration in complex organizations", op. cit.

24 Hogg, MA & Vaughan, GM (1995) *Social Psychology,* Hemel Hempstead, Prentice Hall/Harvester Wheatsheaf

25 Stoner, JAF (1961) *A Comparison of Individual and Group Decisions Involving Risk*, unpublished Master's thesis, MIT School of Industrial Management

26 Janis, IL (1982) *Groupthink: Psychological Studies of Policy Decisions and Fiascos,* 2nd edn, Boston, MA, Houghton-Mifflin

27 Janis, IL & Mann, L (1977) *Decision Making,* New York, Free Press

28 Fishbein, M & Ajzen, I (1975) *Belief, Attitude, Intention And Behaviour: An Introduction To Theory And Research,* Reading, MA, Addison Wesley

29 Edwards, JR (1988) "The determinants and consequences of coping with stress", in CL Cooper and R Payne (eds) *Causes, Coping and Consequences of Stress at Work,* Chichester, John Wiley

30 Simon, HA (1976) *Administrative Behavior,* 3rd edn, New York, Free Press

31 Mintzberg, H (1973) *The Nature Of Managerial Work,* New York, Harper & Row

32 Karasek, R & Theorell, T (1990) *Healthy Work: Stress, Productivity, and the Reconstruction of Working Life,* New York, Basic Books

33 Kahnemann, D & Tversky, A (1984) "Choices, values and frames", *American Psychologist,* No. 39, 341–50

34 Hayes, N (1994) *Foundations Of Psychology,* London, Routledge

35 Kershaw, C, Budd, T, Kinshott, T, Mattinson, J, Mayhew, P & Myhill, A (2000) *The 2000 British Crime Survey,* London, Home Office Statistical Bulletin 18/00

36 McGregor, D (1960) *The Human Side Of Enterprise,* New York, McGraw-Hill

37 Rosenthal, R & Jacobsen, L (1968) *Pygmalion in the Classroom: Teacher Expectations and Pupil Intellectual Development,* New York, Holt, Rinehart & Winston

38 Wheatley, MJ (1994) *Leadership and the New Science,* San Francisco, Berrett-Koehler Publishers Inc

39 Hayes, *Foundation of Psychology,* op. cit.

40 Jones, EE & Davis, KE (1965) "From acts to dispositions: the attribution process in person perception", in L Berkowitz (ed.) *Advances in Experimental Social Psychology,* **2**, New York, Academic Press

41 Jones, EE & Harris, VA (1967) "The attribution of attitudes", *Journal of Experimental Social Psychology,* No. 3, 1–24

42 Ross, L, Amibile, T & Steinmentz, J (1977) "Social rules, social control & biases in social perception processes", *Journal of Personality and Social Psychology,* No. 35, 485–94

43 Heider, F (1958) *The Psychology of Interpersonal Relations,* New York, Wiley

44 Piaget, J (1932/1965) *The Moral Judgement of the Child,* New York, Free Press

seven

I have the resources to do it

managing resources When considering business processes, in Chapter 6, I suggested that processes are made up of activities, each of which has three parts: inputs, transformation and outputs. If we work back through these three elements we might begin by defining an output as something that we want to have that we don't have now. We could then move on to determine the nature of the transformation that needs to take place in order to produce the thing that we want, and this would lead inevitably to a list of necessary inputs. These inputs are the resources that are required if the activity is to be carried out successfully.

Some of the inputs to any specific activity, of course, are likely to be the outputs of another, earlier activity, just as some, if not all, outputs of that activity will be inputs to another, later, one. This "chaining" (concatenation) of outputs and inputs is the essence of a *process*.

It follows that if managers want activities – or "work" in general – performed successfully they must ensure that the necessary resources are available to the people who need them, at the time when they are required. *Available* in this context means that it's both ready for use and "accessible". For example, a computer display – which is an information resource – might be available if it was in an adjacent room but it's accessible if it's clearly in the line of sight of a technician who needs to refer to it. A tool that is somewhere in a cluttered toolbox is available (it's somewhere in the toolbox), but it isn't readily accessible. Similarly, a specific piece of information may well be available in a thick manual, but isn't necessarily very accessible.[1]

who's responsible? It's important to emphasize that the availability and accessibility of resources are management responsibilities. Of course, resources not being available can sometimes be due to genuine external causes – "the lorry was struck by lightning" or "there's been a coup d'état in Andorra" – but very often it's the result of a deliberate policy, or at least, a decision; staffing levels, budgets, secrecy and so on are not usually natural phenomena. This doesn't mean that a manager has to take care of every aspect of workplace practice personally. That would almost certainly become oppressive as well as being prohibitively expensive. Rather, managers must ensure that people are enabled to do their jobs; that obstacles are removed and ineffective practices changed or improved. In the end, that's basically what managers are for.

The first practical step required is to identify the necessary inputs to every task. These inputs, or resource requirements, are likely to fit into one or more of five broad categories:

- people and skills
- raw materials
- partially completed work
- tools and equipment
- information.

staffing levels, budgets, secrecy and so on are not usually natural phenomena

I could also include finance here, but I've left it out because usually money is only(!) a medium of exchange by which items in the other categories can be obtained. This isn't always so. In some situations money may actually be the raw material that is to be transformed into something else, even if this is simply larger amounts of money. Time is another resource that can have a profound impact on the work that is done in any organization, but I won't consider time as an isolated category here because ways of optimizing the use of time, gaining (or buying) time or speeding up the performance of an activity are likely to be very specific to the particular activity under scrutiny. This does not, however, mean that it can be overlooked.

Some of the categories in the list above have their own special features that need to be looked at individually, but there are one or two general considerations that apply to all or most of them.

cutting some slack There are several factors by which resource management can be assessed – in particular, efficiency and effectiveness.[2] Efficiency is often cited as a worthwhile goal for its own sake but this is simplistic; just as, earlier, I suggested that measurement should be seen as a tool used in the process of assessment, so efficiency should be seen as a factor contributing towards *effectiveness*, which is the real goal. Efficiency, in science, is a value-free term describing the ratio of energy used to work produced, or of inputs to outputs. In organizational settings the word is normally used with distinct value-judgement overtones to mean maximum outputs for minimum inputs. All things being equal, this amounts to the minimization of waste, which is certainly something to aim for. However, striving for maximum efficiency can be counter-productive if a short-term or small-scale view is taken. Sometimes effectiveness – which at one level means successfully achieving objectives – can be better served if there is a certain amount of "slack in the system".

sometimes effectiveness can be better served if there is a certain amount of "slack in the system"

The reason for this is that work takes place in variable conditions. Some of the variations can be controlled but others are effectively uncontrollable. Any serviceable product or process must be able to function properly under all the conditions that can reasonably be anticipated if it is to work effectively and this means that it must be able to tolerate a certain amount of these uncontrollable variations, which Genichi Taguchi, whose early career was in telecommunications, refers to as "noise".[3,4]

For example, a photocopier will be used in an office; the temperature and humidity of offices varies quite a lot and some offices can be quite dusty. Static electricity levels can be high. Also, the paper used in photocopiers is of variable quality, subject to variations in size, accuracy of cutting, thickness, moisture content, flatness, surface density, loose fibres, and so on. If the photocopier is to go on working the probable upper and lower limits of all these variables under "normal" conditions must be assessed and the machine designed to go on working so long as conditions remain within these limits. This inevitably means that in offices with conditions that remain close to the average or central values of all these variables much of the machine's capability to cope with the extremes will never be needed. This is wasteful and inefficient on the micro scale, but in terms of overall production it means that a single design can be used for a range of user environments, and that machines will be less likely to fail if normally stable conditions undergo occasional big variations such as a heatwave, a batch of sub-standard paper, or someone leaving the windows open during a rainstorm.

This example clearly relates to the design of a physical product, but Taguchi's principle of "robust design"[5] applies equally to resourcing in general terms: working to very tight tolerances can lead to inflexibility and make the organization vulnerable to fluctuations in the general environment. Tough economic conditions, cut-throat competition and the demand for profits all act to tempt managements into operating as close as they dare to maximum efficiency. The danger of this is that their organizations develop what has been called "corporate anorexia".[6] Anorexics can't see for themselves – although everyone else can – just how thin and ill they are becoming. They think they look fat and, in extreme cases, continue to think so until starvation causes irreparable damage to vital functions. This is a fair analogue of what can happen to an organization that becomes obsessed with efficiency.

I have mentioned one aspect of effectiveness: the successful achievement of objectives. This isn't much good, though, unless you have the "right" objectives in the first place.[7] Doing the wrong thing very efficiently just leads more quickly to disaster.

people planning Ensuring that the right *people* with the right skills (and the right attitudes) are available in the right place at the right time is called human resource planning. In a sense, much of this book is concerned with achieving this desirable situation so here we will consider only the more "mechanical" aspects.

If the nature of the activity is well known, which may be the case with well-established "steady state" processes, then the numbers of people required and the skills they will need to possess are relatively easy to estimate. Resourcing then becomes a matter of anticipating the need far enough ahead to recruit or transfer people who either have the necessary skills already or have the potential to learn them. If training or retraining is necessary then this anticipation requires greater prescience and considerably more investment, but the principle is more or less the same. Unfortunately, it's seldom as easy as this. The volatility of markets and the pace of environmental change often mean that activities can only be planned in the shortest of timescales, which means that the human resource demands are identified far too late for the leisurely process described above to be a realistic option.

One increasingly common response to this problem is to deploy people with the necessary skills temporarily to work full- or part-time on the activity concerned. Usually, these people would retain their place in the

doing the wrong thing very efficiently just leads more quickly to disaster ongoing organizational structure, so they would still have the same line manager and departmental hierarchy, but for the duration of their involvement with the activity they would also have responsibilities to the "owner" of the activity. This is called a *matrix* arrangement, and it has various strengths and weaknesses.

Perhaps the most obvious problem is that traditional hierarchies are disrupted, and people end up with two or more bosses. This *dual subordination* feature of matrix organizations has been described as a complex psychological situation which "puts stress on all three people involved, just as in a love triangle".[8] This understanding isn't new, of course; St Matthew described it very well when he wrote that "no man can serve two masters; for either he will hate the one, and love the other; or else he will hold to the one and despise the other", but of course serving two (or more) masters is just what employees are expected to do in matrix arrangements.

Line managers will probably still be the people who write annual appraisals and have the strongest influence on bonuses, promotion prospects and long-term happiness at work, so people will (again, probably) be most concerned to stay in favour with them. On the other hand, activity owners are the "customers" for the work in the shorter term, and may be influential characters whom it would be unwise to antagonize. Hence the individual may be faced with competing demands, prioritization difficulties and role conflicts.

If the people doing the actual work can find the situation problematical, there are also difficulties for the line managers and the activity owners. Line managers can find their key staff taken away from "business as usual" to work on activities that contribute little to their own objectives – which is a resource issue in its own right – and may resent the diminution of control over their own departments. Activity owners may find that their priorities mean little to the line managers on whom they are dependent for a key human resource and may find themselves waiting for someone else's grace and favour while vital deadlines loom ever closer.

This can lead to power struggles and conflict where boundaries of authority and responsibility overlap, and competition for scarce resources. It can make an organization sluggish because consultation and shared decision-making can slow reaction times down. There can also be difficulties in monitoring and controlling because information sources are multiplied and responsibility can get blurred between the various participants.[9]

All this might make this kind of organizational approach seem distinctly unattractive, so it may seem surprising that matrix organizational structures are extremely common,[10] perhaps even "the most common form found in today's organizations".[11] The reason for this is that despite the disadvantages matrix approaches offer the most satisfactory (or maybe just the least worst) way of utilizing human resources and responding quickly to opportunities.

On the positive side, the benefits of organizing in this way are that resources, especially people, can be utilized more efficiently, and information flow and communication have been found to improve both vertically (up and down the hierarchy) and laterally (between peer groups). Flexibility has been found to improve, partly because people from different departments are frequently in contact with each other and so can make decisions and adapt to each other's needs more readily. Functional experts and specialists are kept together even though projects come and go, so expertise is retained and developed. And motivation and commitment have been found to improve, possibly because people are involved in decision-making.[12]

The one really vital organizational requirement, if high performance is to be achieved, is that the pressure of the conflicting demands must be taken off the person actually performing the work. Line managers and activity owners have to talk to each other and negotiate for the individual's time and priorities without obliging the person to choose between them, otherwise it's likely to end in tears. Senior management can help considerably by providing a genuinely fair and impartial arbitration service, based transparently on organizational priorities, and by being seen to be willing to compensate the "loser" by relaxing or modifying their objectives where appropriate.

parts and labour I will not say too much about the second category of resources, *raw materials*, because this is, after all, a book about people and not about quantity surveying or procurement. I will, however, reiterate that it's a manager's job to ensure that the necessary raw materials are available and accessible, and are deployed with due regard to economy and the avoidance of waste. In order to audit the resource requirements for any given activity (or, on the wider scale, any process or project) a simple but highly effective modelling tool can be applied.

The *work breakdown structure* (WBS) is a hierarchical breakdown of all the work required to achieve a particular outcome. The principle is exactly the same as an organization chart, where whole organizations are composed of divisions, which are sub-divided into departments, comprising units or teams, made up of individuals. The starting point of the WBS is a description of the "complete" output of the activity. This is then "deconstructed" to identify its major components. Each of these is then treated in the same way to identify the parts or sub-components that go to make it up. Although WBS stands for *work* breakdown structure, it's good practice to define its elements in terms of what's produced, rather than what's being done, i.e. to use nouns rather than verbs. This allows for a further level of analysis concerning the tasks or work involved in achieving satisfactory completion of each element.

One objective in building a WBS should be to appoint one "owner" for each of its elements, a named individual who takes responsibility for the outputs defined for that element and *all its sub-divisions*.

To illustrate the process we might take as an example the preparation of one flower bed in a public park or garden. The output of the complete activity is a floral display. This is produced from a selection of plants installed in a prepared flower bed. The prepared bed has to be cleared of the remnants of last year's display, dug over, treated with fertilizer, and raked. Seedlings (which may well be the outputs of an earlier activity) are brought to site and installed to a pre-arranged design in the prepared bed. For this to be successful a supply of water is needed on site. This activity can be represented as a WBS with seven elements, on three levels, as illustrated in Figure 7.1.

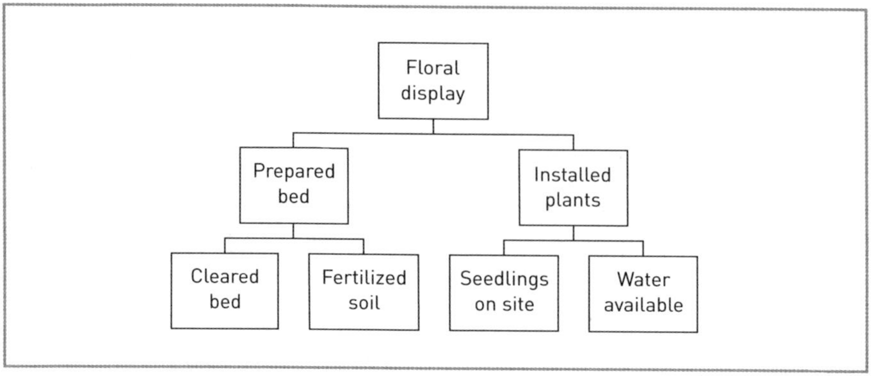

FIG 7.1 ● A work breakdown structure

Clearly though, each of the elements represents several tasks and a variety of resources. The tasks, for example, involved in achieving a "cleared bed" include removing all the old plants, together with any weeds and, presumably, carting them away for disposal off site. What we must do is determine what resources are needed to complete the job: labour, transport and disposal facilities. These have to be quantified. How many people are needed to do the job? What kind of vehicle? Driven by whom? Will the waste go for composting, incineration or landfill? Is it necessary to make arrangements with the owners of the disposal activity for the output of this task (i.e. the waste) to be accepted?

When "building" a WBS it's natural to begin to think about the logical order or sequence in which the various elements will be performed. This isn't what the WBS is for, however; the WBS should be used to *identify* the tasks and resources that will be necessary to achieve the overall objective; putting the tasks into their proper sequence is another, later, step.

Identifying and quantifying the resource requirements for each of the elements in the WBS produces an alternative version of the model known as a *bill of materials* (BOM) in which a complete output – or product – is composed of major assemblies, which are constructed from sub-assemblies, which are built up from components, which comprise various parts (different terminology may sometimes be used for these "levels of completeness"). Which of the two variations is likely to be most useful will depend on the exact nature of the activity; sometimes both will be found helpful. The important thing is for the manager to be fully aware of all the inputs required for the activity to be completed in the most satisfactory way, and to ensure that any obstacles impeding the availability and accessibility of resources are removed. In other words, to make it as easy as possible for people to do the work they are being paid for.

Where the input to an activity is *partially completed work* this is likely to be the output(s) of other people's activities. There is considerable potential for conflict and misunderstanding at the interface points where output is handed over and becomes input to the next activity. Initially, it is the clear responsibility of the two activity owners concerned to ensure that they understand and respect each other's needs. This is a significant management skill and it's at least arguable that managers who fail this "cooperation test" aren't performing adequately. All managers experience their own pressures and priorities, however, and it would be unrealistic to expect that this will never lead to difficulties that the protagonists are unable to resolve by themselves. When this happens the problem needs to be escalated to more senior managers for resolution.

The need here is to lift the decision-making above the level of personal competition. If the outcome is that one manager is enabled to meet her objectives while the other is prevented from achieving his, then it's essential that responsibility for this "failure" is shouldered by the organization and doesn't have any negative implications for the individual manager. Over time, consistent application of this principle will lead to increased cooperation and a much higher "hit rate" of successfully achieved objectives across the organization.

Tools and equipment are a special kind of resource because in many cases they are not "consumed", or used up, as the activity is performed. There are two qualifications to this statement. Equipment that is hired

make it as easy as possible for people to do the work

specifically for the activity concerned and then returned is better considered as a consumable (in fact it's the cost that's consumed but for practical purposes it's much the same thing). Similarly, many kinds of equipment for commercial use suffer from physical depreciation, so using it on the activity will result in some directly attributable costs. Purely time-related depreciation, which would happen even if the equipment was left in a cupboard, is a little more complicated because it raises issues of whether the equipment would have been bought in the first place if that particular kind of activity wasn't being carried out, and whether additional units of the same equipment are needed because of the number of similar activities being undertaken concurrently. What proportion of these costs should be attributed to individual activities is an accounting decision which we won't consider here.

Forethought, planning and good cooperation between activity owners can help considerably in optimizing the use of tools and equipment. An example of this is illustrated in Figure 7.2.

In this simple example, a second concrete mixer is needed for a while because the two activities overlap. If both mixers are hired at a daily rate this probably doesn't matter at all, but if the company owns one mixer it may have to hire a second one for three days and then have its own capital equipment standing idle once Activity 2 is completed. This suggests

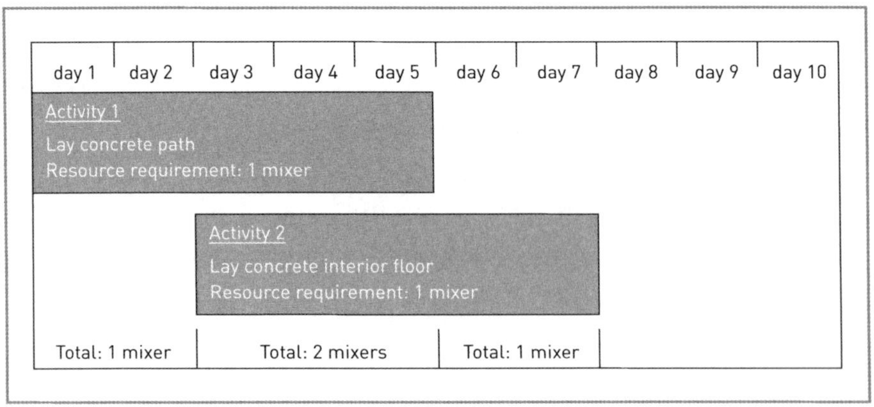

FIG 7.2 ● **Optimizing resources**

that it would be beneficial to delay the start of Activity 2 and have the equipment in continual use for ten days, with no hire charges incurred. Of course, the consequences of delaying Activity 2 in this way would have to be taken into account.

what you know *Information*, which might be defined as "useful data", is an intangible but none the less vital resource for most activities. Earlier, I suggested that access to information is an important source of power in organizations, although it has been argued that access to information contributes to everyone's power by increasing the collective ability to think and to organize.[13] As with any other resource, there's a need to analyze the specific requirements of each activity to define what information is needed for that activity to be performed effectively, but there are some special considerations.

The accessibility of information depends, perhaps more than other resources, on the means by which it is conveyed to those who need it. This needs very careful research and, perhaps, experiment in order to get it right. Also, in general terms it's best to be as free as possible with information because the wider people's understanding of a situation is, the more enabled they are to make decisions about it. The value of this in terms of increased effectiveness and reduced supervision and inspection overheads can hardly be overstated. Earlier, with regard to goals and objectives, I said that if people understand the purpose of their work they often won't need to be given detailed instructions because they will apply their own intelligence, skills and creativity to the task, making hundreds of daily low-level choices and decisions sensibly and without the need for constant close supervision. They can only do this if they have information readily accessible to them, not only narrow, task-related information but also the kind of contextual information that helps to make the task make sense.

There are two valid reasons to restrict the accessibility of information. One is that if it gets out it will do some kind of harm. In other words, it needs to be kept secret. Realistically, this is limited to certain kinds of commercially or politically sensitive information and a really objective assessment will often show that either it doesn't matter very much if it gets out or that it does matter, but the competitors already know about it anyway. Secrecy can be extremely damaging when applied inappropriately. As an example, the second world war proto-computer, codenamed Colossus, was built largely at his own expense by the British Post Office engineer, Tommy Flowers, working at Bletchley Park on principles developed by the mathematician Alan Turing. In wartime, of course, secrecy was essential but Flowers was required to continue to observe absolute secrecy about the work when he returned to the Post Office after the war and he never developed his designs for commercial purposes. This development went ahead in the less obsessively secretive USA, with the result that the computer industry flourished in America instead of in its birthplace in England.[14]

Sometimes the need for secrecy is more personal, where possession of information confers power or influence that an individual doesn't want to relinquish, or perhaps free access to information would reveal unethical or even criminal behaviour. It hardly needs to be said that the interests of the organization will usually be better served if these things are brought out into the open.

The second reason for restricting access to information is more positive: too much information can be overwhelming. Avoiding this kind of "information overload" needs careful handling because if people feel things are being kept from them they are likely to become suspicious and distrustful, which isn't an atmosphere that is conducive to excellent performance. A reasonable compromise is to ensure that all the information people would find useful is highly accessible, while all other information except that which genuinely needs to be kept confidential *can* be accessed, but people have to make a positive effort to get at it. Of course, this starts with some kind of audit of the information people need and, as with other assessments of people's jobs, it's a good idea to ask the people who have to perform the task rather than make assumptions on their behalf.

if essential resources are missing it's a failure of management, not of the employees

No-one can do an excellent job if they don't have access to those resources that are required for the job's performance. Ensuring that resources are available is a prime management responsibility; if essential resources are missing it's a failure of management, not of the employees. On the other hand, good stewardship is another key management responsibility and inefficient or wasteful deployment of resources is an unnecessary cost burden on the organization's functioning.

Striking a sensible balance between these two requirements will be easier if resource needs are properly analyzed and action is taken to match supply to demand.

"I have the resources to do it" checklist

To what extent are processes you know about in your organization designed to cope with occasional variations?

Is any form of matrix arrangement operated in your organization?

If so, are you aware of any issues/difficulties arising from it?

Is any conscious action taken to make such arrangements work smoothly?

If you have to escalate disputes over resources to higher management for a decision, is the outcome usually fair to everyone?

What resources, including information, do the people who report to you need in order to do their jobs to the standards that you require?

Would they produce the same list as you? How do you know?

What resources (including information) that you personally need to do a good job are often not accessible to you?

What can you do to make things easier for yourself and your people?

notes and references

1 Harbour, JL (1996) *Cycle Time Reduction,* New York, Quality Resources

2 Thompson, JL (1997) *Strategic Management,* London, Thompson Business Press

3 Taguchi, G (1986) *Introduction to Quality Engineering: Designing Quality Into Products and Processes*, Dearborn, MI, American Suppliers Institute

4 Peace, GS (1993) *Taguchi Methods: A Hands-On Approach,* Reading, MA., Addison-Wesley

5 Phadke, MS (1989) *Quality Engineering Using Robust Design,* Englewood Cliffs, NJ, Prentice Hall

6 Kirwan-Taylor, H (2002) "Are you suffering from … corporate anorexia", *Management Today,* December, 24

7 Thompson, *Strategic Management,* op. cit.

8 Harrison, FL (1992) *Advanced Project Management,* 3rd edn, Aldershot, Gower

9 Larson, EW & Gobeli, DH (1987) "Matrix management: contradictions and insights" *California Management Review*, **xxix** (4), 126–38

10 Kliem, RL & Ludin, IS (1992) *The People Side of Project Management* Aldershot, Gower

11 Wysocki, RK, Beck, R & Crane, DB (1995) *Effective Project Management,* New York, John Wiley

12 Larson & Gobeli, "Matrix management", op. cit.

13 Husar, R (2002) *Information as a Resource,* School of Engineering and Applied Science, Washington University in St Louis, available at: http://capita.wustl.edu/CAPITA/People/RHusar

14 Clarkson, J (2004) "Jeremy Clarkson's inventions that changed the world – the computer", BBC2 Thursday 22 January. For a summary, see: www.bbc.co.uk/pressoffice/pressreleases/stories/2003/12_december/23/invention_synopses.shtml#computer

eight

the environment is right

organizational culture If a good friend of yours had just been offered a job in your organization, what advice would you give him or her about how to survive and thrive there?

If you treated this question with the seriousness and rigour that it deserves you should now have a highly pragmatic working model of the organization's *culture*. This model, however, will be rather superficial; it reflects the very common definition of culture as "the way we do things around here". This definition, with its implications of distinctiveness – "the way *we* do things is different from the way other organizations do them" – is helpful, but incomplete, as well as being superficial. Culture goes deeper than mere actions. It's been described as a "distinctive constellation of beliefs, values, work styles and relationships that distinguishes one organization from another".[1] Those beliefs and values are powerful influences on individual and collective behaviour, amounting to a kind of "software of the mind"[2] or mental programming that can determine not only what we do but also what we perceive to be the *right* things to do and even what we think.

There are many other ways of defining or modelling organizational culture, and we will explore several of them in the following pages. First, though, it's legitimate to ask why culture matters. Many writers and researchers have investigated relationships between culture and performance and it seems clear that the two are linked. Culture has been called "a soft, holistic concept" that has "hard consequences",[3] or even the "psychological assets of an organization, which can be used to predict what will happen to its financial assets in five years' time".[4]

Extensive research in the early 1990s by what was then the Institute of Personnel Management concluded that management strategies to manage performance or the quality of service or production would succeed or fail depending largely on the culture of the organization, and that an understanding of culture "and the commitment to make any necessary changes were prerequisites for almost any successful management strategy".[5]

Inconveniently, though, it isn't at all clear just what cultural attributes will make an organization successful, although adaptability seems to be quite important. Some attributes which may contribute to success under some circumstances can become handicaps when conditions change. For this and other reasons we will look at culture from a variety of perspectives in order to try to build a balanced understanding.

personality plus One particularly useful way of looking at it is to think of an organization's culture as being like an individual's personality. Of course, like any analogy this only works up to a point. All the same, there are many similarities and considering culture from this metaphorical perspective will enable us to clarify some terms that will recur repeatedly as we examine this topic.

The term "personality" is a convenient label for a range of distinguishing characteristics, including:

- mental abilities
- sociability

- emotional stability
- impulsiveness
- conscientiousness
- temperament (which covers things like activity level, attention span, adaptability and irritability).

Personality has been defined as: "the distinctive patterns of thought, emotion, and behaviour that define an individual's personal style and influence his or her interactions with the environment",[6] which is rather strikingly similar to the definition of culture quoted above.

These ideas help to describe the phenomenon of personality, but they rather invite the question "where does it come from?"

There seem to be two primary influences in the formation of personality: genetic factors and things that are learned. It's important not to oversimplify this dual influence model because the two factors are inextricably combined; "living organisms construct themselves out of the raw materials provided by both genome and context".[7] With this caveat, though, it's useful on the practical level to think of genetic factors as forming the "hard wiring" that determines what is possible and, perhaps, influences an individual's preferences in a variety of ways, whilst the learnt or environmental factors may be thought of as the "software" that is "installed" and "upgraded" throughout life.

Evidence for the genetic contribution seems quite strong. Some studies of twins[8] have found that identical twins who had been separated at or soon after birth and brought up apart had very similar sets of personality characteristics (technically, a correlation of +0.49, which is significantly more than you would expect to occur by chance) and identical twins brought up together showed only slightly higher levels of similarity (a correlation of +0.52). In contrast, non-identical twins, i.e. siblings born at the same time but not sharing identical sets of genes, showed much lower correlations (+0.21 for those brought up apart and +0.23 for those brought up together). The implication of this is that upbringing, i.e. learned factors, had much less impact than genetic factors on what the individuals were "like". The validity of these studies has been challenged[9] and it's been claimed that very little human psychology is more than 50% inherited,[10] so just how important the genetic "hard wiring" is in determining personality isn't absolutely clear, but it must be seen as playing a role, even if we can't be sure how big that role is.

The second source of personality characteristics is social learning. This is based on the principles of reinforcement and conditioning which were introduced earlier. Social learning theory[11] extends the concept of conditioning by showing that people can learn not only from things that happen to them, but also from observing what happens to others and how they respond. A major force in social learning is the positive reinforcement we derive from the approval of others and from "belonging" and the negative reinforcement arising from disapproval and exclusion. So an important factor in the development of personality is that we quickly learn the "right" things to do and say and, inevitably, the right things to think and to believe.

under the influence This adaptation of our behaviour under the influence of other people occurs at three levels.[12] The lowest level is *compliance*, which means going along with what we think, or are told, is required, without necessarily believing it's the right or best thing to do. For example, if someone is holding a knife to your throat you will probably comply with their request to hand over your wallet. You will not, though, see giving your credit cards to complete strangers as a behaviour that you wish to continue in the longer term. Compliance tends to last only as long as the external influence that is driving it persists – a point that was mentioned in the discussion of rewards and motivation.

Identification is the next level. This means adopting the behaviours (style, manners, speech, dress code, typical actions, etc.) of another person or group because we admire them and want to be more like them, to seem like them, or to be accepted by them. Because this is more of a voluntary behaviour it tends to last rather longer, as long as we

compliance tends to last only as long as the influence driving it persists

continue to admire the reference group or person, or still want to be accepted by them. The concept of a role model comes into this process at the level of identification.

The deepest level is *internalization*, which means changing our ideas, values and behaviours because we have come to believe that the new ways are better and more valid. Once the level of internalization is reached the behaviours or values concerned can be said to have been incorporated into personality; they become *our* behaviours and *our* values, rather than someone else's that we are merely copying. Identification, and possibly, but less likely, compliance, may be intermediate stages in this process.

Although the process of social learning depends on our observations of other people's behaviour and events going on around us, what we observe isn't wholly objective or necessarily accurate. Human perception is a dynamic process by which we try to make sense of the world around us as best we can.[13] This dynamic process takes the raw data input from the five senses and filters, processes, augments and alters it to give it meaning, using established patterns or categories with which we are already familiar. This means that our perceptions can never be 100% objective; a proportion of what we perceive as "reality" is always coming from inside our heads rather than from the "real world" outside, as illustrated in Figure 8.1.

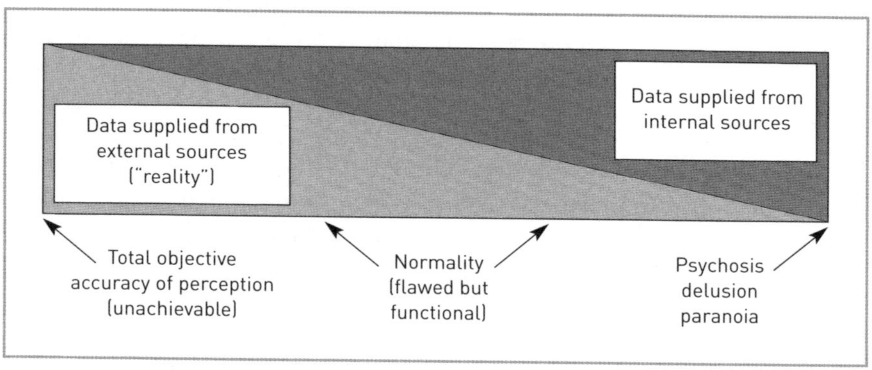

FIG 8.1 ● **Perceptions of reality**

Because of this dynamic aspect of perception, and because people *interpret* their environment continually, what has already been learned and experienced will affect new learning and experience. It does this first by influencing *what* we look for – which can determine whether things are perceived at all – and secondly by changing *how* things are perceived. In other words, future development of personality will be affected strongly by the way it has developed up to now.[14,15] The subjective nature of what we usually think of as "reality" is illustrated in the model shown in Figure 8.2, which also demonstrates the interconnectedness or mutual dependency of perception and mental processes.

The argument that an individual's personality is formed partly through genetic "hard wiring" and partly through life experiences and learning is certainly an oversimplification and there are other views about how personality is formed. There is also disagreement about how stable the characteristics are likely to be over time; clearly, if characteristics are acquired in the first place through learning then they must be susceptible to change through the same mechanism. However, it may be of more practical importance to consider the extent to which individuals' personality characteristics, as they are now, influence or determine their behaviour.

Earlier I suggested that personality can affect how we perceive our environment, and even *if* we perceive certain things at all. It follows that

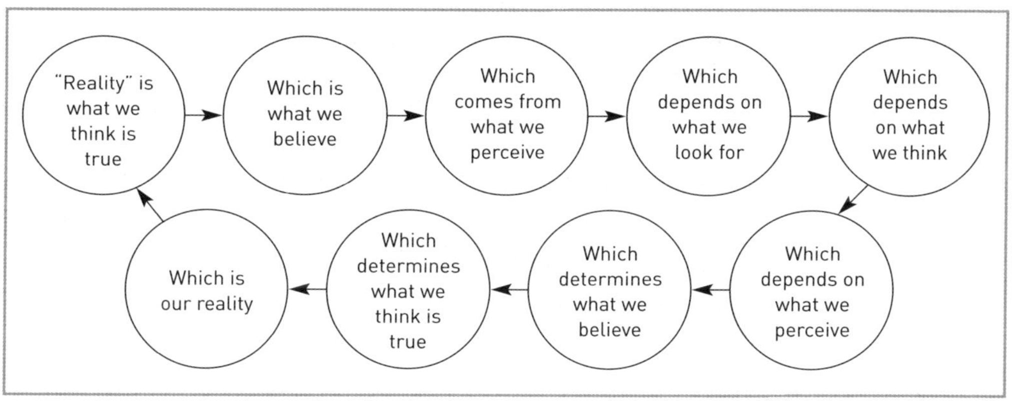

FIG 8.2 ● Model of perception

Source: Based on words by Gary Zukav [16]

when we are faced with a choice between alternative courses of action our decisions may be affected by our personality in two ways: first, we may not fully understand the range of available choices because we may fail to perceive certain options, and secondly the relative attractiveness of the various options that we *do* perceive to be available is also likely to be influenced by personality factors. This raises a question that has exercised philosophers for centuries: just how free is free will? For now it may be best to limit ourselves to considering its implications for decision-making, personal and organizational.

If the analogy of individual personality and organizational culture is valid – or more importantly, if it's *useful* – it should be possible to draw direct parallels between specific aspects of the two concepts. To do this it will be helpful to consider how the organization was first established: the people involved, the things they considered important, their views of right and wrong, and the commercial, social and/or legal context at that time. We should then try to establish what learning experiences have shaped and influenced the development of the organization's culture over its lifetime up to now. Armed with this information, we would be in a position to explore how the present-day culture of the organization – the way we do things around here – is affected by these two influences.

everyone has attitude

The analogy of individual personality with organizational culture can also be helpful when we consider beliefs and values, which were identified as elements in the "distinctive constellation"[17] of organizational culture. We can also mention *attitudes* here because these three concepts are intimately linked. In fact this causes some difficulties because the three concepts are so inter-related that they tend to be defined in terms of one another. It may be helpful first to consider that, as adults, each of us probably has tens of thousands of beliefs, hundreds of attitudes, but only dozens of values.[18]

A *belief* may be defined simply as "the acceptance of some proposition"[19] without implying any particular attitude about that proposition. For example, you may *believe* that Hampshire is an English county, but not feel any emotional engagement with that fact. Some beliefs, though, certainly will affect attitudes and values directly; religious or philosophical beliefs are obvious examples. It can work the other way, too. Negative *attitudes* towards, for example, certain kinds or categories of people can make us more ready to *believe* bad things we hear or read about them.

Attitudes are a little harder to define than beliefs. One authoritative definition[20] describes attitudes as "learned orientations or dispositions" towards things or situations that lead us to respond favourably or unfavourably towards those things or situations. This is quite complex because it combines three kinds of components: thinking or *cognitive* elements, feelings and value judgements (*affective* elements), and the actions that result (the *behavioural* element).

Most definitions of attitudes agree that they are learned, either from direct experience or from observing others, education, the media, and so on. The process of reinforcement, or conditioning, is at work here, following the *Law of Effect,* which says that actions that are reinforced tend to be repeated, whilst actions that are not reinforced tend to die out.[21] One of the kinds of reinforcement associated with attitude formation arises from the process of Compliance–Identification–Internalization, described above;[22] having the "right" attitudes helps you fit in and having the wrong ones can get you excluded.

Attitudes may also serve a more inward-facing, personal function; for example, an individual who has inner fears about getting too close to someone else may develop cynical attitudes about close relationships in general. This is called *externalizing* the fear, which means finding an apparently genuine and rational reason outside ourselves to explain and justify the way we feel. An attitude may be meeting any or all of these needs so attitudes can be very hard to change.

At this point it will be useful to define *values*. Values are regarded as a rather abstract concept representing an individual's ideals about what is

having the "right" attitudes helps you fit in

good or desirable, and underpinning his or her behaviour and goals. Key characteristics of values are that they are enduring[23] guiding principles, and that they are *transsituational*,[24] an admittedly ugly piece of jargon but one that does convey the sense in which values are independent of specific situations. This suggests that values should be thought of as pre-existing reference points that are influential in the formation of attitudes when the need arises, as well as helping to guide our choices between alternative possible behaviours.

In this sense, attitudes may be thought of as the means by which generalized values are applied to specific situations; attitudes are values in action.

It is possible for the same underlying value to give rise to a variety of specific attitudes. So, someone who had acquired the underlying *value* of honesty might develop *attitudes* towards such things as telling lies (which might – but might not – be different for different categories of lie, ranging from kindly intended "white lies" through to outright perjury), or "liberating" small items from the workplace, or tax evasion, or theft, or shifting the blame when things go wrong, or taking the credit for someone else's work or ideas.

In fact, any new situation requires us to formulate an attitude about it. For this to happen, all the processes described above will come into play. However, although the pressures of reinforcement and social factors such as compliance, identification and so on may be very strong, trying to maintain an attitude that conflicts with an underlying value can be psychologically disturbing. The mind has mechanisms to protect us against this potentially damaging disturbance.

tell it on the mountain

One such mechanism, which may have quite profound effects on our perceptions, was described and explained after a researcher[25] became fascinated by an event involving a religious cult, whose leader prophesied the destruction of a major city and gathered her followers on a hill-top to await the event. When the catastrophe failed to occur the cult members might have concluded that their leader had got it wrong but that would have implied that they had been gullible, not to say stupid, to have been so convinced of her infallibility. Instead, they came to the belief that it was their prayers that had saved the city, thus re-balancing the "dissonance" between their belief in their leader and the reality that her prophesy had not come true. They had succeeded in "cognitively reconstructing reality".[26]

To test this idea out,[27] students were paid to perform an extremely tedious task: turning a large number of wooden pegs through quarter-turns for half an hour. The students then had to help recruit more participants by telling them that the task was really worthwhile, important and interesting. One group of students, who had been paid $20 each, did as they were asked but afterwards maintained their original view that the task had been excruciatingly boring and pointless. Another group, who had been paid only $1 each, however, appeared genuinely to believe in the value of what they had been doing. This difference was explained by attributing the $1 group's attitude to a need to justify to themselves their seemingly irrational action in lying about the task for such a trivial sum, whilst for the $20 group the payment was sufficient justification without any need to adjust their cognitions.

The conclusion to be drawn from this is that when there is conflict between two related cognitions – such as attitudes – tension or "dissonance" will result. This tension will be dealt with either by changing one of the cognitions or by adding another to "explain" the discrepancy. This "cognitive dissonance" theory has been supported by a number of studies subsequently. Cognitive dissonance theory matters because it describes a psychological mechanism that can affect what we perceive, and therefore what we believe, or "take to be true".

Organizations, as well as individuals, have values, attitudes and beliefs and these have a profound effect on what the organization can do, and what it sees as the right things to do. Sometimes organizations can hold and practise values that would shock their individual members if applied at the personal level. Thus it's quite possible for directors who are, in private life, humane and caring individuals, to sit around the boardroom table and make decisions that will have catastrophic consequences for other people, destroying livelihoods, damaging environments and even leading to injury or death, because the value of profit and shareholder return takes priority *in that context*. Cognitive dissonance theory helps to explain how this is possible.

Understanding what processes of reinforcement and learning might have produced these cultural phenomena and the effects they have on decision-making can be very enlightening and will certainly repay the time and effort involved. It can also help to clarify the compatibility or incompatibility of our own personal values, attitudes and beliefs with those of the organization.

literary device Considering culture as the organization's "personality" in this way is a *metaphorical* perspective. A metaphor is a literary device in which one thing is described as something else. Usually, the reader or listener is well aware that the description isn't meant to be taken literally. For example, if we read that "the sea was molten gold" or that "the north wind was an icy dagger" we (probably) don't imagine that these statements are actually or literally *true*. Metaphors like this do, however, provide a great deal of perfectly valid – i.e. *true* – and certainly useful *information* in a very few words by creating powerful images in the mind.

In his book *Images of Organization*[28] Gareth Morgan makes very effective use of the power of metaphor as an aid to understanding organizational life: a way to bring order to and make sense of the highly complex, messy and jumbled collection of elements that we typically see when we first look at an organization. Morgan recommends using different metaphors to identify or highlight key aspects of the situation and then to make use of the different interpretations to build understanding, evaluating the significance of the insights provided by each different metaphorical perspective. Just taking one metaphor won't do, because "any realistic approach to organizational analysis must start from the premise that organizations can be many things at one and the same time",[29] so to use this approach you need to try several metaphors for size and see which ones prove helpful. I've picked the following examples from among Morgan's collection of organizational metaphors.

The organization is a *machine*. If we think about the characteristics of a machine we might identify features such as: standardized, replaceable "parts"; tightly defined functions; fixed, formal relationships; control systems; and fixed, imposed procedures. Organizations that operate this way may, in fact, be called "mechanistic" and, like machines, they may not work well outside their pre-defined parameters.

The organization is an *organism*. The characteristics of living organisms might include: living; growing; interacting with its environment; a "life cycle"; evolution; perhaps reproducing?; learning; eventually dying. We might also use such biological imagery as "healthy" to describe an organization, and we might think of organizations as belonging to various "species". Understanding the organic nature of an organization can help us to manage – or, at least, cope with – its untidiness and unpredictable development patterns.

The organization is a *brain*. Brains acquire information from the environment, via "senses". They process that information and have storage and retrieval capabilities. They take decisions, and they interact with the environment. They are also powerful cybernetic devices; that is, they are self-regulating and respond to feedback. Brains have also been found to have "holographic" properties. This is itself a metaphor; holograms are formed by interacting laser beams that create an "interference pattern" that scatters the information being recorded on a photographic plate. It has been observed that, if a hologram is broken, any single piece can be used to reconstruct the entire image. In neuroscience, this metaphor describes the apparent capability of the brain to distribute stored memories so that they can potentially be retrieved from any part of it (or several parts, at least). Organizational culture is distributed through the organization in a similar way, so that everything that's done in the organization is affected to some extent by the culture in ways that can't be directly controlled by any individual or group.

The organization is a *political system*. Of course, to some extent all groupings of people are political systems. Some of the characteristics of political systems are: power; control (of decisions, resources, information, boundaries, etc.); category groupings (by gender, class, ethnicity, religion, education, language, etc.); conflicting interests; alliances; factions and in-fighting. Some common kinds of political structure, which may have parallels in organizational life, include: autocracy (rule by one person), oligarchy (rule by a group of people), democracy (rule by "the people"), tyranny (technically, this should mean rule by an autocrat who seizes power unlawfully, but the term is usually taken to mean an oppressive or despotic regime), and anarchy, which means no-one rules at all.

The earlier discussion of leadership may have some relevance in evaluating the strengths and weaknesses of these various structures in the organizational setting. The main point here, though, is to reach some conclusion about what you've actually got (as opposed to what would be nice to have) and formulate strategies for either improving it or making the most of it.

The organization is a *psychic prison*. This sounds rather poetic and needs some explanation. First, it's worth remembering that according to the philosopher Epictetus "wherever anyone is against his will, that to him is a prison".[30] Here, the term "psychic prison" is a metaphor that describes the restrictions on the freedom of thought and imagination that organizations can impose on their members. Some of the psychological processes that help us to "belong", to fit in and to work together, can also act as powerful constraints through which an organization, group or team can impose restrictions on the freedom of its members to act or even think independently. Groupthink is just one example of these processes. This extends beyond behaviour to influence attitudes and values, and even the ideas it is possible for us to have. In the seventeenth century Richard Lovelace wrote "stone walls do not a prison make, nor iron bars a cage", knowing that such physical restrictions are quite superfluous if the real restraints are in our minds.

Society, of course, is based on continual compromise between personal freedom and conformity to norms in return for social benefits. As Edmund Burke put it: "liberty must be limited in order to be possessed".[31] However, allowing an organization to become a psychic prison is a recipe for disaster. Members may not realize how restricted their perspectives have become, in which case they will be unable to consider an adequate range of options when decisions have to be made. On the other hand, they may perceive themselves to be under restraint and resent it, in which case the "resistance" mechanisms discussed earlier may start to show themselves.

The organization is a *process of change*. It may seem odd to think of or describe a "thing" – in this case an organization – as a "process", but in nature we find examples of "process structures" that don't have any rigidity or solid shape and yet still maintain their form over time.[32] An example of this kind of phenomenon is a whirlpool, which clearly does have a physical existence. It can be seen, heard, felt, measured, photographed and in fact subjected to many kinds of scientific analysis or study. It has power, sometimes to devastating effect. It's definitely real! And yet the whirlpool only exists as a characteristic of *water* in a certain state of movement and subject to various influences that force it into certain "actions". These produce the form that we see. The analogy here is that the organization is also a kind of process structure, produced when its members are subjected to a combination of influences. If we think about the "form", in the sense described above, of a particular organization we can then begin to understand what influences are making it the way it is. From there it's a relatively short step to wondering whether any of these influences are susceptible to control and, if so, what effects that might have.

The organization is an *instrument of domination*. It would be unusual for an organization to declare openly that domination – enabling one person or group of people to exercise power over others – was actually its *purpose*, but some organizations do make use of domination in one form or another as an operational policy, and some individuals may come to derive significant personal satisfaction from the ability to dominate others that the organizational setting affords them.

some organizations make use of domination as an operational policy

Power may be exercised over employees or subordinates through such means as rewards, opportunities, penalties or intimidation, or over markets through innovation, efficiency, cheap labour, ubiquity or patents, or over competitors by efficiency, economic muscle or dirty tricks, or over politicians by means of lobbying, political contributions, deals, bribery or blackmail, and even over whole societies through trade agreements, patents, political influence, bribery, being a monopoly employer, and so on. These are only examples; there are sure to be many more kinds of "victim" and many more ways in which domination is exercised. Also, some of these strategies are often considered legitimate, others are not, and some of them may be acceptable in one place and unacceptable elsewhere.

The value of looking at an organization through the "lens" of this metaphor is that we can examine the behaviour of the organization or members of it and consider where it's leading.

working the system

So far we have considered organizational culture from a variety of *metaphorical* perspectives: first as the organization's personality, and then through some of Gareth Morgan's imaginative imagery. Now we will take a more *analytical* approach, considering various aspects, or dimensions, of organizational culture's make-up.

At the very beginning of this book I referred to organizations as *systems*, pointing out that systems have characteristics that are only present in the whole, and are not found among the component parts. The technical term for this is that systems have "emergent properties". We will now look a little deeper into what constitutes a *system* and some other phenomena arising from the systemic nature of organizations.

Aristotle was probably thinking mainly of living organisms – which are classic examples of systems – when he suggested that "the whole is more than the sum of its parts", and it is a biologist – Ludwig von Bertalanffy – who is often considered to be the "father" of modern systems thinking during the mid twentieth century. Figure 8.3 illustrates this concept.

Essentially, a *system* in this context means any group of components which, when assembled together, make something with an existence in its own right. Which components we choose to consider is a matter of

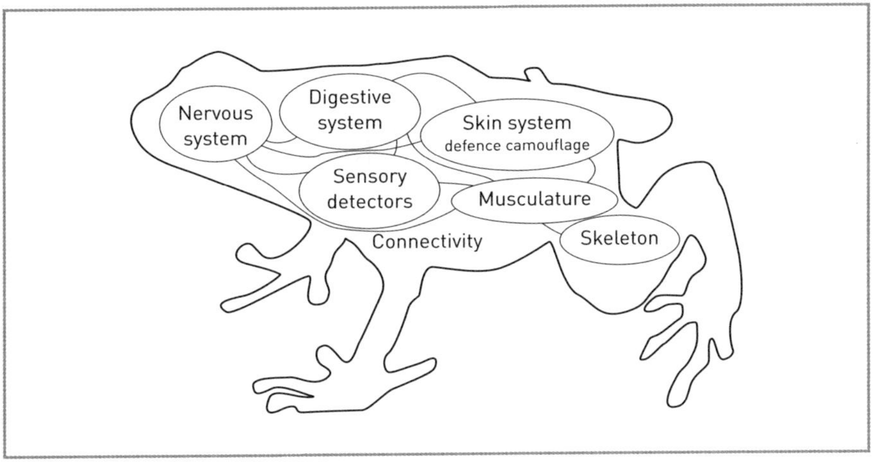

FIG 8.3 ● **A living organism as a system**

judgement, because systems may well be composed of sub-systems that could themselves be seen quite legitimately as systems, too. We will examine this further as we go on.

The systems that are of primary interest in the study of organizations are human activity systems. These, too, can be seen as being composed of system elements, which interact with each other and together make up something with an identity of its own.

Because it's possible to perceive almost anything as a system provided that certain minimum criteria are present, it's important to define the system boundary at an early stage: what is an integral part of the system and what lies outside it? A "viable" system should have several basic properties.[33] First, it must have some purpose or objectives; then it needs measures of performance, and the monitoring and control mechanisms to keep track of them; there must be decision-taking procedures; and the system must have the resources that it requires to function. These are really categories of elements; there might be several or many elements of each kind in any system. The elements are all interconnected and it's likely that the system "in focus" – i.e. the one under consideration – may itself be an element in a bigger system; that is, it may be part of a hierarchy of systems. The basic concept is shown in Figure 8.4.

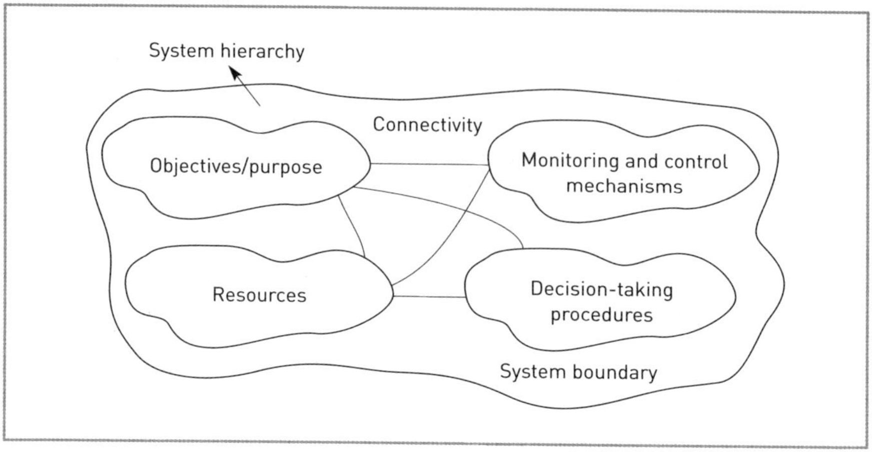

FIG 8.4 ● A basic system map

To illustrate this, we might take a small customer reception centre as our system in focus. We might describe the system in the following terms: the system boundary is defined by the responsibilities and authority structure of the department; the department is part of a wider organization, on behalf of which it interacts with customers, deals with queries, takes orders, etc., so it is one element in a bigger system. There are various elements in our system in focus, such as a manager, operators, IT systems, defined procedures, performance targets and communications, and they all interact with each other in a variety of ways. Of course, this is a highly simplified overview; in real life you might expect to identify many more elements.

If you tried to draw even a simple "system map" in a similar way for your own department, including all the interactions between the elements, you would probably find it took a lot of time and thought and it's likely, however well you know your department, that you would get some of the elements and relationships wrong – missing some out and assuming others that aren't really important.

If you now tried to estimate the *direction* of each relationship – whether element A influences element B, or if it's the other way round, or perhaps it works both ways – and the *strength* of those influences – just how much each element is affected by the others – you might find it a major challenge. But assuming you were able to do this comprehensively and accurately, and if you were to ignore all the influences from outside the system boundary, you would now be in a position to estimate what the effects would be if just one of those factors were to change slightly. For example, if an existing relationship were to end, or a new one begin, or if any of the relationships should increase or decrease in strength, or change direction.

What we have just been considering is the basis of *complexity theory* – better known perhaps as chaos theory – as it applies to the study of organizations. Chaos, in the sense I am using the term here, doesn't have its usual colloquial implications of "utter confusion or a complete lack of any form".[34] What it means is that the relationships between many elements of our system in focus become so complex that a very small change can begin a "chain reaction" that for all practical purposes is quite unpredictable.

An example of this principle, so familiar that it almost counts as folklore, is the idea of the butterfly fluttering its wings in Brazil and causing a typhoon in China. This is, of course, rather silly (isn't it?) but it's conceptually quite sound; a minute "change of state" – in this case an infinitesimal disturbance of air currents – may disturb a delicate balance of forces and so prompt another, very slightly more significant change, and so on until something really major occurs. An equally familiar example might be the old nursery rhyme that goes something like this:

For the want of a nail the shoe was lost

For the want of a shoe the horse was lost

For the want of a horse the rider was lost

For the want of a rider the message was lost

For the want of a message the battle was lost

For the want of a battle the kingdom was lost

And all for the want of a nail.

Chaos theory in action!

Now you wouldn't expect the behaviour of organizations to be utterly unpredictable or unstable – chaotic – all the time. The key to instability lies in how sensitive systems are to small changes. Chaos as we are discussing it here occurs when the equilibrium, or stability, of a system is very finely balanced, so that there is very great potential for small changes in one or more of its elements to cause major changes in the whole system.[35]

Feedback, positive or negative, is a vital factor in understanding chaos. Negative feedback acts to suppress trends, whilst positive feedback enhances and accelerates trends. The control unit in a domestic heating system reacts negatively as the ambient temperature rises, turning the heating off and thus suppressing the trend towards high temperature. When the room cools down the control again functions negatively, switching the heating on and thus suppressing the trend towards low temperature. Negative feedback in this sense promotes stability. Positive feedback works the opposite way. For example, in human interactions praise or reward for good work may act to reinforce behaviour patterns and so lead to even better performance. Positive feedback promotes change. Within a system, the interactions of feedback may be highly complex and/or contradictory, and the effects can be very unpredictable.

Fortunately, there are positive aspects to the unpredictable behaviour of systems. First, unpredictability is not absolute; there are "recognizable patterns or categories of behaviour" within which there is "endless individual variety".[36] A graphic example of this is the image of a marble rolling around in a bowl: "locally unpredictable, globally stable".[37] Where the marble will roll is not predictable, but we can be sure it won't pass through the sides or base of the bowl, or defy gravity and rise vertically.

Also systems, including organizations, may operate at their most robust and effective level at the interface between stability and disorder, the "edge of chaos",[38] because of the richness of interfaces and the exchange of information which occurs across these interfaces. It's in this "optimal transition zone"[39] between complexity and chaos that change and development occur at the maximum speed without being thrown into total disorder by trivial events.

We will leave the notion of chaos there. Clearly, unpredictability has massive implications for such routine organizational preoccupations as strategy and planning, and you may want to give these implications some serious thought. Indeed, you may come to the conclusion that activities like these merit rather *less* serious attention; you should draw your own conclusions. Systems concepts, though, are fundamental to the understanding of organizational behaviour.

pigeon holes There are several other ways of looking at organizational culture, each of which has the potential to add something to our understanding of culture in general, or to help in understanding a specific organization's culture with a view to improving some aspect of performance.

Many authors have suggested ways of categorizing organizational cultures, based on prominent characteristics. Of course, no real-life organization would actually fit any notional category very closely, but it can help to understand a specific culture if we have a model of a *culture type* in a "pure" form with which to compare it. Some of the descriptions, or labels, for the various culture types found in the management literature can be quite imaginative. Charles Handy[40] for example uses the names and characteristics of various ancient Greek gods to illustrate his typology. Others have talked about the "tough guy" culture and the "bet your company" culture[41] or the "guided missile", "Eiffel Tower", "family" and "incubator" cultures.[42]

I will make use of one fairly representative taxonomy of culture types, by W.E. Schneider,[43] to illustrate this approach. He identifies four basic culture types, based on a matrix with the vertical axis running from "Actuality", meaning an orientation towards what *is*, to "Possibility", meaning an orientation towards what *could be*. The horizontal axis goes from "Personal", meaning an orientation towards people as individuals, to "Impersonal", indicating an orientation towards the whole organization as an entity. The model is illustrated in Figure 8.5.

Some cultures seem to emphasize teamwork, partnership and cooperation. They tend to foster positive relationships and find it quite natural

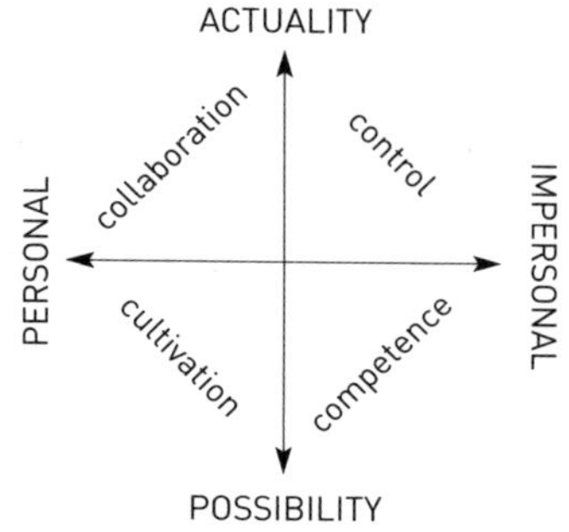

FIG 8.5 ● Four culture types

to build and make good use of diversity, which suggests that they gravitate towards the "Actuality/Personal" quadrant of the matrix. These are called "Collaboration" cultures. They tend to be versatile and adaptive. Individual talent is fostered, in practice, although it may not always be recognized, and employees often feel a sense of ownership and pride. On the negative side, when faced with a ruthless adversary, Collaboration cultures may be disadvantaged by slow decision-making, short-term thinking, and vulnerability to groupthink.

Cultures that are more oriented towards the "Actuality/Impersonal" quadrant are called "Control" cultures. These are based primarily on people's need for power. They tend to be hierarchical, with formal systems and centralized goal definition. There is often an emphasis on reward and punishment (usually linked to goal achievement). Control cultures tend to be stable and secure, but they can be arrogant, and individual flair and innovation can be stifled.

Cultures that are based on the achievement motive are likely to prize and emphasize personal and organizational excellence. These "Competence" cultures tend towards the "Impersonal/Possibility" quadrant. Cultures like this are often the sources of technological advance but they may foster technical excellence at the expense of pragmatism: "we can, therefore we will!" People may feel insecure in competence cultures; you have to keep showing how competent you are and maybe you're only as good as your last success.

The last quadrant of this matrix – the "Personal/Possibility" area – is where cultures based on trust and commitment are found. These "Cultivation" cultures are characterized by flexible relationships and are amenable to change and adaptation. They are likely to value their people's aspirations and hopes, and are good at tapping and utilizing individual talent. Perhaps as a consequence of this, people may well feel fulfilled, inspired and "enlivened". The down side, and there has to be one, is that Cultivation cultures may lack direction and focus. They can be blind to "hard" data, and poor at decision-making if too many options are available, and they can be weak at completing/finishing.

Of course, the four quadrants of this matrix represent only tendencies, or especially noticeable groupings of characteristics. Any individual organization might have a mixture of characteristics, although you may feel that some combinations would be rather unlikely. Also, it's quite feasible for parts of the organization to have noticeably different cultures. You may well have noticed this if you have ever moved to another department within the same organization, and found that it "felt" quite different, and things were done in different ways.

A slightly different perspective, which to some extent complements the one above, also uses a quadrant model but with a vertical axis from "Flexibility and Discretion" at one extreme to "Stability and Control" at the other. The horizontal axis has "Internal Focus and Integration" at one end and "External Focus and Differentiation" at the other. Because these labels represent opposing views about what is "right" in the context of organizational structure and management, this model is called the "Competing Values Framework".[44] The four quadrants of this model show how different organizational values are associated with different forms of organizations.

A set of values that tends towards flexibility and discretion, and towards integration and an internal focus produces a "Clan" culture. This has a lot in common with extended family units, characterized by teamwork, cohesiveness, shared values and goals, while the individual is valued and nurtured.

Value-sets that tend towards integration and internal focus on the horizontal axis but towards stability and control on the vertical one produce a "Hierarchy" culture. This is pretty much the traditional form of bureaucracy, which was originally a neutral description of an observable organizational structure, rather than a term of abuse. In fact, Max Weber, who coined the term in the late nineteenth century, regarded bureaucracy as an efficient and humane way of structuring organizations and it has, on the whole, served quite well for a long time. The characteristics of a hierarchy culture are formal rules and procedures, managers who are good coordinators and organizers, and restrictions on individual initiative.

Values that tend towards stability and control, but towards external focus and differentiation on the horizontal axis, produce a "Market" culture. The energies of this type of organization are directed towards winning orders and making deals; the basic measure of work is the "transaction", and success consists in getting the best of every negotiation.

The fourth quadrant, oriented towards external focus and differentiation and towards flexibility and discretion, is called "Adhocracy". In this kind of organization risk-taking is encouraged, individuality is fostered, and organizational structures change constantly to meet the needs of the moment, or of the near future.

Both these models essentially describe different sets of characteristics that their authors find particularly significant or noteworthy, so both could usefully be applied to any organization in order to gain a better understanding of how it functions, culturally.

what you see is what you get? There are some other ways to look at organizational culture, each of which in its own way has the potential to increase understanding.

When we first try to examine an organization's culture, some aspects of "the way they do things around here" are actually visible, although the meaning of what we see may not be clear.[45] These are the "artefacts": the creations, the technology in use, perhaps the art which is on display, and the visible and audible behaviour patterns of the people.

Below this superficial level lie the culture's values: the "sense of what ought to be, as distinct from what is".[46] The recognition of a culture's values represents and requires a greater level of awareness on the part of the observer. At the deepest level of all lie the culture's basic assumptions, about its relationship to its environment, about such concepts as reality, truth, human nature, human activity and human relationships.[47] It can be very difficult for people who are members of the organization to recognize these basic assumptions, and outsiders can usually only hope to infer them from observation of the "higher" levels.

Some understanding of the values held by the organization can be gained by checking the prevailing attitudes to certain issues. These "functional values" may differ in six principal ways.[48]

First, how important and how widely respected are position and hierarchy. This indicates whether the culture tends towards being hierarchical or towards informality. Then, how willing the organization is to "accept imprecision" or to take risks indicates its tendency towards risk tolerance or towards risk aversion. Is greater value placed on "macho" behaviour or on caring/nurturing behaviour? Does there seem to be a preference for working in and being judged as groups or as individuals?

Where the organization is located on the theoretical–practical axis is shown by the degree of interest in and comfort with concepts and theories. Finally, organizational thinking may tend to focus on long-term or on short-term timescales and issues.

strong stuff

At one time the "strength" of an organization's culture was thought to be a major asset. In their book *In Search of Excellence* Tom Peters and Robert Waterman[49] showed that a number of "excellent" – i.e. financially successful – companies had very "strong" cultures where everyone knew how to behave and was strongly influenced by "the way we do things around here". For a while this perspective on the value of strong cultures was generally accepted but has since been rather discredited, as we will see shortly.

The notion of culture strength seems to have three components.[50] *Pervasiveness* refers to how widespread, or shared, the culture is, and also to the numbers of people who have internalized the beliefs and values rather than simply complying with them. *Range of control* refers to how many aspects of behaviour and how many beliefs and values the culture sets out to influence. *Consonance* refers to what's often called "said and done policy": how well the organization's explicitly stated values and beliefs match the genuine values and beliefs that really drive behaviour. These three elements determine how strong the culture is, or the amount of pressure it exerts on people in the organization; for example whether members feel compelled to follow the dictates of culture or if they feel that the culture only "mildly suggests that they behave in certain ways".

In practical terms, this model can be used to form judgements about an individual organization's culture through some simple questions (simple to ask, that is; getting the answers may be anything but).

Range of control covers such things as: What behaviours are directed or influenced by the culture? What beliefs? What attitudes? And which are not?

Pervasiveness can be addressed through questions like: Is more or less everyone affected by the culture? If not, who isn't? And why not? Are the values internalized? Or just complied with?

Consonance can be judged by considering to what extent you can detect discrepancies between the organization's *espoused* values (those it claims to hold) and its actual behaviour (which may betray its real values) and asking how much does it matter?

Peters & Waterman's view was that, when an organization's members shared beliefs and values, rules and regulations would become unnecessary.[51] In other words, behaviour is controlled by the members themselves. This is probably true in the sense that it's an accurate observation of what happens. What doesn't seem to have turned out to be quite right is the prediction that this would be an unqualified advantage for such an organization. In fact, most of Peters & Waterman's "excellent" companies failed to sustain their performance; just five years after their book was published "two-thirds of those companies had hit trouble in varying degrees".[52] A later study of over 200 US companies concluded that "the statement 'strong cultures create excellent performance' appears to be just plain wrong" and advised that strong cultures "can lead a firm into decline as well as success".[53]

The reason for this seems to lie in the homogeneity of strong cultures; the social control, the compliance–identification–internalization axis, and the common interpretation of environmental factors all lead the organization's members to see things, to behave, and even to think in similar ways. Survival in a rapidly changing world, however, requires a variety of perspectives, new ideas, and a willingness to adopt new beliefs, attitudes and values more suited to current conditions. It seems that a strong culture is an advantage only so long as the rest of the world, including the competition, cooperates by not changing too much

it's what you know

To "survive and thrive" in an organization requires a considerable amount of knowledge, of various kinds.[54] First, there's the kind of knowledge that is commonly held and includes definitions and descriptions. This is called *dictionary knowledge*. Then there's knowledge about cause-and-effect relationships, processes and how to do things. This is called *directory knowledge*. *Recipe knowledge* covers "recommendations, improvements, and repair strategies" and is "composed of cognitions about what should be done to improve things or what should be done in case something goes awry".

Finally, *axiomatic knowledge* covers the "basic assumptions that have influenced an organization's existence".

Cultural knowledge of this kind has to be absorbed – or learned – by newcomers if they are to fit in to the culture in which they find themselves, but equally the accumulation of knowledge is a vital part in the process by which culture develops and changes. This happens in various ways, including the importation of knowledge into the organization by the newcomers themselves.

getting the balance right

Hopefully, the preceding pages have shown that there are many dimensions and facets to the way organizations work. Increasingly, there is a recognition that managers need to pay attention to all, or at least many, different aspects of organizational life if the highest standards of performance are to be achieved. This has led to the development of various "balanced" models of management, two of which we will look at briefly now.

The European Foundation for Quality Management (EFQM)[55] has developed a complex model, used as the basis for awarding an annual prize for "excellence" to competing organizations. The model is divided into two sections. The first, called "enablers", consists of five categories:

- leadership
- people
- policy and strategy
- partnerships and resources
- processes.

The second section, called "results", has four categories:

- people results
- customer results
- society results
- key performance results.

Points are awarded for performance against targets in each of the categories. Even if they don't win the prize, organizations that achieve a minimum score can be deemed "excellent".

Working from a slightly different perspective, Robert Kaplan and colleagues developed what they call their *balanced scorecard*, intended to improve strategic management by providing a more sophisticated performance measurement system.[56,57,58] Traditionally, management measures have tended to focus on financial factors, such as economic value added or return on capital employed. The balanced scorecard doesn't dismiss these but it supplements them with new measures concerned with the creation of "value" for customers, the enhancement of internal processes, including innovation, and the creation of new capabilities in employees and systems.

It's claimed that the balanced scorecard approach leads to improved consensus and clarity about strategic objectives, better communication of strategic objectives to business units, departments, teams and individuals, better alignment of strategic planning, resource allocation and budgeting processes, and clearer feedback about the effectiveness of strategy and its implementation. Support for these claims has come recently from an extensive investigation by The Work Foundation.[59] After talking to a thousand chief executives the foundation concluded that the highest performing organizations balanced their priorities across five performance categories: customers and markets; shareholders; stakeholders; employees; and creativity and innovation. Firms scoring highest on an index calculated from these factors were over 40% more productive than those at the bottom.

Models like the Balanced Scorecard and EFQM represent a new orientation in management thinking, which owes a great deal to systems concepts. Previously, commercial organizations tended to perceive their principal activity to be "making profits". However, profits – like happiness – tend to be elusive when pursued directly. They are more likely to come as a side-effect, or spin-off benefit, of some other activity, such as "meeting customers' requirements" or perhaps "making a better mousetrap".

Balanced management approaches recognize that organizational success or effectiveness is most likely to be a product of nurturing *all* the major elements of the organizational system. This is likely to be the case regardless of whether, overall, success is measured in profits, or market share, or new patents, or degrees awarded, or numbers of homeless people housed, or any other criteria.

profits – like happiness – tend to be elusive when pursued directly

If the perspectives on organizational culture described in this section seem complex and perhaps occasionally contradictory it's because human social interactions are subject to a vast array of influences. Trying to understand how a large unit like a modern organization actually functions is never going to be easy; it has occupied the careers of an army of academics and consultants for the best part of a century and the current state of knowledge can be summed up as "the more we learn about it the more complicated it seems to get".

Much of the research into culture has been based on the study of small groups, which is probably a good place to start but does provoke the criticism that the interactions in a larger organization are exponentially more complex, so generalizations from the small group scenario must be treated with a certain amount of caution. It is also true that multiple sub-cultures can exist within any large organization, each with its own system of assumptions, values, beliefs and attitudes. These sub-cultures may be in conflict or competition with each other, and may not support the aims of the senior management of the organization.

Also, we all belong to other cultural systems besides that (those) of our workplace, such as ethnic, linguistic, class or professional contexts, to name just a few examples. When we come to work we bring with us to the organizational setting the values and assumptions of these other cultures and these contribute to the development of the organizational culture, as well as creating tensions where the different cultures don't mesh together too well.

People are adaptable, however. We can cope, most of the time, with belonging to more than one culture-group even if they are significantly different, so long as we avoid overload. Organization members can help each other – and thereby be helped themselves – by recognizing and appreciating differences and respecting the tensions that inevitably arise when overlapping cultures don't quite synchronize. Greater awareness of what's going on in your own organization's culture, which the models and perspectives described here can enhance, helps to reduce friction and anticipate issues before they become serious problems. The job of managers is to ensure that "the way we do things around here" helps rather than hinders people in their jobs and provides a satisfying quality of working life.

organizational climate If organizational culture can be summarized, however inadequately, as "the way we do things round here", organizational climate is shorthand for "what it feels like to work here".

Straw polls I have taken at workshops and seminars suggest that most managers would agree with the proposition that what it feels like to work in an organization is likely to make a difference to the quality and/or quantity of what gets done, and it's certainly the case that recent studies have shown a link between the way people are managed – which is an important factor in climate – and the "bottom line" performance of organizations. For example, an overview by the Chartered Institute of Personnel and Development[60] of more than 30 studies carried out in the UK and US during the 1990s left "no room to doubt" that there is a positive, cumulative relationship between people management and business performance: "the more effective the practices, the better the result". Another study sponsored by the same institute[61] examined variations in profitability and found that an emphasis on quality could account for about 1% of the variations, strategy for about 2%, and research and development activity for 6%, but up to 20% could be attributed to various human factors.

There's less consensus, however, about the actual characteristics of an organizational climate that would be likely to lead to better results. Attitudes on this may range across quite a wide spectrum, but the two extremes can be marked with some quotes.

from Rome to Padua First, an ancient one: "Let them hate, so long as they fear", from the Roman statesman Accius (150 to about 90 BC). It sounds even more menacing in Latin: *Oderint, dum metuant.* You may think this is a bit extreme, applied to twenty-first century work organizations. Or perhaps you have come across – as I have – organizations or departments where people were genuinely afraid of the boss and had come to detest him or her. I've adopted the label *the Accius orientation* for this end of the climate spectrum because it seems to encapsulate the attitudes and beliefs of a certain kind of manager.

Then we have the "urban myth" apocryphal response of a sales manager to a naïve enquiry: "yes, we do have an incentive scheme: people who meet their targets get to keep their jobs". Or the remark attributed to Henry Ford: "if they're having fun then they should be paying *me*".

Finally, the comment by one manager I interviewed as part of a major research project: "I think the motive of fear is very relevant, even today ... perhaps even more so ... the finger is pointed at you if you don't perform".[62]

The idea that a bit of fear is a useful management tool isn't at all uncommon. There are many organizations where the approach to "keeping people on their mettle" is to make them aware that there will be penalties for poor performance, however that is defined. Another manager who was on the receiving end of such an approach and who clearly believed it to be quite legitimate told me: "I don't think the fear caused bad decisions. It kept me on my mettle, I think".[63]

Conal Walsh[64] reports on one giant US corporation where: "twice a year, 15% of the workforce were ritually sacked, to be replaced by new arrivals, and a further 30% warned to improve". Clearly, this approach is designed to ensure that over time the quality of the workforce gets better and better. This company's approach to people management isn't unique, especially in countries with minimal employee protection legislation. Not so long ago we might well have been reading articles in certain sections of the management press extolling the virtues of this "tough" management stance and pointing to the company's commercial success. However, in view of events in 2002 we may feel rather less enthusiastic. Walsh goes on: "The company's cut-throat working culture destroyed morale and internal cohesion but also made workers afraid to question their superiors, let alone blow the whistle on sharp practices. This, in the end, would be Enron's undoing".

This kind of general orientation towards employees is broadly in line with Douglas McGregor's[65] Theory X, which I described in Chapter 2, although Theory X can also manifest itself through more benign, paternalistic, attitudes than those just described.

At the opposite end of the spectrum is a view that has much more in common with McGregor's Theory Y. Another historical quote sums this up for me. In Shakespeare's *The Taming of the Shrew* Tranio says to Lucentio: "No profit grows, where is no pleasure ta'en". This linking of enjoyment, satisfaction and interest with the beneficial outcomes of an activity is key to this orientation, which I call *the Padua Paradigm*, because *The Taming of the Shrew* is set in Padua.

Other reasons for managers to adopt a "Padua" perspective are that, as Charles Handy[66] tells us, "a culture of excitement, of question and experiment, of exploration and adventure cannot survive under a reign of fear", and that "no one can put in his best performance unless he feels secure", according to W. Edwards Deming,[67] who was perhaps the foremost exponent of total quality management (TQM) and whose crucial role in the Japanese economic recovery earned him an honour from the Japanese emperor.

Psychologist Michael Eysenck[68] explains that security and freedom from fear are important in good performance because anxiety can adversely affect the learning or acquisition of information and also the ability to retrieve it when it's subsequently needed.

a climate of success

So, we have two extreme positions, the coercive and the nurturing, both of which, and probably almost everything in between, are to be found in real life management attitudes. This clearly invites the question "which view is 'right'?" If managers want their organizations to be successful, is it more effective to make sure that everyone knows their jobs are on the line, or is it better to create a climate where people feel safe and enjoy their work?

In my own research[69] I have found a very clear answer to the question posed above: a certain kind of organizational climate is strongly associated with successful work outcomes. I interviewed 44 managers, at various levels of seniority, from 17 organizations, all of them major, nationally recognized companies, institutions or government bodies from a range of industry sectors. They were asked about the last completed project in which they were involved. I probed both the project outcomes, which were analyzed rigorously, and the interviewees' subjective experiences.

I was particularly interested in finding evidence of several positive and negative factors that I knew from previous research were likely to be significant in determining the overall perception of climate. The positive factors are:

- intrinsic satisfactions derived from the work itself;
- genuine participation in defining goals and objectives;
- freedom to express your own ideas;
- freedom to express concerns;
- freedom to question (especially decisions and policies determined by more senior people);
- freedom to try new concepts and approaches.

The negative factors are two distinct kinds of threat: *purposive* threats means consciously applied threats that are deliberately aimed at individuals to coerce their behaviour, or possibly even from malice.

Environmental threats covers threats arising from natural events, from events in society that aren't being consciously directed by anyone, or from policies that are decided without any thought for – perhaps even without any knowledge of – the people affected. This kind of perceived threat can produce feelings of personal insecurity and uncertainty. It may also, significantly, lead to doubts about what might be called the *continuance of context*: enthusiasm for a current task or project is very likely to be undermined if there seems a real possibility that it will be stopped, by management decision or external forces, before it's completed.

As I assessed these factors I was able to calculate a climate index, or coefficient, produced by adding the positive factors and subtracting the negative ones. When the 44 individual climate indices were compared with their corresponding assessments of project success the correlation was startling. Even if no allowance was made for known special factors (i.e. good excuses) affecting the project outcomes the correlation was +0.7, which is very high indeed. The closeness of the relationship is illustrated by the two lines on the graph in Figure 8.6.

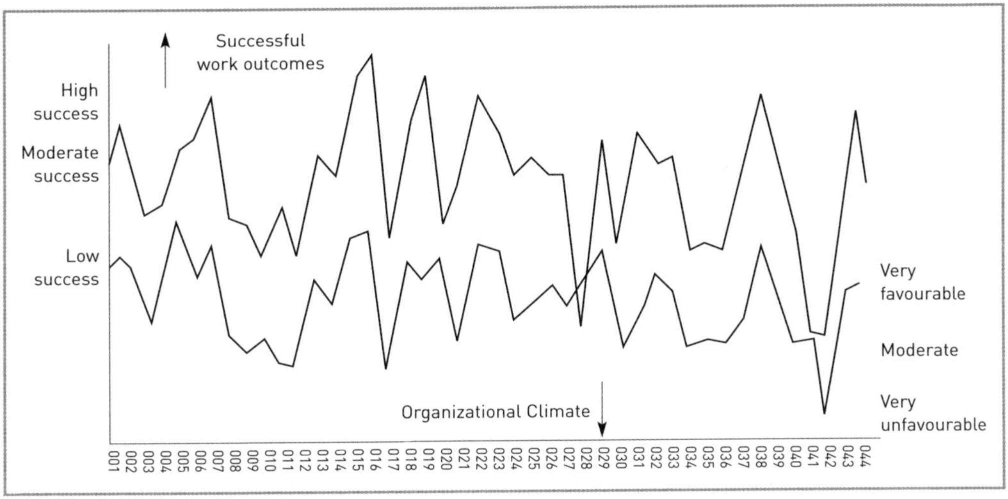

FIG 8.6 ● Organizational climate and work outcomes

There are good economic as well as humanitarian reasons why this matters. A poll in 2001 by Gallup[70] found that more than 80% of UK employees were not "engaged" at work. Engaged employees, in the Gallup survey's terms, are "loyal and productive. They not only get their work done effectively, but they are also less likely to leave and more inclined to recommend their company to friends and family". Disengaged employees, on the other hand, are "not psychologically bonded to their organization". They are "less collaborative than their colleagues, less innovative, less tolerant of change and more vocal about their many dissatisfactions". Commenting on other aspects of the Gallup survey, Richard Scase[71] remarks that despite an "explosion in management education" and widespread knowledge of people management theory and models, "employees and managers still do not trust each other". There's some evidence that this syndrome is particularly acute in the UK. A survey carried out across twenty European countries[72] found that the UK was nineteenth in terms of employees' commitment to their organizations. Only 59% said that they would recommend their company as a good place to work. Nearly half of them said they would leave if they could.

From this research my colleagues and I were able to design a questionnaire that we could use in our consulting work to help analyze an organization's climate (Figure 8.7, p. 199). In fact, the questionnaire is quite simple to use without specialist training. It consists of 24 statements in plain English, each of which addresses one of the factors that contributes to the climate index. There are eight of these factors, so each of them has three statements devoted to it. Respondents are asked to say whether they (A) strongly agree, (B) tend to agree, (C) tend to disagree or (D) strongly disagree that each statement is "true of my organization". Every member of the organization or department is asked to complete a questionnaire, which should be returned anonymously for analysis.

The results of the survey are analyzed using two tables (which can be found at the end of this section). Table 1 (Figure 8.8, p. 201) is a look-up table that converts the A, B, C or D answer for each statement to a numerical value of 0, 1, 2 or 3. The 24 numbers are then added up to provide an overall climate index with a maximum value of 72. This gives a broad indication of the perceived climate in the organization or department; the higher the index, the more favourable the climate. In very general terms, a score above the mid-50s suggests a climate that is likely to be helpful in achieving successful outcomes. Scores below this level suggest that some attention is required to climate factors, and a very low score indicates that urgent and serious effort is needed.

Table 2 (Figure 8.9, p. 202) allows a more detailed analysis of the eight individual factors. All the factors that contribute to the perception of climate are inter-related and interactive, so you would expect them to get roughly similar scores. It would be unusual for any factor to be significantly out of step with the overall pattern, so if this occurs it needs to be investigated. It may indicate a new or developing situation which requires attention. To show whether this is the case Table 2 transfers the value for each individual statement to one of eight columns, according to the climate factor it addresses. The appropriate column for each statement has a clear box, the other boxes being obscured. The values in each column are added up to produce a total of 0 to 9 in each case.

Clearly, there is little point in collecting information unless you intend to act on the messages it conveys. In fact, the process of collecting information – in this case by asking people to complete questionnaires – is never neutral. People always make assumptions about why you are doing it and it often raises expectations that something is going to change, which is likely to be unsettling and can lead to disappointment and suspicion of bad faith if the anticipated action doesn't happen.

Management action following an organizational climate assessment should normally aim at improving all eight factors shown in Table 2, but if any factor seems significantly lower (or higher) than the others this should be dealt with first. The most likely reason is that something has changed recently, so it's worth looking for evidence of such changes to begin with. The personal style of senior people has a major influence over most of the climate factors. Perhaps a new manager with a different style has recently been appointed and his or her impact has lowered – or of course, raised – the rating in a particular area. It's likely that the other factors will follow this trend over time, so a negative change is an advance warning and an opportunity to take gentle, supportive corrective action. If the anomaly is positive, there's an opportunity to draw attention to the systemic nature of climate ratings, and to encourage attention to the other factors. Environmental threats, though, can affect the whole range, and an adverse change in this factor is an alarm signal that shouldn't be ignored.

Whether an individual factor calls for special attention, or whether the ratings are low across the board, practical action needs to address specifics rather than generalities.

Examples of environmental threats may include economic, competitive, political or technological problems that could affect the future success of the organization. Anything which causes people to have concerns about their future is likely to have a negative impact on their work. It may not be possible to reassure people about these things – and such reassurances may not be believed anyway – but ways of shielding staff from external threats should, at the very least, be on the agenda for senior management attention. More controllable forms of environmental threat include reorganizations, which can feel very threatening to employees who have little or no say in what is proposed or implemented. The effects on climate of any proposed changes should be considered explicitly as part of the planning process and positive action should be taken to minimize the uncertainty and powerlessness that many people feel at such times. When the costs and benefits of change proposals are being weighed up, the negative effects on *continuance of context* should be realistically included in the analysis.

Disagreements or disputes among senior managers, about policy or support for specific initiatives or even on a personal basis, can be a significant form of environmental threat with a negative impact on organizational climate. Senior people don't have to involve subordinates in these disagreements and it's usually best if they avoid doing so, but consulting with all the stakeholders before deciding on a policy is still generally a positive and helpful thing to do; there's a judgement to be made here, which is where senior people earn their salaries.

Purposive threats are consciously applied threats that are directed at individuals to coerce their behaviour. The idea that threats of various kinds are justified on the grounds that they promote better performance is quite widespread, but my research[73] found clear negative correlations between levels of purposive threat and successful work outcomes. The implication of this is that threats should never be used as a management technique. This means, of course, that bullying, coercion and all forms of hostility and aggression are quite unacceptable. It also means, perhaps counter-intuitively, that inducements such as bonus payments and PRP shouldn't be close-coupled to specific objectives because the possibility of their being withheld is often perceived as a form of threat. Overall, rewards should be perceived as fair in relation to overall contribution; this is not by any means an easy outcome to achieve because the perceptions involved are very subjective, but it's certainly worth a lot of management effort. Being seen to be trying to be fair will help to influence perceptions positively.

threats should never be used as a management technique

The remaining climate factors are the positive ones: intrinsic satisfactions derived from the work itself; participation in defining goals and objectives; free expression of ideas; free expression of concerns; freedom to question, especially decisions and policies determined by more senior people; and freedom to try new concepts and approaches.

Actively promoting an organizational climate in which people have maximum involvement in defining their own targets and goals, in which they feel free to question, challenge and contribute to the decisions of more senior people, in which their suggestions and ideas are actively sought, valued and treated with respect, and in which intrinsic satisfactions are to be found can produce significant "bottom-line" benefits. Promoting these characteristics means continual and sustained effort, and is primarily a matter of individual management style. Senior managers have a vital role to play in improving the climate of their organizations because they have the power to demonstrate the behaviours that they require from their people. If the middle manager who demonstrates the Accius orientation ("let them hate, so long as they fear") is seen to win promotion whilst another who favours the Padua Paradigm ("no profit grows where is no pleasure ta'en") is sidelined, then an unmistakable message is sent out across the organization; actions speak very much louder than words.

Organizational climate has a profound and direct influence on work outcomes. Whilst there are no guarantees, and individual cases can vary widely, there are very clear correlations which show that certain features of organizational climate are far more likely than others to be associated with success and excellence. Threats and coercion are linked to low success rates, as are uncertainty and insecurity. A climate of trust, respect, tolerance and satisfying work, on the other hand, is clearly associated with successful achievement of organizational aims.

To sum up, the key messages are:

- *Never* use purposive threats.

- Be very cautious in the use of rewards; aim for fairness based on overall contribution rather than "incentives" close-coupled to specific outcomes.
- Plan change carefully; be aware of the effects on people at all levels.
- Work hard to minimize uncertainty and insecurity.
- Seek consensus among senior people; don't involve staff in top management disputes and conflict if it can be avoided, but don't be secretive and distrustful either.
- Empower people; don't steal their decisions.
- Promote maximum participation in goal-setting.
- Actively seek feedback; even if you don't much like what it tells you.
- Recognize and reinforce these behaviours in people who report to you and *never* reward contrary behaviours; the damage will be very hard to repair.

the Organizational Climate Assessment (OCA) instrument The questionnaire and the two analysis tables are reproduced below in Figures 8.7, 8.8 and 8.9. It would be useful first to try completing the questionnaire yourself, in confidence, and analyze the results to find out how you perceive the climate of your organization. Then, if you are sure you can do so without adverse effects (see above) get other people in a specific part of the organization to complete a questionnaire and analyze the aggregated results. Once you have identified an issue you can then move on to consider what action you could take to improve the climate of that part of the organization.

Here is the questionnaire (Figure 8.7):

This is true of my organization	A Strongly agree	B Tend to agree	C Tend to disagree	D Strongly disagree
1 The organization is gioing through a lot of changes at the moment				
2 Lots of good ideas come from quite junior people				
3 If the top people disagreed between themselves about anything the rest of the staff probably wouldn't know about it				
4. Your boss decides what your targets should be				
5 Most people get a lot of satisfaction from their work, quite apart from the pay				
6 People who don't meet their targets are in trouble				
7 It's quite OK to tell your boss you think s/he's got it wrong				
8 If people aren't performing too well we look for their strengths and help them to find a more suitable job placement				
9 Junior people know that their concerns are taken seriously at senior management level				
10 Our industry is quite volatile				
11 If it wasn't for the money a lot of people here would find something more interesting to do				
12 You need the broader perspective of seniority to formulate practical suggestions				
13 People know what they have to do, but how they do it is largely up to them				
14 People have a big say in fixing their own objectives				
15 People get paid for solving problems, not for sharing them around				

FIG 8.7 ● Organizational Climate Assessment Questionnaire

This is true of my organization	A Strongly agree	B Tend to agree	C Tend to disagree	D Strongly disagree
16 There's a right way to do everything: it's in the manual				
17 If you disagree with policy decisions it's best to keep it to yourself				
18 If something's bothering anyone here there's always someone they can talk to about it				
19 People seem to like working here				
20 We keep up with the latest developments in best practice				
21 Rewards are linked directly to objectives				
22 Managers like you to point out the down-side of their decisions: it helps to avoid costly mistakes				
23 Working practices are based on inputs from people at all levels				
24 People can negotiate changes to their objectives at any time to take account of changing circumstances				

FIG 8.7 ● **Continued**

The two analysis tables follow:

Table 1 For each statement, convert the A, B, C or D answer to a numerical value using the table, and enter the answer in the box on the right. Then add up the scores to produce a climate index (maximum possible value: 72).

Table 2 For each statement, take the numerical value from the box in Table 1 (Figure 8.8) and enter it in the clear box in Table 2 (Figure 8.9). Then add up the scores for each column (maximum possible value: 9).

Statement	Answer				
	A	**B**	**C**	**D**	
1	0	1	2	3	
2	3	2	1	0	
3	3	2	1	0	
4	0	1	2	3	
5	3	2	1	0	
6	0	1	2	3	
7	3	2	1	0	
8	3	2	1	0	
9	3	2	1	0	
10	0	1	2	3	
11	0	1	2	3	
12	0	1	2	3	
13	3	2	1	0	
14	3	2	1	0	
15	0	1	2	3	
16	0	1	2	3	
17	0	1	2	3	
18	3	2	1	0	
19	3	2	1	0	
20	3	2	1	0	
21	0	1	2	3	
22	3	2	1	0	
23	3	2	1	0	
24	3	2	1	0	
				Total:	

FIG 8.8 ● OCA Table 1

	i	ii	iii	iv	v	vi	vii	viii
Statement	Value							
1								
2								
3								
4								
5								
6								
7								
8								
9								
10								
11								
12								
13								
14								
15								
16								
17								
18								
19								
20								
21								
22								
23								
24								

Totals:								
	i	ii	iii	iv	v	vi	vii	viii

FIG 8.9 ● OCA Table 2

The eight columns in Table 2 (Figure 8.9) represent the following climatic elements:

i. Freedom to express ideas

ii. Freedom to express concerns

iii. Freedom to question, especially decisions and policies determined by more senior people

iv. Genuine participation in defining goals and objectives

v. Intrinsic satisfactions derived from the work itself

vi. Freedom to try new concepts and approaches

vii. Environmental threats

viii. Purposive threats

All eight columns would normally show similar, though probably not identical, total scores. Any column that is markedly different with, say, a variation of more than 2 or 3 points from the others, may be an indication of something significant and needs to be looked into.

The research that underpins the OCA instrument showed very clearly that organizations can expect to benefit from an organizational climate that supports the well-being and, if it isn't too emotive a term, the happiness of their employees. Work itself can make an important contribution to this well-being, providing intrinsic rewards and satisfactions for individuals if they are committed to the work objectives, which is more likely if they have participated in determining what those objectives should be.

High scores in the OCA indicate an optimum organizational environment for successful work outcomes, but achieving such an environment means continual effort on the part of management. Whenever a choice of alternative actions is available managers need to choose the option that moves their organizations towards, rather than away from, the ideal. The impact on effectiveness of each such choice may be in many cases quite modest. Just occasionally it may be very significant indeed. In the great majority of cases, though, the impact is likely to be positive. Applied consistently, the management orientations that help to build a positive organizational climate can be expected to lead to more effective work outcomes, more satisfied and fulfilled people, and more successful organizations.

the psychological contract In a general sense, people's perception of the climate of their organization has a lot to do with the perceived fairness of the interactions between them and it. How we see this depends, of course, on what we think we are entitled to receive from the organization, and what we believe we have an obligation to give in return. This is known as the *psychological contract*, described by Denise Rousseau[74] as "individual beliefs, shaped by the organization, regarding terms of an exchange agreement between individuals and their organization".

It might seem that the term "contract" isn't quite appropriate here. The film producer Sam Goldwyn famously said (or maybe he didn't) that "a verbal contract ain't worth the paper it's written on" and what we are talking about here is not only unwritten but usually unspoken as well. Because of this the two sides to the bargain may have very different ideas about its terms. All the same, several writers have defended the use of the word "contract" by pointing out significant features of contractual agreements that seem to apply to, or have parallels in, the psychological landscape of the workplace.

An essential feature of all contracts is that they involve an *offer* to do or to provide something in *exchange* for what English law calls a *consideration*, i.e. a payment in money or in kind. When the offer is *accepted* a contract normally exists, provided that both the offer and the acceptance were *voluntary*.

This last point is a vital attribute of contracts; you can't be forced to make a contract. To be valid, the commitments in any contract must be made freely.

protect and serve The main reason why contracts are entered into is that the parties to them expect to benefit in some way, either positively or through protection against loss. This means that changes to the contract, potentially, may mean that one or other of the parties loses out in some way. Largely for this reason contracts don't usually allow changes to their terms unless such changes are mutually agreed. However, contracts are seldom perfect because it's very difficult, if not impossible, to cover every eventuality at the time of the agreement. Over time missing elements have to be filled in and the terms of the contract interpreted to apply to new situations. So, even though it may be risky and inconvenient, some change is very likely to occur over the lifetime of a contractual relationship.

The workplace psychological contract may fulfil most of these criteria. The one thing it manifestly is not is *explicit*. Both parties are likely to have ideas about the *offer* they are making, and about the *consideration* they expect to receive in return. Unfortunately, because the terms aren't made explicit the ideas both parties have about these things may be very different, but there's a strong possibility that neither side will be aware of this. Now, if you conscientiously deliver what you believe to be your side of a bargain, but the other party fails to deliver what you believe to be theirs, you are quite likely to feel that you've been cheated.

It will be helpful to look at how these very subjective perceptions of the "terms" of the psychological contract become established.

There seem to be two sets of processes at work here. First, there are social cues we pick up that we interpret as indicators of the organization's intentions towards us or in matters that concern us. In other words, we observe the behaviour of "the organization" – which in practice means the behaviour of people whom we regard as representative of the organization – and we derive certain messages about what is expected of us and what we should expect in return. This presents some problems. We have already discussed some of the psychological processes, such as fundamental attribution error and a range of heuristics, which can influence our perceptions, and these distortions can easily affect our interpretation of people's behaviour in the specific context we are considering here. Another difficulty may stem from the differing behaviours of individuals who, in the employee's perception, are representing the organization.[75] So the attractive picture painted by the interviewer when you applied for the job may not match the reality of how your eventual line manager seems to interpret the "deal".

The other group of processes that help to determine how an individual will construe the "contract" operate within the individual concerned. These might include his or her perceptions, values, attitudes and ways of processing information, all of which may lead the employee to interpret actions or situations as representing some kind of "promise" or statement of intent. Some of the familiar artefacts of organizational life, such as policy statements, HR documentation, procedure manuals, and so on play their part here, as may observing what happens to other people who are perceived as being party to the same deal.[76]

continuous renewal In fact, the ability to manipulate, or at least influence, the employee's perceptions of the contract's terms arises mainly because the contract isn't fixed at a particular point in time, as a written contract would be, but develops and changes as the employee and the organization interact in the course of their working relationships. Whilst formal contracts of employment tend to be fairly stable, relatively speaking, the psychological contract is continually being reshaped, changed and revised; "virtually any change in the way work is organized, either physically or socially, will have an impact on it".[77]Also, the implicit mutual expectations and perceived obligations covered by the psychological contract tend to spread out to cover more and more aspects of the relationship between the employee and the organization the longer people remain with an organization.

Perceptions are liable to change over time. A study in the early 1990s[78] found that employees' feelings about the terms of the psychological contract shifted over the first two years with an organization so that they came to feel that they owed less to their employer while their employer owed them more. Expectations play an important role here. If the organization has high expectations of what employees can and should contribute the employees may well respond with excellent performance. However, awareness of this contribution may well lead employees to expect more in return, beyond simple financial reward, such as job security, respect, jobs that are challenging and satisfying, and training and development opportunities.[79]

All this suggests that managers need to be constantly aware of the changing and developing understanding of the terms of the contract on the part of employees, and actively try to "surface" the expectations both sides have. For example, employers' requirements might be likely to include loyalty and flexibility,[80] and perhaps working harder, or at least longer, than the formal contract of employment demands. More than half of the employees in one study[81] felt obliged to do this in order to "get the work done", which suggests that employees were willing to accept inadequate staffing levels as part of the "deal". Fear of losing jobs if the extra work wasn't done was apparently not a significant concern in this study but another survey carried out soon afterwards on behalf of the Institute of Personnel and Development[82] suggested that working harder did not in many cases directly result in increased pay but might have affected job security, which suggests that the psychological contracts of the people in the survey were moving towards terms which were less favourable to them and more favourable to their employers (if we assume that employees "working harder" would necessarily be beneficial to their organizations, which is quite a bold and rather simplistic assumption to make).

keeping the bargain In return for this flexibility employers traditionally provided security, particularly in the case of managers.[83] This has become increasingly hard to provide over recent years and in difficult and uncertain economic conditions even the best-intentioned managements may be unable to deliver their side of the bargain.

Different understandings by the parties involved have the potential to create conflicts and resentments when expectations are not fulfilled. Trust plays an important role here; if levels of trust are high then there may be quite substantial reserves of tolerance, which can buffer both sides against short-term problems. "In fact, one way to tell when a relationship is under stress is when the timescale over which the 'balance sheet' is balanced, shortens. In such situations the participants begin to expect almost immediate repayment of favours done".[84] Trust, as we have already seen, depends to a large extent on predictability and may continue so long as neither party is surprised by the behaviour of the other.[85] The kinds of relationships in which trust will thrive are those where the parties are able to understand each other's point of view, where there are strong interpersonal relationships and frequent contact between the people involved. Trust is harder to sustain if what Denise Rousseau[86] calls "an external pattern of violations" exists – for example, where the organization itself is being forced to change for some reason – where one side seems to have strong incentives to breach contracts or perpetrators perceive themselves to have no alternatives, such as in times of crisis.

If the psychological contract is hard to define, fragile, and a source of potential conflict, how much does it matter? Several writers have argued that the state of the psychological contract has direct implications for organizational performance. A positive psychological contract has been found to be strongly linked to higher commitment to the organization, higher employee satisfaction and better employment relations.[87]

Researchers working in the 1990s tended to be rather pessimistic about the state of the psychological contract in the organizations they studied. Some of the problems were associated with large-scale downsizing and redundancies, and the consequent uncertainties experienced by those who remained as well as the bitterness felt by those who found themselves rejected by the organizations they had previously regarded as "theirs". In more stable economic conditions there are opportunities for organizations to repair the damage and learn from the mistakes of the past and there is some evidence that this is happening in the UK. David Guest and Neil Conway, who have conducted regular surveys on the subject over several years, say that in mid 2002, "broadly speaking, the results suggest that a rather traditional psychological contract is alive and well",[88] with around three quarters of those who believed they had been "promised" various things saying that the promises had largely been kept, although stress levels were rather worrying and employee satisfaction wasn't showing much sign of improvement, especially in the public sector.

The overall message that comes out from research into the psychological contract is to make its terms as explicit as possible. This can only be done if it is the subject of regular discussion in an atmosphere of trust and mutual respect, in other words, a favourable organizational climate.

workplace stress Stress has been called "one of the most inaccurate words in the scientific literature"[89] because people use the word to refer to causes, process and effects, as well as other things like concentration and effort. For example, you sometimes hear people say that some stress is necessary for good performance. The scientifically accurate term here should be *arousal*, rather than stress, but even then the statement is misleading, because there's an optimum level of arousal for any task, and the more complex the task the more relaxed and unpressured the worker should be for best performance.[90,91] I could be rigorous in my use of language here and use the term *stressors* to refer to causes, *stress* to mean the process itself, and *strain* to refer to the physical and mental consequences, but it may actually be more helpful to acknowledge that other people may be using the word "stress" with one or more of a variety of meanings.

Stress has the potential to do serious damage to individuals, apart from making them miserable, which you may think is quite important in itself. Stress is linked to heart disease and a wide range of other diseases including cancer – most probably by adversely affecting the body's immune system – and with a variety of mental health problems. It's important to recognize that because of these associations sometimes *stress kills people*. It's also associated with increased accident rates, mistakes, low productivity and high staff turnover. So broadly speaking stress is something to be avoided.

risk and opportunity The experience of stress begins with a *demand* – physical, mental or a combination of both – which is placed upon an individual. The demand may take the form of danger or it may come as an opportunity. For our remote ancestors attacks by predators would have been a frequent source of danger-demand, and opportunity-demands like unwary small animals coming within stone-throwing range would have presented themselves from time to time. Survival and health would depend on being able to respond appropriately. In the modern workplace demands are likely to be generated by tasks, workloads, relationships, career-related opportunities, and a variety of organizational factors that we will come to later.

Once a demand is perceived (and if it isn't perceived it won't trigger the process we're discussing here) physical and mental responses are initiated to deal with it. This process of response is what is technically called arousal. It involves a range of physiological and mental changes that have evolved to enable us to deal with the demand and so, at the most basic level, to survive. Typically, routine physiological functions are either speeded up or slowed down in preparation for "fight or flight".[92] The bronchioles of the lungs dilate, increasing the capacity for the exchange of gases. Sugars are released into the bloodstream from the liver, increasing the energy supply to the muscles. The hormone adrenaline is released from the adrenal glands and natural pain-killing and mood-enhancing chemicals called endorphins enter the bloodstream. Heart beat increases to pump more blood to the brain and limbs, providing more oxygen and nutrients, and the pupils of the eyes dilate for maximum visual acuity. Functions that are not urgently needed, such as the digestive processes, are slowed down to conserve energy.

These physiological changes are accompanied by psychological responses; we are likely to experience feelings of fear, excitement or anger. Physiological arousal can prompt any of these emotions. Which one dominates depends to a large extent on our interpretation of the situation; a non-threatening opportunity is likely to be exciting, a threat we believe we can overcome may make us angry, and a threat we believe could do us harm is likely to make us feel afraid.[93,94] These emotions play a vital role in the instant decision whether to fight or run away.

crisis management Significantly, this complex arrangement of physiological and psychological responses is best suited to dealing with *acute* demands, rather than chronic ones (*chronic* = continuing over an extended period of time). If they are closely followed by intense physical activity, e.g. "fight" or "flight", the chemical balances of the body soon return to their normal states, known as *homeostasis*. If there's little or no physical activity to use up the "emergency" resources that the body has made available and the high state of arousal continues for a long time, then damage can result; we're not designed to run in emergency mode for more than short periods.

we're not designed to run in emergency mode for more than short periods

Hans Selye, considered to be the "father of stress research", describes this process in his General Adaptation Syndrome[95] (see Figure 8.10). This is quite a helpful model and it has been very influential in subsequent research into the mechanisms and effects of stress, but it isn't perfect. The main criticism is that it's too static; it ignores the capacity that people have to *cope* with stressful situations. People don't usually passively accept the stressful things that go on in life; healthy people, and other living things too, *respond* in a variety of ways to handle the threats and opportunities the world throws their way.

Coping behaviours fall into two main categories: adjustment *to* the situation and/or adjustment *of* the situation. Remember, though, that the "situation" is itself a construct of our perceptions! Adjustment *of* the sit-

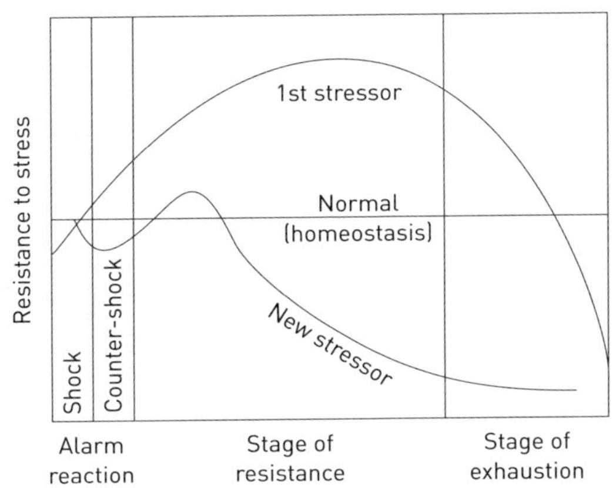

FIG 8.10 ● **Selye's GAS**

Source: Gray, JA (1991) *The Psychology of Fear and Stress*, 2nd edn, Cambridge, CUP, p. 61. © Cambridge University Press.

uation is fairly straightforward; fighting is one way of doing it and running away is another. In other words, dealing directly with the perceived stressor so that either it's not there any more or it's no longer stressful. Of course, you can't successfully effect adjustments of the situation unless you have – or believe that you have – some level of *control*. Whilst many factors are involved in the experience of stress and how damaging that experience might be for any individual, this one factor emerges as by far the most significant; that is, the extent to which the person feels him or herself to have control over the situation. Many studies have found that people who, for example, have a say in decisions that affect them have lower levels of stress damage than those who are not involved in decision-making.

Adjustment *to* the situation, on the other hand, is a psychological process of changing our perceptions so that the situation seems less threatening. This may be done by trying to understand the situation better – seeking more information – or it may be done by denying that the stressful situation exists, or "cognitively reconstructing reality".[96] Cognitive dissonance theory has already been discussed in respect of attitudes and values. When situations are "cognitively reconstructed" in this way, what is going on is effectively a reduction in the severity of the mismatch, or *dissonance*, that we perceive between what *is* and what *ought to be*. This "denial" response could, of course, have serious consequences if it leads to a failure to take practical steps to handle the problem, such as not getting away from danger, or not seeking treatment for injury or disease.

am I coping?

Whatever strategies we adopt to cope with stressful situations – and we are likely to make use of several in combination – we will probably have perceptions about how well those strategies are working. These perceptions feed back into the overall experience of stress. Stephen Williams[97] represents this dynamic interaction in what he calls a "simplified mechanistic model", illustrated in Figure 8.11.

In this model sources of pressure would be likely to produce negative effects if it were not for the counterbalancing function of our coping

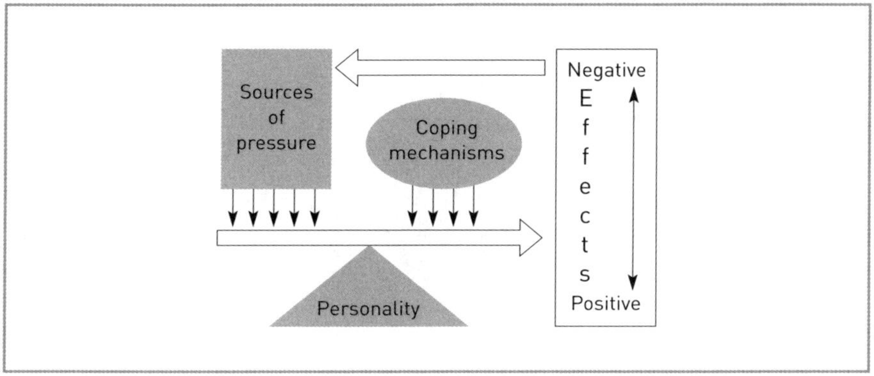

FIG 8.11 ● The four-way stress model

Source: Williams, S (1994) *Managing Pressure for Peak Performance*, p. 42. © Kogan Page Ltd.

skills. An increase in the force exerted by either factor would tend to increase or decrease the likelihood of negative effects. Clearly, the position of the fulcrum – personality – makes a lot of difference here; if it isn't in the middle one side of the contest is going to be severely disadvantaged. We will consider this aspect shortly.

It's worth emphasising at this point that, although any one of us can suffer harmful effects from stress, most people, most of the time, don't. Alan McLean[98] tells us that for stress to become a problem three factors have to come together. A person may be *vulnerable* to suffer from stress for some reason at a particular time, the *context* in which the individual is placed at that time may be potentially stress-inducing, and/or something stressful – a demand or *stressor* – may occur. Any two of these factors can be present with no ill-effects; it's only when all three come together at the same time that stress-related problems are likely to occur. Figure 8.12 illustrates this three-factor model.

the stressful workplace Some of the kinds of *demand* that tend to occur in the workplace have already been mentioned. Almost anything can constitute a demand and therefore become a potential stressor if it's perceived as such by the person who experiences it. No-one else

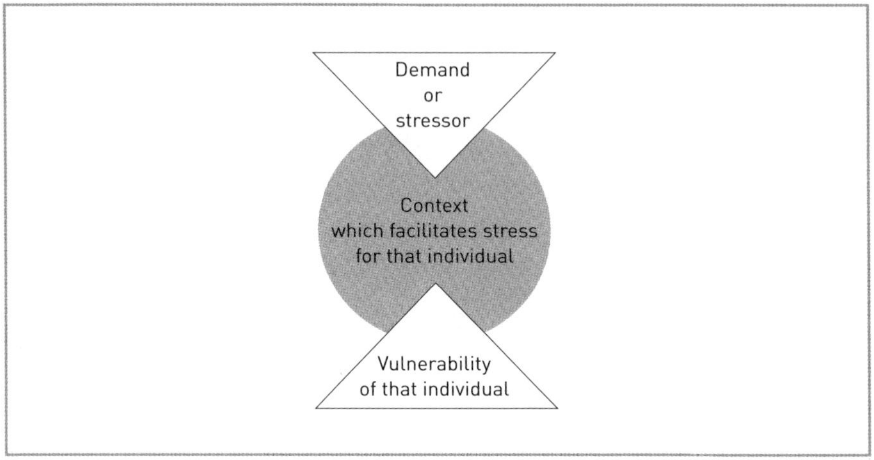

FIG 8.12 ● Three-factor stress model

can say "that isn't a stressor" because no-one else is in a position to know. Common workplace stressors[99] include such things as:

- The *physical demands* of the job (such as noise, vibration, humidity, ventilation, temperature variation, lighting, hygiene, climate).
- *Task factors* (such as shift or night work, workload, long hours, new technology, repetitiveness, monotony and boredom, experience of risk and hazards).
- *Role factors* (such as role conflict, role ambiguity, responsibility for people and/or things).
- *Relationships and interpersonal demands* (for example, with supervisors, colleagues and/or subordinates).
- *Career factors* (such as job insecurity, or "status incongruity", meaning under or over promotion).
- *Organizational structure and climate* (especially how much participation in decision-making there is).

It will be helpful to say more about some of the items in this list but they tend to crop up as factors in vulnerability and context, which I will move on to now.

There are many things that might make someone more vulnerable to the effects of stress at a particular time. An obvious possibility, illustrated by Selye's GAS,[100] is that they are already dealing with another, unrelated, demand. Most of us wouldn't know what demands, in this sense, our colleagues are currently dealing with, any more than our bosses, peers or subordinates know what potentially stressful demands we have in our own lives. This should make us all rather cautious about making assumptions concerning the possible impact on other people of demands that we are able to control.

Characteristics inherent in an individual's personality are also thought to contribute significantly to their vulnerability. In the see-saw model of coping it is clear that if the fulcrum – personality – were not in the centre coping would either be harder, and the individual would therefore be more vulnerable to stress damage, or coping would be easier and damage would be less likely to occur. We will look briefly at some of the personality factors that have been associated with vulnerability.

ideal recruit

Many managers in organizations would probably be quite pleased to discover the following characteristics in an employee or in a job applicant:

A strong commitment to work and much involvement in their job, a well-developed sense of time urgency (always aware of time pressures and working against deadlines) and a strong sense of competition.

In 1974 the results of a major study were published[101] which found a strong correlation between a group of observable behavioural characteristics, which were called the "Type A behaviour pattern" (TABP) and the development of coronary heart disease. It will probably come as no surprise that the defining characteristics of the TABP are those shown above,[102] although I cheated a bit by leaving out "a marked tendency to be aggressive".

Stephen Williams[103] comments that these behavioural characteristics are highly regarded in the Western world. Recruitment and promotion systems tend to reward Type A behaviour, and interviewers see some of these traits as positive indicators of success. In fact, William says research evidence indicates that people who show the TABP *don't* actually perform any better than other people and they show less ability to cope with pressure, resulting in more health problems.

Some of the other observable characteristics of Type A people might sound positively alarming: "drivenness, extremes of competitiveness, aggression, easily aroused irritabilities, work orientation, preoccupation with deadlines, and a chronic sense of time urgency. Type A individuals appear to be guarded, alert, and intense, with rapid and jerky body movements, tense facial and body musculature, and explosive speech".[104]

The TABP isn't universally regarded as a straightforward indicator of vulnerability, partly because links between TABP and actual physical heart damage (up to and including death) have only been observed in about half of the studies.[105] It may be that it's only some of these characteristics that are associated with ill health, not the whole "package". Irritability, and anger and hostility have been suggested as being the factors that increase vulnerability, and these, in turn, may be associated with an absence of trust in one's fellow human beings.[106]

The apparent, superficial, attractiveness to organizations of some aspects of the Type A behaviour pattern, and the evident risks of being subjected to stressors if you are one of the people who show these characteristics, have obvious implications for selection and promotion practices. Organizations have responsibilities to their employees and it may be that these behavioural traits may one day be taken as evidence of vulnerability, which organizations overlook at the risk of being held accountable for any adverse consequences.

who's in control? People who have an "internal" *locus of control* tend to believe that *they* make things happen, whereas people with an "external" locus of control tend to think that things happen *to* them.[107] Just why people should come to feel this way can be explained by social learning theory. Of course, external or internal loci of control can be self-fulfilling prophesies, because people who think they *can* control their environments and what happens to them tend to make more effort to do so. "Internals" may be better at learning, seek new information more actively and make better use of it, and seem more concerned with finding things out than with social demands or situations.[108] Partly because of the efforts they make to control what happens to them, it's suggested that internals experience less stress than externals and they apparently report fewer negative life events than externals.[109]

All this might suggest that it's "better" to have an internal locus of control than an external one. There is a down side, though; when things do go wrong externals can hold someone else responsible, but internals have no-one to blame but themselves, and this is potentially psychologically damaging. Most people, of course, aren't extremely "external" or excessively "internal", but exist fairly comfortably around the middle of the spectrum with just a moderate tendency towards one or the other, and this shouldn't lead to too many problems.

Similarly, people with certain personality characteristics have been found to be less likely to become ill, either physically or mentally, in high stress situations.[110] The first of these characteristics is "commitment", meaning a belief in one's own value, the value of the things one is doing and a tendency to get fully involved in work, family and social life.

The second characteristic is "control", which means pretty much what "internal locus of control" means in the preceding paragraphs, and the third is "challenge", meaning the belief that "change, rather than stability, is the normative mode of life".[111] People with these characteristics – called *hardiness* – tend to find opportunities to make decisions, set goals, and engage in complex activities. They also seem to be capable of evaluating any given event in the context of an overall life plan, so single events don't take on a significance that is out of proportion to their real impact on life.[112] All this seems to make them less vulnerable to stress damage, perhaps because they have confidence in their coping mechanisms and so are less likely to feel that they have lost control over what happens to them.

Several other personality characteristics have been identified which seem to be associated with ill health more frequently than pure chance would predict. Optimistic people seem to stay healthier than pessimists[113] and hostility, repressed hostility or potential for hostility has been associated with cardiovascular symptoms.[114] Neuroticism (moodiness, anxiety and instability) seems to be linked with higher vulnerability to stress damage, as does having an extrovert (outward-looking, sociable) personality.[115]

These factors, as well as TABP, locus of control and hardiness, all seem to have much in common and to overlap to some extent. There has been a lot of debate about whether they are directly linked to vulnerability, or whether they are just symptoms of a common underlying factor. The "strongest candidate" for this common factor would appear to be "negative affectivity".[116] If this is right, it would seem that hostility and distrust towards other people may be bad for your health!

In practical terms there's very little that managers can do to change personality characteristics that may make people more vulnerable to stress damage, but they can observe these characteristics and acknowledge them as contributors to the three-factor (context + stressor + vulnerability) model of the risk of such damage. If almost anything can be a potential stressor, and vulnerability is both hard to assess and even harder to change, that leaves *context* as the factor in this model that managers can most easily control, or at least influence.

a healthy environment There are a number of factors in the work context or environment that have been identified as promoting or exacerbating stress. Many of these are avoidable, which has led researchers Robert Karasek and Töres Theorell[117] to write scathingly about "the work environment where stressors are routinely planned, years in advance, by some people for other people". Perhaps the most basic factor in the work environment that may help to reduce the incidence of stress damage is that the subject should be taken seriously; an organiza-

hostility and distrust towards other people may be bad for your health

tion that recognizes and actively looks out for a potential danger is far more likely to take steps to avoid it, so just being *aware* of stress and its consequences is likely to be beneficial.

Secondly, undertaking an audit of the physical environment may enable managers to reduce, or even eliminate, some of the factors that have been found to be common stressors. Some of those that seem to get mentioned most frequently[118,119] include the following:

- density and crowding
- lack of privacy
- high noise levels
- vibrations and/or soundwaves
- temperature extremes
- air movement
- background colour and illumination
- chemicals
- dust
- badly designed machinery/equipment
- badly designed premises.

Several of these factors are common features of modern, open-plan office environments, as well as the more obvious factory or workshop setting.

At least as important as the physical environment is what is termed the psychosocial environment. Bullying, which the Health and Safety Executive[120] defines as "persistent unacceptable behaviour … by one or more individuals working in the organization against one or more employees … perceived by the person experiencing it to be offensive, abusive, intimidating, insulting or involving an abuse of power" is almost certain to be stressful and should be unacceptable in any twenty-first century organization. Harassment – "unwanted conduct"[121] – is very similar to bullying.

It should be quite possible to eliminate any kind of bullying and harassment from the workplace. Simply making it clear that both are unacceptable and won't be tolerated would go a long way towards solving the problem. Unfortunately, things don't seem to be improving much with escalating workloads fostering a "kill or be killed" atmosphere in UK workplaces where bullying, deceit and backstabbing are on the increase, according to a new study by the Roffey Park Institute.[122] This clearly needs to be addressed by managements with concern for their employees, and for the long-term future of their organizations. Managements should also be aware of and take steps to deal with any physical risks, including potential violence, that may be associated with doing a job.

An audit of the physical environment of the workplace can quickly identify many, if not all, of the potential stressors, and this is probably the place to begin tackling what could be a very significant source of personnel-related costs, poor work, and physical and mental health problems.

A significant factor in the psychosocial environment may be the level of insecurity that individuals feel about their jobs: whether or not their employment will continue, whether or not they would be able to find another job, whether the nature of what they have to do will change (for the worse), whether their physical environment will change (for the worse), whether they will have a new (and worse) boss, and so on. The stress literature doesn't really tells us whether change itself is stressful or whether the stress levels that are seen to be associated with change are due to the uncertainty and lack of control which often go with it,[123] but these factors contribute to the organizational climate as well as being potentially serious stressors.

organizing stress out Whilst the physical and psychosocial environments are very significant sources of workplace stress, it is probably the organization of the work itself that has the greatest potential to cause harm. Role-related problems – role ambiguity, role conflict and role overload – have all been found to be potentially stressful. However, there is a widespread view among researchers that uncertainty is a significant factor in making them stressful: uncertainty about what one should do, about how one is evaluated, about priorities, and so on. Uncertainty is greatly reduced if people are fully involved in decision-making processes; after all, there's no great uncertainty about what you should do if you participated in determining your objectives and priorities in the first place. Similarly, if you've had an input into how your work will be evaluated, uncertainty about this won't be a problem to you.

There are clear links between personal "decision latitude" at work and heart disease symptoms,[124] which suggests that having some freedom to decide how you will do your work, knowing what's going on and how it affects you, and especially having some input into the decisions, can help to reduce the experience of stress and the harm it may do to you.

Participation in decision-making doesn't go quite as far as having *control*, so it isn't a complete answer to stress, although it will almost certainly be beneficial. It's the feeling of not being in control which is the major factor in the experience of stress. One of the commonest ways in which we may feel we have lost control is when there seems to be a mismatch between what we have to do and our capacity to do it. This may happen simply because there's too much to do in the time available, or it may be because the work is beyond the individual's capabilities, because of conflicting, incompatible requirements, or because of inadequate resources.

Too much work can often mean working excessive hours, which can lead to health and relationship problems, but people who control their own schedules, the self-employed for example, tend to suffer less harm from working long hours.[125] The introduction of flexitime often leads to only minor changes in actual behaviour, but has been found to have a positive effect on well-being.[126] The increase in control over their own schedules that people feel when they work flexitime is enough to improve health, even if the control is not actually exercised.

When people work may be as significant as how long they work. Work patterns that disrupt or conflict with life's normal – "circadian" – rhythms, like rotating shifts, and permanent night-work in particular, have been linked to a variety of detrimental effects on psychological and physical health, as well as behavioural and social problems.[127]

It may not be just the quantity or the schedule of work which causes problems: having work that is too difficult, or demands skills or knowledge that someone doesn't have, can also be a significant source of stress. Managers have a legal responsibility under the Health and Safety at Work regulations to ensure that employees are not asked to perform work that is beyond their capability to perform safely. This is usually taken to mean that people must be adequately trained so that accidents are avoided, but being asked to do things for which we lack the necessary skills, knowledge or resources is stressful and potentially harmful, as well as being a reliable recipe for poor results.

However, being overloaded, either in terms of quantity or of difficulty, isn't the only kind of harmful "demand mismatch". Having too little work, or work that is too easy, or that doesn't utilize someone's level of training or education, can be equally stressful.[128]

Of course, the allocation of work in a modern organization is seldom totally under an individual's own control. Tasks may be handed down by a line manager, or by one or more "internal customers", or by automated equipment like the automated call distribution (ACD) systems that control work distribution and pace in many call centres. This, and the electronic performance monitoring that is also a feature of these environments, have been linked to high stress rates and high staff turnover.[129] Managers have responsibility for being *aware* of the demands on their staff, but this may not be all that easy if the work comes direct to them from other sources. The combination of fast-paced work and the need to resolve conflicting priorities, which happens when several people give the same employee large amounts of work with short deadlines, is associated with a higher risk of psychiatric disorder, poor physical fitness or illness.[130]

health and efficiency You will probably have noticed that I haven't said much here about "stress management" programmes, and helping people to deal with their stress through such facilities as counselling, help lines or gym memberships. This is not because I believe that these things have no value, but rather because stress researchers are on the whole unimpressed with stress reduction approaches that focus on the individual, which they tend to see as "victim blaming". The best first-aid facilities in the world don't compare with preventing injuries in the first place.

Over the last few pages we have looked at the nature of stress and some of its potential causes. In a tough world, some people reading this may have been wondering "so what? Why should an organization fighting to survive in a fiercely competitive environment have to devote time and resource to worrying about people who can't keep up?" To help answer this we will look at some of the personal, organizational and economic consequences of stress.

The link between workplace stress and physical illness has been observed over many years. For example, in 1958 it was found that over 90% of young heart disease patients suffered stress at work, whereas only 20% of a comparable group of healthy people did so.[131] Similarly, in the early 1990s twelve out of fourteen studies of heart disease were found to be clearly linked with workplace stress,[132] leading the authors to estimate that 23% of deaths from heart disease in the USA were potentially preventable if the stress levels in the "worst" jobs were reduced to average levels. Heart disease is only one of the health outcomes of stress; many other diseases and health issues, such as gastro-intestinal disorders, immune system failures, neurological problems,[133] and psychological problems such as anxiety and depression,[134] are also attributable to workplace stress and accident rates have been shown to rise in step with stress levels.[135]

These are just examples of a considerable body of evidence relating physical and mental ill-health to workplace stress. Links between stress and health problems might not be of very great concern if the occurrence of such problems was unusual. Unfortunately this is far from being the case. Research has consistently suggested that more than one in four of the working population is suffering from some kind of stress-related disorder at any one time.[136,137] Apart from the human consequences this has direct implications for employing organizations because sickness, however caused, means absence from work, reduced productivity, low creativity, lethargy and high staff turnover. Estimates of the cost to industry of these problems are necessarily difficult to quantify, but the HSE estimates that 6.5 million working days were lost in Britain in 1995 due to stress, depression, anxiety or a physical condition ascribed to work-related stress – with an average of 16 days off work for each person suffering from the condition.[138] In 1992 it was suggested that for every day lost to strikes 30 days were lost to stress-related causes,[139] a ratio that is very unlikely to have decreased since then. All these figures of course take no account of the cost to organizations of the people who do turn up for work, but under-perform while they are there because of stress-related problems.

Managers have legal responsibilities to provide safe systems of work and this includes "taking steps to make sure employees do not suffer stress-related illness as a result of their work".[140] Several pieces of legislation may apply to this requirement, including:

- The Employment Rights Act 1966
- The Health and Safety at Work Act 1974
- The Disability Discrimination Act 1995
- The Protection from Harassment Act 1997
- The Working Time Regulations Act 1998
- The Management of Health and Safety at Work Regulations 1999, especially:

    The duty to assess

    The duty to prevent

    The duty to train and ensure capability

UK courts have been increasingly willing to hold managers responsible for ill-effects arising from work-related stress, especially where problems have been identified but not adequately dealt with. The only way organizations can be confident that they are doing all that is reasonably possible to protect the health of their employees from these hazards is to undertake rigorous risk assessments at regular intervals.

The Health and Safety Executive[141] sets out a five-step risk assessment process:

1. Identify the hazards.
2. Decide who might be harmed, and in what ways.
3. Evaluate the risk:
   - Identify what action you are already taking.
   - Decide whether it's enough.
   - If not, decide what else you need to do.
4. Record the significant findings of the assessment.
5. Review the assessment at appropriate intervals.

An excellent next step in confronting stress in your own workplace, with all its attendant human and commercial consequences, would be to prepare a business case for your senior management team, showing the need to carry out a stress risk assessment and detailing the actions required to do it. It would also be wise to order the two HSE publications mentioned above:

- *Tackling Work-related Stress*, HSE Books (2001)
- *5 Steps to Risk Assessment*, HSE Books (1998)

and a newer one:

- *Real Solutions, Real People – A Manager's Guide to Tackling Work-related Stress,* HSE Books (2003)[142]

and visiting the HSE's website at www.hse.gov.uk/stress/stresspilot/index.htm and making use of all the tools, advice and information that are available to you.

In this chapter I've tried to show how the culture of the organization ("the way we do things around here"); the organizational climate ("what it feels like to work here"); the psychological contract (the "exchange agreement between individuals and their organization") and the stress levels that are attributable to the work context all contribute to an overall experience of the working environment which can have a profound effect on both organizational effectiveness and individual wellbeing.

To the extent that awareness is a prerequisite for improvement, the general understanding that's provided by research and the specific understanding that comes from careful analysis of your own organizational context can combine to help get the environment "right", to the great benefit of everyone concerned.

"The environment is right" checklist

What factors in your organization's origins continue to shape its character today?

What learning experiences have shaped and influenced its culture over its lifetime?

What are the most significant values, attitudes and beliefs in your organization?

What processes might have produced these?

What effects do they have on decision-making?

How well do your own values, attitudes and beliefs match those of the organization?

What tensions/conflicts are there?

Do you know whether there are other people who feel as you do?

What metaphors are most helpful to you in understanding the way your organization functions?

What metaphors would you use to explain your own department to an outsider?

If you are planning to make some change in your own department's operations, what elements of your "system" will be affected by your intended action?

How can you guard against unintended effects?

How would you describe the dominant "culture type" of your organization?

How well does its culture suit the conditions in which it currently has to operate?

What feasible or foreseeable change(s) in those conditions would make the culture more of a liability than an asset?

What are the "basic assumptions" that influence the character of your organization?

What key objectives do you think should appear on a balanced scorecard to make your organization or department more effective?

How favourable to effectiveness is your organization's (or your department's) climate? (You can use the OCA instrument to find out.)

What action could you take to improve the climate?

What are the terms of your own psychological contract with your organization?

What are the terms of the "contract" between you and the people who report directly to you?

What demands (potential stressors) are you currently dealing with?

What demands are each of your people dealing with?

Would your organization regard someone who showed the Type A Behaviour Pattern as an attractive potential recruit?

What stressors are there in the physical environment of your own workplace?

▶

How would you know if someone was being bullied or suffering harassment in your workplace?

What job-related dangers are there in your workplace?

How much control do people in your organization have over their work schedules?

Could this be increased?

What would you include in a business case for your senior management to show the need for a stress risk assessment?

notes and references

1 Harrison, R (1972) "Understanding your organization's culture", *Harvard Business Review,* **50** (3), 119–28

2 Hofstede, G (1991) *Cultures And Organizations,* London, Harper Collins

3 ibid.

4 ibid.

5 Baron, A & Walters, M (1994) *The Culture Factor,* London, IPD

6 Atkinson, RL, Atkinson, RC, Smith, EE & Bem, D (1993) *Introduction To Psychology,* London, Harcourt Brace

7 Rose, S (2003) "Natural conclusion", *The Guardian Review,* 19th April, 13

8 Bouchard, TJ (1984) "Twins reared apart and together: what they tell us about human diversity", in S Fox (ed.) *The Chemical and Biological Bases of Individuality,* New York, Plenum

9 Joseph, J (2002) *The Gene Illusion,* Llangarron, pccs Books

10 James, O (2003) "Children before cash", *Guardian,* May 17, 21

11 Bandura, A (1977) *Social Learning Theory,* Englewood Cliffs, NJ, Prentice Hall

12 Kelman, HC (1958) "Compliance, identification and internalisation: three processes of attitude change", *Journal of Conflict Resolution,* No. 2, 51–60

13 Gregory, R (1977) *Eye And Brain,* London, Weidenfeld and Nicholson

14 Rogers, CR (1961) *On Becoming a Person: a Therapist's View Of Psychotherapy,* London, Constable

15 Kelly, GA (1955) *The Psychology of Personal Constructs,* New York, WW Norton

16 Zukav, G (1992) *The Dancing Wu Li Masters*, New York, Perrenial Classics

17 Harrison, "Understanding your organisation's culture", op. cit.

18 Rokeach, M (1968) "The nature of attitudes", in *International Encyclopedia of Social Sciences,* Vol. 1, New York, Macmillan/Free Press

19 Morgan, CT & King, RA (1971) *Introduction to Psychology,* London, McGraw-Hill

20 Rokeach, M (1968) *Beliefs, Attitudes and Values,* London, Jossey–Bass

21 Thorndike, EL (1911) *Animal Intelligence: Experimental Studies,* New York, Macmillan

22 Kelman, HC (1958) "Compliance, identification and internalisation: three processes of attitude change", *Journal of Conflict Resolution*, No. 2, 51–60

23 Rokeach, M (1973) *The Nature of Human Values,* New York, Free Press

24 Schwartz, S & Sagiv, L (1995) "Identifying culture specifics in the content and structure of values", *Journal of Cross-Cultural Psychology,* No. 26, 92–116

25 Festinger, L (1957) *A Theory of Cognitive Dissonance,* Evanston, USA, Row, Peterson

26 Edwards, JR (1988) "The determinants and consequences of coping with stress", in CL Cooper & R Payne (eds) *Causes, Coping and Consequences of Stress at Work,* Chichester, John Wiley

27 Festinger, L & Carlsmith, LM (1959) "Cognitive consequences of forced compliance", *Journal of Abnormal and Social Psychology,* No. 58, 203–10

28 Morgan, G (1986) *Images of Organization,* London, Sage

29 ibid.

30 Epictetus c.55–c.138 AD *The Golden Sayings of Epictetus,* various sources. The *Golden Sayings* can be found on-line at Authorama Public Domain Books: www.authorama.com/the-goldensayings-of-epictetus-32.html

31 Burke, Edmund (1777) *Letter to Sheriffs,* II, 274, various sources

32 Wheatley, MJ (1994) *Leadership and the New Science,* San Francisco, Berrett-Koehler Publishers Inc

33 Checkland, P (1984) *Systems Thinking, Systems Practice,* Chichester, Wiley

34 Stacey, RD (1991) *The Chaos Frontier,* Oxford, Butterworth Heinemann

35 Stacey, RD (1992) *Managing Chaos,* London, Kogan Page

36 van de Vliet, A (1994) "Order from chaos", *Management Today,* November, 62–5

37 Gleick, J (1987) *Chaos: Making a New Science,* London, Heinemannn

38 Kauffman, S (1995) *At Home in the Universe,* Oxford, OUP

39 Mariotti, J (1996) "A new science for business strategists: complexity, chaos, and the 'natural laws' of business", *Industry Week,* October 21, 12

40 Handy, C (1985) *Understanding Organizations,* 3rd edn, Harmondsworth, Penguin

41 Deal, T & Kennedy, A (1982) *Corporate Cultures,* London, Penguin Business

42 Trompenaars, F (1993) *Riding the Waves of Culture: Understanding Cultural Diversity in Business,* London, Economist Books

43 Schneider, WE (1994) *The Reengineering Alternative: A Plan for Making your Current Culture Work,* Burr Ridge, IL, Irwin

44 Cameron, KS & Quinn, RE (1999) *Diagnosing and Changing Organizational Culture,* Reading, MA, Addison-Wesley

45 Schein, EH (1985) *Organizational Culture and Leadership,* Oxford, Jossey-Bass

46 ibid.

47 ibid.

48 Pay, P (1994) "Organizational dis-functions", *EFMD Forum,* No. 94/1, 19–21

49 Peters, T & Waterman, R (1982) *In Search of Excellence,* New York, Harper and Row

50 Payne, R (1991) "Taking stock of corporate culture", *Personnel Management,* July, 26–9

51 Peters & Waterman, *In Search of Excellence*, op. cit.

52 Kennedy, C (1991) *Guide to the Management Gurus,* London, Business Books

53 Kotter, JP & Heskett, JL (1992) *Corporate Culture and Performance,* New York, The Free Press

54 Sackmann, S (1991) *Cultural Knowledge in Organizations,* London, Sage

55 EQA (2002) *The European Model for Total Quality Management,* Eindhoven, The Netherlands, The European Foundation for Total Quality Management

56 Kaplan, RS & Norton, DP (1992) "The balanced scorecard – measures that drive performance", *Harvard Business Review,* January–February, 71–79

57 Kaplan, RS, Lowes, A & Norton, DP (1996) *The Balanced Scorecard,* Cambridge, MA, Harvard Business School Press

58 Kaplan, RS & Norton, DP (2000) *The Strategy-focused Organization,* Cambridge, MA, Harvard Business School Press

59 The Work Foundation (2003) *The Missing Link – From Productivity to Performance,* London, The Work Foundation

60 Caulkin, S (2001) *Performance Through People,* London, CIPD

61 Patterson, M, West, M, Lawthom, R & Nickell, S (1998) *Impact of People Management Practices on Business Performance,* Issues in People Management series, No. 22, London, IPD

62 Gray, RJ (2000) "Organisational climate and the competitive edge", in L Lloyd-Reason & S Wall (eds) *Dimensions of Competitiveness: Issues and Policies,* Cheltenham, Edward Elgar Publishing

63 ibid.

64 Walsh, C (2002) "Fallen idols of the free market", *Observer,* 28 July, Management, 8

65 McGregor, D (1960) *The Human Side of Enterprise,* New York, McGraw-Hill

66 Handy, C (1990) *The Age of Unreason,* London, Arrow Books

67 Deming, WE (1986) *Out of the Crisis,* Cambridge, MA, MIT CAES

68 Eysenck, MW (1983) "Anxiety and individual differences", in GRJ Hockey (ed.) *Stress and Fatigue in Human Performance,* Chichester, John Wiley

69 Gray, "Organisational climate and the competitive edge", op. cit.

70 Buckingham, M (2001) "What a waste", *People Management,* 11 October, 36–40

71 Scase, R (2001) "Why we're so clock wise", *Observer,* 26 August, Business, 9

72 ISR (2002) "UK workforce is 'one of the least committed in Europe'", *People Management,* 12 September, 11

73 Gray, "Organisational climate and the competitive edge", op. cit.

74 Rousseau, DM (1995) *Psychological Contracts in Organizations,* London, Sage

75 Arnold, J (1996) "The psychological contract: a concept in need of closer scrutiny?", *European Journal of Work and Organizational Psychology,* **5** (4), 511–20

76 Rousseau, *Psychological Contracts in Organizations*, op. cit.

77 Makin, P, Cooper, C & Cox, C (1996) *Organizations and the Psychological Contract,* Leicester, BPS Books

78 Robinson, SL & Rousseau, DM (1994) "Violating the psychological contract: not the exception but the norm", *Journal of Organizational Behavior,* No. 15, 245–59

79 Kolb, DA, Rubin, IM & Osland, JS (1995) *Organizational Behavior an Experiential Approach,* Englewood Cliffs, NJ, Prentice Hall

80 Hallier, J & Lyon, P (1996) "Managing to look after number one", *People Management,* 2 May, 38–9

81 Guest, D, Conway, N, Briner, R & Dickman, M (1996) *The State of the Psychological Contract in Employment,* Issues in People Management Series, No. 16, London, IPD

82 Kessler, I & Undy, R (1996) *The New Employment Relationship: Examining the Psychological Contract,* London, IPD

83 Hallier & Lyon, "Managing to look after number one", op. cit, 38

84 Makin *et al., Organizations and the Psychological Contract*, op. cit., 130

85 Rousseau, *Psychological Contracts in Organizations*, op. cit, 14,

86 ibid., 133

87 Guest *et al., The State of the Psychological Contract in Employment,* op. cit.

88 Guest, D & Conway, N (2002) "Don't hurry, be happy", *People Management,* 21 November, 28–31

89 Williams, S (1994) *Managing Pressure for Peak Performance,* London, Kogan Page

90 Yerkes, RM & Dodson, JD (1908) "The relation of strength of stimulus to rapidity of habit-formation", *Journal of Comparative Neurology and Psychology,* No. 148, 133–46

91 Hockey, GRJ & Hamilton P (1983) "The cognitive patterning of stress states", in GRJ Hockey (ed.) *Stress and Fatigue in Human Performance,* Chichester, John Wiley

92 Cannon, WB (1929) *Bodily Changes in Pain, Hunger, Fear and Rage,* New York, Appleton

93 Ax, AA (1953) "Physiological differentiation of emotional states", *Psychosomatic Medicine,* No. 15, 433–42

94 Funkenstein, DH (1955) "The physiology of fear and anger", *Scientific American,* May, 74–80

95 Selye, H (1952) *The Story of the Adaptation Syndrome*, Montreal, Acta Inc. The diagram is by Gray, JA (1991) *The Psychology of Fear and Stress*, 2nd edn, Cambridge, CUP, 61

96 Edwards, "The determinants and consequences of coping with stress", op. cit.

97 Williams, *Managing Pressure for Peak Performance*, op. cit, 42

98 McLean, AA (1985) *Work Stress,* Reading, MA, Addison-Wesley

99 Sutherland, V & Cooper, C (1988) "Sources of work stress", in JJ Hurrell, LR Murphy, SL Sauter and CL Cooper (eds) *Occupational Stress: Issues and Developments in Research,* London, Taylor and Francis

100 Selye, *The Story of the Adaptation Syndrome*, op. cit.

101 Friedman, M & Rosenman, RH (1974) *Type A: Your Behavior and Your Heart,* New York, Knoft

102 Cox, T (1993) *Stress Research and Stress Management: Putting Theory to Work,* Sudbury, Health and Safety Executive

103 Williams, *Managing Pressure for Peak Performance,* op. cit.

104 Powell, LH (1987) "Issues in the measurement of the Type A behaviour pattern", in SV Kasl (ed.) *Stress and Health: Issues in Research Methodology,* Chichester, John Wiley

105 Payne, R (1988) "Individual differences in the study of occupational stress", in CL Cooper and R Payne (eds) *Causes, Coping and Consequences of Stress at Work,* Chichester, John Wiley

106 Powell, "Issues in the measurement of the Type A behaviour pattern", op. cit.

107 Rotter, JB (1966) "Generalised expectancies for internal versus external control of reinforcement", *Psychology Monograph,* 80–94

108 Phares, EJ (1976) *Locus of Control in Personality,* New Jersey, General Learning Press

109 Krause, N (1986) "Stress and coping: reconceptualizing the role of locus of control beliefs", *Journal of Gerontology,* **41**, 617–22

110 Kobasa, SC (1979) "Stressful life events, personality, and health: an inquiry into hardiness", *Journal of Personality and Social Psychology*, **37** (1), 1–11

111 Kobasa, SC (1985) "Conceptualisation and measurement of personality in job stress research", NIOSH Symposium *Measures of Job Stress* Workshop, 21–23 October, New Orleans, NIOSH

112 Kobasa, SC & Puccetti, M (1982) "Personality and social resources in stress resistance", *Journal of Personality and Social Psychology,* **45** (4), 839–50

113 Payne, "Individual differences in the study of occupational stress", op. cit.

114 Cox, *Stress Research and Stress Management*, op. cit.

115 Pratt, J (1976) *Perceived Stress Among Teachers,* Unpublished MA thesis, University of Sheffield

116 Payne, "Individual differences in the study of occupational stress," op. cit.

117 Karasek, R & Theorell, T (1990) *Healthy Work: Stress, Productivity, and the Reconstruction of Working Life,* New York, Basic Books

118 Burke, RJ (1988) "Sources of managerial and professional stress in large organizations", in CL Cooper and R Payne (eds) *Causes, Coping and Consequences of Stress at Work,* Chichester, John Wiley

119 London Hazards Centre (1994) *Hard Labour: Stress, Ill-health and Hazardous Employment Practices,* London, London Hazards Centre

120 HSE (2001) *Tackling Work-related Stress,* Sudbury, HSE Books

121 ibid.

122 McCartney, C & Holbeche, L (2003) *The Roffey Park Management Agenda 2003,* Horsham, Roffey Park Institute

123 Cox, *Stress Research and Stress Management*, op. cit.

124 Karasek & Theorell, *Healthy Work*, op. cit.

125 Coe, T (1993) *Managers Under Stress,* Corby, Institute of Management

126 Landy, FJ (1992) "Work design and stress", in G Keita and S Sauter (eds) *Work and Well-Being: An Agenda For The 1990s,* Washington, DC, American Psychological Association

127 Sauter, SL, Murphy, LR & Hurrell, JJ (1992) "Prevention of work-related psychological disorders: a national strategy proposed by NIOSH", in G Keita and S Sauter (eds) *Work and Well-Being: An Agenda For The 1990s,* Washington, DC, American Psychological Association

128 Fletcher, BC (1988) "The epidemiology of occupational stress", in CL Cooper and R Payne (eds), *Causes, Coping and Consequences Of Stress At Work,* Chichester, John Wiley

129 Arkin, A (1997) "Hold the production line", *People Management,* 6 February, 22–7

130 HSE, *Tackling Work-related Stress*, op. cit.

131 Russek, HI & Zohman, BL (1958) "Relative significance of heredity, diet and occupational stress in CHD of young adults", *American Journal of Medical Sciences,* 235, 266–275

132 Landsbergis, PA, Schurman, S, Israel, B, Schnall, PL, Hugentobler, M, Cahill, J & Baker, D (1993) "Job stress and heart disease: evidence and strategies for prevention", *New Solutions,* **3** (4), 42–58

133 Cooper, CL (1994) "The costs of healthy work organizations", in CL Cooper & S Williams (eds) *Creating Healthy Work Organizations,* Chichester, John Wiley

134 HSE, *Tackling Work-related Stress*, op. cit.

135 Cartwright, S, Cooper, CL & Barron, A (1993) "An investigation of the relationship between occupational stress and accidents amongst company car drivers", *Journal of General Management,* **19** (2), 78–85

136 Willcox, R (1994) "Positive health screening at work", in CL Cooper and S Williams (eds) *Creating Healthy Work Organizations,* Chichester, John Wiley

137 Smith, A (2001) "Perceptions of stress at work", *Human Resource Management Journal,* **11** (4), 74–86

138 HSE, *Tackling Work-related Stress*, op. cit.

139 Banham, J (1992) "The cost of mental ill health to business", in R Jenkins & N Coney (eds) *Prevention of Mental Ill Health at Work,* London, HMSO

140 HSE, *Tackling Work-related Stress*, op. cit.

141 HSE (1998) *5 Steps to risk assessment,* Sudbury, HSE Books

142 HSE (2003) *Real Solutions, Real People – A Manager's Guide to Tackling Work-related Stress,* Sudbury, HSE Books

9 nine

I can do it better next time

the learning organization

Learning in the organization must be equal to or greater than the rate of external change. If not, the organization faces decline or extinction. (Reg Revans)

Over recent years, management writers have increasingly focused on the concept of "organizational learning", for the reason succinctly defined above by Reg Revans.[1] The commercial value of being or becoming a learning organization is, quite simply, that it gives you competitive advantage over anyone who isn't as good at it as you. It may, in fact, be the single most important factor in achieving an edge over the competition.[2,3]

All this may seem little more than common sense; surely organizations that are good at learning would be expected to do better than those that aren't. There are, though, some difficulties in first defining what a learning organization actually is, and then in developing the characteristics of such an organization back in our own real-world workplaces.

In Chapter 3 we considered the process of learning, as experienced by individuals, but organizational learning cannot be quite the same. As individuals we are all equipped from birth with the most powerful integrated ICT (information and communications technology) device yet identified: the human brain. Our brains, with their five sensory systems and network of connecting nerves, give each of us a staggering capacity to monitor our environment, process, to store, retrieve and evaluate the data gathered from this monitoring, and formulate short- or long-term responses, all in a highly coordinated, centralized way. Every experience we have ever had is automatically added to our data banks; it only needs the right trigger to summon the data back to enrich our responses to new situations.

By comparison, an organization, with limited sensory faculties at the organizational level and made up of individual components with only tenuous information sharing and transfer mechanisms, isn't in the same league. All the same, organizational learning is possible, even if it's bound to be an extremely crude, pale imitation of the learning of which individuals are capable.

collective consciousness The label "learning organization" tends to get used quite loosely, so it would be helpful to try to pin it down. David Garvin[4] says it means "an organization skilled at creating, acquiring, interpreting, transferring and retaining knowledge, and at purposefully modifying its behaviour to reflect new knowledge and insights". This definition is pitched exclusively at the whole-organization level, almost as though the organization has a brain of its own. But of course, it hasn't; the organization's capacity to learn depends on the brains of its individual members. For the organization to learn its people have to "continually expand their capacity to create the results they truly desire", as Peter Senge puts it.[5]

the organization's capacity to learn depends on the brains of its individual members

On the face of it, this seems to suggest that organizations whose members "learn" – whatever that means or implies in terms of the quality and quantity of learning involved – will be or will become a learning organization almost automatically. This is far from being the case. Undoubtedly, individual learning is a vital prerequisite but that alone won't be enough. If it were, managers could stand back and just let it all happen, because, as Senge points out, "we are all learners. No one has to teach an infant to learn; not only is it our nature to learn but we love to learn".

For learning, at any level, to occur the organizational context has to be supportive of the learning process. Cultural factors play a big part in this; history, structure, power and relationships, norms, rules, beliefs and values all have the capacity to help or hinder individual learning.[6] Context can be a very powerful constraint, as Senge points out with his observation that people, however different, tend to produce similar results when they are placed in the same system.

Where this takes us is to the conclusion that organizations cannot simply rely on individuals' willingness to learn for themselves, but must take active steps first to encourage individual learning and then to channel and utilize that learning at the wider organizational level. Clearly, every manager, at every level, has the responsibility for this because they have the power to facilitate the learning of their people – which was discussed in some detail in Chapter 3 – but perhaps even more crucially they have the power to coordinate individual learning and construct organizational learning from these separate components.

There's widespread agreement in the learning organization literature that this is a three-stage process. First, the organization has to monitor its environment, make observations, and acquire data and information. Secondly, it must interpret that raw data in the light of its own context, needs and priorities. Finally, the organization must put the interpreted information to use, beginning new behaviours and changing or ceasing old ones.

This sounds very much like Kolb's experiential learning cycle, which we considered in Chapter 3, but with an organizational rather than individual slant. The first stage, in which information is acquired, maps quite neatly on to Kolb's *concrete experience* phase. The second stage, in which the information is interpreted and perspectives and attitudes are formed, relates to the *reflections* and *formation of abstract concepts* phases of the Kolb cycle, and the third stage, in which these new interpretations are applied or used, is the equivalent of Kolb's *experiment* phase. This is quite helpful and reassuring, because it indicates that the learning process is quite consistent, whether at the individual or organizational level.

keep channels open So, for any meaningful learning to occur at the organization-wide level there must first be mechanisms in place for events to be detected and understood. In other words, effective communication channels must be open for information to reach the decision-making centres. Whatever your level in your organization, you are unavoidably a conduit for this information flow.

Because, just like the rest of us, their personal data-processing capabilities are finite senior managers must rely on other people to tell them what they need to know, and this means that what they are told will have been interpreted and filtered before it reaches them. This interpretation and filtering is part of the daily workload of every junior and middle manager, and may be so routine and natural that it isn't recognized for what it is. The people at the top have to rely on and utilize the intelligence and expertise of people further down the hierarchy to ensure that they get the information they need, but this can only be effective if everyone has a grasp of the organization's objectives and feels commitment and goodwill towards the upper echelons, and feels safe in providing accurate information. Nothing is easier than blocking, delaying or distorting information flows; it's the traditional power base of middle managers.

Similarly, allowing too much data through can effectively paralyze, or subvert, decision-making. When the Whitehall mandarins in the BBC "Yes, Minister" series wanted the minister's assent to measures they thought he wouldn't much care for, they would place the relevant papers in the middle of a pile of routine, tedious material. When the minister opened his red box he would carefully read the first few papers, but then the boredom would take its toll and he would negligently skim through those in the middle of the pile, including the controversial one. As he got near to the bottom of the box the prospect of finishing his evening's work gave him renewed energy, and the last few papers again received their due attention. Senior managers are likely to act in much the same way, and the ruse is even more effective if the paperwork is computer-generated.

Nancy Foy, in her study of STC,[7] found a "power culture" where mistakes were routinely punished and bad news was never allowed to reach senior managers. The result of this was that senior people never found out that they had made a mistake and consequently never thought about changing what they did or the way they did it. Some organizations still actively discourage this upward flow of information. The idea of senior people who can't be challenged and won't tolerate disagreement or unsolicited advice conjures up for me an image of a pompous CEO, surrounded by obsequiously smiling and nodding minions as he strides majestically towards an open manhole. The case of Enron, mentioned in Chapter 8, shows just how destructive this mindset can become. You can quickly test the "danger level" in your organization by asking how senior people find out about what's going on, and how likely it is that the observations or concerns of very junior employees will ever be discussed in the boardroom.

a word to the wise

Assuming that the organization has succeeded in establishing the information flows that will enable events and environmental changes to be detected by some coordinating function, the next requirement is for evaluation, or *reflection*, to use Kolb's term. This is a resource-hungry activity since reflection is, by its very nature, a quiet, detached, contemplative activity. It's important, though. Peter Senge asks[8] how we can expect people to learn when they have little time to think and reflect, individually and collaboratively. He goes on: "I know of few managers who do not complain of not having enough time. Indeed, most of the managers with whom I have worked struggle unceasingly to get the time for quiet reflection".

A few years ago, I was asked to carry out a review of the operations of a division within a major UK company. Unusually, the division was headed up by not one manager but by a triumvirate known (inevitably) as the three wise men. It was perceived that the division wasn't performing as well as it should and I was asked to find out why. As I talked to people in the division, their suppliers and their customers, I found the usual mix of everyday issues but the only really significant and consistent theme was that people found it hard to get the attention of the "three wise men" when guidance and direction on strategic policy was required, or disputes needed to be resolved. Either the bosses were unavailable or the time they could give to the issue was severely restricted. They were just too busy.

When I reported back to the triumvirate I was not surprised to be kept waiting for nearly an hour because their previous meeting was over-running, and the half-hour allocated for my presentation was reduced to ten minutes, not nearly enough to explain things properly. It was very clear that the three managers were both pleased and gratified by my findings, which they interpreted as a perception by their people that they "worked too hard". They had missed the point entirely. As heads of the division their primary function was to provide direction and coordination. With their daily working lives so cluttered with detail they were, in fact, failing to do their jobs, although they may well have been doing several other people's jobs instead. They needed more time to listen and to reflect, and the people who worked for them needed, but weren't getting, their support.

Medieval society used to maintain communities of monks to do its thinking for it while the rest of the population got on with the work. Modern organizations, many of which have already been cut and downsized to the point where they can barely sustain life, are likely to regard think-tanks, or the equivalent, as luxuries they can't and don't wish to afford. Some compromise needs to be reached. Organizational learning needs in any case to permeate the whole organization, beginning with individual learning and extending right up to the behaviour of the entire enterprise, so it needs to be embedded in the daily life of the organization and not sequestered in the corporate equivalent of a closed monastic order. The people who can really make sense of events are the same people who make the day-to-day decisions of management, but they do need to step back from the hurly-burly just for a moment while they do it. If you really haven't got the time to do this then perhaps your roles need to be re-examined.

Don't be too quick to assume that you are too busy to think, though. It may be that you need to re-prioritise, perhaps to delegate or perhaps just to be less ready to take on responsibilities which should really be other people's. Merrill and Donna Douglass[9] suggest a simple but very powerful model for prioritizing the work you have on your desk right now. They advise you to look at each task or activity and allocate it to one of four boxes (you could take this literally, and have four in-trays), as illustrated in Figure 9.1.

If a task is important *and* urgent, do it now. If it's important but not urgent, allocate a specific time to do it so that it will be dealt with before it becomes urgent. If it's not important, but is urgent (i.e. if it's going to be done it needs to be done soon) make a conscious decision about whether to do it or not. After all, if it isn't important why do it? It may be something you want to do, or that you feel is useful or desirable for some reason, which is quite a legitimate decision to take. If so, schedule it in after the important and urgent things have been done. Otherwise, don't do it (but you may need to tell someone you aren't going to do it, and this may be important and/or urgent). The things that aren't either important or urgent sound like prime candidates for ditching. If you don't feel you can do this, do they really belong in one of the other three boxes?

	Important	Not important
Urgent	1	3
Not urgent	2	4

FIG 9.1 ● Importance/urgency matrix

back to basics In a learning organization the habit of reflection is endemic. This doesn't mean that everyone spends vast amounts of time gazing into the middle distance, but it does mean that people routinely think back over events and assess their significance. And pass on their ideas to others. A learning organization is a thinking organization.

It is certainly the case that "double-loop learning",[10] discussed in Chapter 3, has the greatest possible significance and value at the organizational level. It isn't necessarily easy for organizations to re-examine their "governing variables" – the underlying bases or principles on which actions or strategies are founded – but unless this is done learning at the wider level will be severely curtailed, at best. "Nothing undermines openness more surely than certainty. Once we feel as if we have 'the answer', all motivation to question our thinking disappears".[11] At the organizational level learning just won't thrive without a culture of inquisitiveness and openness and a willingness by managers to tolerate challenges to basic assumptions and questioning of accepted viewpoints. You have a part to play here, both by being courteously inquisitive and questioning in your own interactions with colleagues and bosses, and by encouraging these behaviours in the people who report to you.

The place where double-loop learning begins is at the first, information gathering stage of the organizational learning process, because it's all too easy for information to be screened out and rejected if it conflicts with established perspectives. Then the frames of reference within which information is interpreted, in the second stage, must be continually revised and tested; they can get out of date and new developments can show that they have been wrong all along. This can be very difficult; it's easier and more comfortable to view the world through the old familiar spectacles, but that's a recipe for failure.

So, the process of interpreting what has happened or, in Kolb's terms, of *reflecting* on it and formulating conceptual understanding demands an

a learning organization is a thinking organization

open mind and a readiness to see things from new perspectives. This is hard, and it can seem threatening to senior people who are used to issuing instructions and having them received deferentially, and perhaps didn't get where they are today by encouraging people to offer them alternative perspectives.

Systems thinkers suggest that new methods of interpretation and analysis are needed if better and deeper levels of understanding are to be attained. According to Peter Senge[12] any complex situation can be explained at several levels. The most superficial level simply examines and seeks to explain *events*. This is the commonest way in our culture of trying to understand the world. At a deeper level, we can try to identify and understand *patterns* of behaviour, which will begin to show longer-term trends and allow us to assess their implications. The third level of explanation is the level of *system structures*. This "structural" explanation is, according to Senge, the least common but the most powerful. It focuses on finding out what is causing the patterns of behaviour. It's important to seek the deepest possible level of explanation because problems are not likely to be adequately dealt with by simply addressing their symptoms. Only by dealing with underlying causes can problems be eliminated. This isn't always a very welcome suggestion. Short-term, symptom-suppressing solutions can be very appealing; there is always another issue awaiting attention.

fire! ready! aim!

Systems concepts also caution us against the too-ready assumption that there are simple, linear relationships between cause and effect. According to Matthew Miles and Michael Huberman,[13] "the case can be thoughtfully made that causality is not a workable concept when it comes to human behaviour", which may be a rather uncomfortable thought. It's possible to take a more positivist view of this issue, because the reasoning that lies behind Miles & Huberman's observation is that the problem isn't so much an absence of causes, but rather an excess of them, which makes it effectively impossible to identify cause–effect linkages. It's rare in social research, which includes organizational research, to find a single cause having a specific effect. It's far more common to find that an effect is the outcome of not just one cause but of a complex network of determinants, many of them interrelated.[14] The only effective way of dealing with this complexity is to look for inter-relationships rather than linear cause–effect linkages.

Interpretation, then, is quite a complex process that can't be rushed. It depends on recognizing incoming data and then analyzing it with imagination because objective analysis may well be elusive. Above all, if you can't reflect you probably won't learn, so being too busy may be a recipe for failure.

The third stage of organizational learning, in which organizations put their interpreted information to use, is loosely equivalent to the *experiment* phase of the Kolb learning cycle. This gets progressively more difficult to put into practice, because it involves taking risks, which is utterly contrary to the instincts of senior managers and most organizations' procedures.[15] It's easy to see why this would be so; allowing experimentation and risk-taking means accepting that things will go wrong sometimes, and on the whole we don't want things to go wrong. But this is a key management paradox; occasional failure is the price of general success.

This means that organizations won't succeed in promoting learning unless they accept that people are fallible and imperfect, so there must be the freedom to fail without incurring punishment or penalty. This doesn't mean that people should be free to be careless, reckless or negligent. Excellent performance is always linked with accountability, and there need to be systems or incentives in place that encourage the "identification, analysis, and review of errors".[16] When things go wrong – as they sometimes will – the review that takes place should ask whether the risk was a reasonable one to take, given what was known at the time (and whether enough effort was made to find out as much as possible before

a key management paradox: occasional failure is the price of general success

the risk was taken). If so, then the outcome was a genuine learning experience and the participants should be praised, not blamed.

Often, management's focus is on auditing compliance with procedures that have been found to work in the past (or sometimes, ones that have been found not to work, but somehow people can't quite bring themselves to let go). The profusion of "quality" standards now found in UK industry and commerce is firmly based in this philosophy. However well-intentioned these standards may be, their effect can often be to discourage experimentation and stifle learning. The desire always to have clear, "hard" measures against which people's actions can be checked and approved or disapproved is perhaps one of the defining weaknesses of current organizational practice. Management is much more subtle, and more difficult, than that.

learning to be a learning organization

If we accept the view that a learning organization is one that is in touch with its environment so that information flows inwards continually, in which that information is interpreted to produce new perspectives and better understanding, and in which that enhanced understanding is applied, resulting in new activities and behaviours, then we need to find ways to transform our existing organizations so that they at least begin to demonstrate the characteristics of a learning organization.

Mike Pedler, John Burgoyne and Tom Boydell, in their book *The Learning Company*,[17] identify eleven characteristics of the learning organization, many of which imply specific actions to implement them. They say that learning organizations have, first, a "learning approach to strategy". This means that they carefully structure their policy making and strategy formulation to encourage learning, for example, "deliberate pilots and small-scale experiments are used to create feedback loops".

They also practise "participative policy making", involving as many members of the organization as possible in the decision-making process, especially at the strategic and policy-making levels.

In the learning organization "information technology is not just about automation but is used to inform people about critical aspects of the business in order to encourage and empower them to act on their own initiative". One specific aspect of this is to structure reporting systems, budgeting and accounting to help people understand the function served by finance in the organization.

Learning organizations show a high degree of "internal exchange", which means that learning from other departments is normal and people see themselves as part of a learning network as well as regarding themselves as each other's customers and suppliers.

A learning organization's reward systems are very flexible, to support the autonomy and empowerment that goes with the learning orientation. Roles, processes and procedures are seen as temporary structures that can be changed to meet job or customer requirements.

Environmental scanning is carried out by "people who have contacts with the outside world of users, suppliers, business partners, neighbours and so on", and processes are in place for this information to be channelled back into the organization and disseminated to where it's most needed. "Inter-company learning" is encouraged through such means as benchmarking, joint ventures and other alliances.

A "learning climate" is promoted where "leaders and managers facilitate their own and other people's experimentation and learning from experience, through questioning, feedback and support".

And finally, resources and facilities for self-development are made available to all members of the organization and "not just the favoured few".

The reference to "a learning climate" is interesting. Many of the characteristics that Pedler, Burgoyne & Boydell identify in a learning organization are very similar to characteristics of organizational climate that have been positively associated with successful work outcomes, as discussed in Chapter 8. This is unlikely to be a coincidence.

house style

The comparison of organizational learning with Kolb's experiential learning cycle suggests that organizations, like individuals, may have preferred learning styles, each of which has its strengths but also its potential pitfalls. Mike Pedler and Kath Aspinwall[18] have identified five organizational learning styles:

Some organizations have a style that features "habits" and standard procedures, which can be beneficial because the procedures often survive even though individuals come and go. The down side is that the habits may persist and degenerate into unthinking repetition when they are no longer useful. Pedler & Aspinwall call this the "Blind Automaton Syndrome".

Others favour memory as a learning style. These organizations may become adept at "collecting, storing and disseminating experience, data and knowledge" but risk relying on solutions to "yesterday's problems" and falling prey to the "Resistance to Change Syndrome".

Organizations that lean towards "modelling" may be good at "imitating, cherry picking and benchmarking best practice internally and externally" but can find themselves over-valuing ideas from outside, undervaluing home-grown solutions and losing confidence in their ability to innovate internally: the "Others Lead, We Follow Syndrome".

Organizations that like to experiment may be innovative but may find themselves "fixing what ain't broke", trying out too many ideas and neglecting core business in favour of experimentation: the "Flavour of the Month Syndrome".

Finally, enquiry-oriented organizations are often good at "reflecting on experience, being open-minded and curious, with a wide awareness of the organization, its context and environment", but too much of this can take the eye off the ball, losing focus and neglecting detail: the "Ivory Tower Syndrome".

The basic principles of creating or developing a learning organization are fairly straightforward, but putting them into practice isn't easy. It demands real dedication to continuous improvement and active encouragement of everyone you can influence to do the same.[19] This is quite an onerous requirement, since it involves continuous attention to what's going on in the organization (or, at least, that part of it you can personally influence) and active encouragement of the processes of learning described above.

The four key conditions for sustained organizational learning, according to Bob Garrat,[20] are:

- People in organizations are naturally learning while working, but they need help to learn both regularly and rigorously from their work.
- Such learning needs both robust organizational systems and a positive organizational climate to move the learning to where it is needed.
- Learning is seen to be valued by the organization in achieving its objectives.
- The organization is so designed as to be able to transform itself continuously through its learning to the benefit of its stakeholders.

Perhaps not many organizations fully meet these conditions but, as with most advice of this kind, it provides a benchmark with which our own, imperfect, real-life organizations can compare themselves. The issue is, how would your organization need to change in order to satisfy these four "key conditions", and what is the first step towards attaining this goal?

> Organizational learning is the key to staying healthy, alert and responsive to risks and opportunities.
>
> Becoming a "learning organization" is an arduous process, demanding dedication and constant vigilance. It involves creating a climate where individual learning is fostered and encouraged, and in which that individual learning is coordinated, absorbed and utilized effectively at the wider organizational level. The reward comes in the form of significantly increased competitive advantage and enhanced control over the impact of environmental and developmental change.

organizational change Having read as far as this it's possible that you have reached the conclusion that your own organization seems to have all the characteristics that have been identified as generally positive and conducive to excellent performance by its members, and few or none of those that have been shown to be generally negative and tending to suppress energy and initiative.

On the other hand, you may have felt that there are some aspects of the way things are done that could be improved. Also, regardless of how good your organization is at getting things done, the external environment in which it has to operate is unlikely to be standing still and it may be that what needs to be done today is different from the things you were doing so well last month, or last year. Being very good at doing the wrong things doesn't lead to success. This means that, one way or another, something may need to change.

It's hard to study the literature on organizational change without being left with two clear impressions: first, that change is inevitable and, second, that it's probably a good thing. We'll examine these two propositions in reverse order, on the grounds that if something is inevitable we have to find a way of coping with it regardless of whether it's good or bad.

Much of the recent literature on change seems to relish the fast, and apparently accelerating, pace of change as it affects organizational life. Constant change, it seems to be telling us, means dynamism, energy and life at the cutting edge. Change, it seems, is at the very heart of an organization's business success: the more you change the better you'll get on. Robert Kriegel and Louis Patler went so far as to advise: "If It Ain't Broke, Break It",[21] reasoning that the way you are doing things now is bound, by definition, to be inferior to the way you could be doing them, so if you're happy with the status quo you urgently need to be shaken out of your complacency.

the future? we're in it now

All this has a certain degree of credibility, but needs to be treated with some caution. As long ago as 1970, Alvin Toffler was warning about impending "Future Shock"[22] resulting from increasing transience, novelty and diversity. Transience refers to the shorter relationships we tend to have: with *things*, because new developments mean we replace things more frequently; with *places*, because we tend to move around more than previous generations; with *people*, because, according to Toffler, our relationships tend to be more functionally based than in the past, and anyway increased mobility tends to lead to more and shorter interpersonal relationships. We have shorter relationships now with *organizations*, because they tend to be less stable than in the past, and finally with *ideas*, because knowledge and beliefs are constantly being challenged and revised. Toffler says that these factors combine to create a kind of overload, similar in many ways to the culture shock that people may experience when they move to a new country or society, but with the major difference that it may sometimes be possible for migrants to go back home if they find they can't settle in their new environment but none of us can go back to an earlier age.

Change can be stressful for individuals, although this broad statement needs to be taken in context. It's often said that "people don't like change" but there are situations where this clearly isn't true. In the workplace context, a pay rise – a change in remuneration – isn't usually unwelcome. Similarly, for someone doing boring or unpleasant work a change to something more interesting is likely to be accepted with enthusiasm. Most of us quite like going on holiday, which often means a radical, if temporary, change from familiar or habitual lifestyles, and the need for variety is embedded in our language: "a change is as good as a rest", "variety is the spice of life", etc.

The real problems for individuals of change in the workplace arise primarily from the perceived uncontrollability of change. Earlier I pointed out that the "psychosocial environment" is affected by the level of insecurity that people feel about their jobs, the work they have to do, their physical environment, their boss, and so on, quoting Tom Cox's view[23] that the stress associated with change "is due to the uncertainty and lack of control which it often represents". This is largely because people tend to anticipate that changes that are planned and implemented without their participation will probably result in their being left worse off in some way. Another major source of problems is the concatenation of changes: the sequencing of changes one after another so that the cumulative strain exceeds people's tolerance levels and "change overload" or "change fatigue" occurs.

Change is also a factor in organizational climate that can affect work outcomes; a stable working environment is more likely than a turbulent one to be associated with successful results.[24] This can become especially clear when frequent changes in an organization lead people to lose confidence in the *continuance of context*; there's little point in putting your heart and soul into a task or project if there's a real possibility that someone "up there" will pull the plug on it before it's finished.

All this suggests that it's naïve to see change as an unqualified boon.

As for being inevitable, the prevailing view in the literature is summed up by Derek Ayling: "surviving change is like getting old – there is only one alternative".[25] This applies to organizations as much as to individuals. To be successful, organizations have to adapt, continually, to changes in the competitive environment.[26]

projected returns Throughout the 1990s the number of major changes in UK business steadily and rapidly increased,[27] with most businesses undergoing a major reorganization at least once every three years.[28] Unfortunately, many of the changes which are initiated in organizations didn't – and don't – turn out the way they were intended. Despite the enormous enthusiasm for change that perhaps characterized the 1990s, the failure rate of change initiatives has been staggering.[29] Fewer than half of the 800 reorganization initiatives examined in a CIPD survey delivered the required improvement in internal flexibility or increased customer responsiveness.[30] It isn't clear whether this dismal lack of success is a reason for the apparent widespread distaste for risk-taking in UK organizations,[31] or whether it's risk aversion that contributes to failure.

Actually, projects in general – and all projects are concerned with change in some sense – have a fairly dismal record of delivering what

frequent changes lead people to lose confidence in the continuance of context

they promise. The failure rate of over 50% is quite consistent with more general reviews of project success,[32] or, if anything, a cause for some optimism; other reports suggest that things are much worse. The National Audit Office examined 23 public sector projects in 1996 and almost all of them were delivered late, with an average slippage of 31 months and a total overspend of £700 million.[33] Some examples of well-known projects that overran budget and/or schedule include: Eurofighter, which was three years late and £1.25 billion overspent in the UK alone; the British Library, which overran its costs by almost 300% and was years late in completion; the Stock Exchange Taurus project, which had to be aborted; the London Ambulance computer system, which collapsed disastrously when implemented; and the Channel Tunnel, again spectacularly over-budget.[34] This is nothing new. Professor Peter Morris, who has researched project failures extensively, says that in the early 1980s he collected data on all the 1449 projects he could find in the public record. Of these, only twelve had out-turn costs below or on budget. He later repeated the exercise with over 3,000 projects, with similar results.[35]

What these reports of failure often don't take into account, though, is that such notions as "late" and "over budget" represent only one side of an equation. If a project takes twice as long and costs twice as much as the original estimates it could well be that the original schedule and cost estimates were hopelessly unrealistic in the first place. It's well known in project management circles – if not often stated explicitly – that commercial contracts commonly go to bidders whose estimates are highly "optimistic", relying on specification changes during implementation to justify the cost and schedule increases that won't be subject to such fiercely competitive tendering and so can be priced more realistically and make the job profitable.

Internal projects often follow a similar pattern. Corporate apparatchiks quickly learn that the way to get their pet project approved is to overestimate the benefits while understating the costs and timescales. The really close scrutiny usually comes at the front end, when approval is being sought, and anyway it's usually possible to explain away any overruns further downstream. Some of the responsibility for this must rest with managements who, consciously or unconsciously, set the rules of the game and send out signals to their people that they actually wish to be misled.

It's also important to recognize that eventually projects are evaluated by the "products" or outcomes they leave behind. Once the project has been completed, schedule and cost problems tend to be forgotten and the quality – or usefulness – of what's been delivered becomes the key factor.[36] For this reason, any evaluation should take a wider view of the impact a project has had, including any side-effects, and the views of the various stakeholders before assessing its success,[37,38] These stakeholders may have differing requirements and are likely to have different perceptions of what constitutes success. An example of this principle in action is Concorde, the development of which was massively over budget and took years longer than scheduled. A whole generation revered this aircraft as an outstanding technical achievement, and as an icon of national pride, even despite a tragic accident in which many lives were lost. Development costs and schedule long ago became irrelevant and there was widespread regret when it was finally taken out of service.

don't cut the wrong corner The practical importance of this cannot be overstated. Traditionally, the objectives of any project have been represented in the form of a triangle, showing time, cost and quality (or schedule, budget and specification), illustrated in Figure 9.2. This is a useful metaphor because, just as a change to one of the angles of a

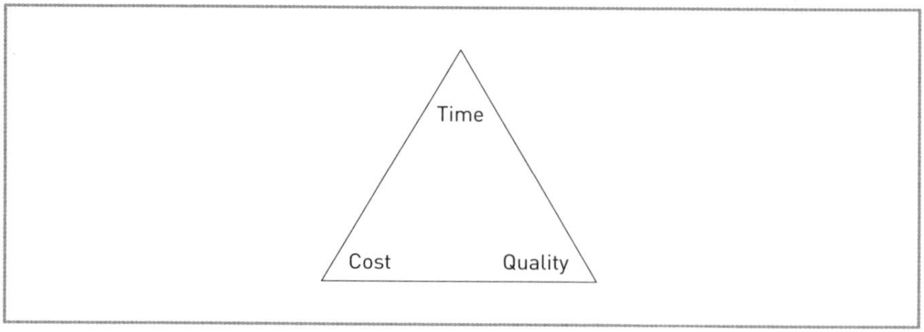

FIG 9.2 Time-cost-quality triangle

triangle must mean changes in the other two, so the three criteria of project success are inextricably mutually dependent.

When projects seem to be slipping or costs escalating, the almost irresistible temptation is to cut corners, to economise, and the angle which this mainly affects is "Quality", or specification. What research tells us, though, is that the quality of the project outcomes – how useful people find whatever it was that the project actually did for them – is the one factor that will really count after a little time has passed; and that is the thing that's been sacrificed in order to meet schedule and budget targets.

At this point it's necessary to acknowledge that project-based approaches to organizational change, quite apart from questions about how to assess their effectiveness, are under challenge by alternative perspectives. The contending schools of thought, although there are many subtle nuances of approach, are broadly on the one hand those who see change as a project to be planned and managed, and on the other those who argue that change shouldn't be seen as a series of linear events within a given timescale, but rather as a continuous process.[39] The latter perspective is called the "emergent" approach to change. On the whole its supporters tend to be defined more by their scepticism towards planned change than by any commonly agreed alternative.

My own view is that this is a rather sterile and unhelpful debate. Many years as a manager and as a consultant have led me – perhaps through a process of action learning – to the belief that if you want things to be different you have first to work out how to get from where you are now to where you want to be, and then put those plans into action. So I believe that the planned approach has validity. If you don't go through this process of planning and implementation you probably won't just stay where you are, because the world doesn't stand still. What is more likely is that you will find yourself and/or your organization being swept along by events in directions you can't control towards destinations you can't envisage.

Even if you do make plans, however, planning at most deals with intentions. It isn't actually possible to know how the world will be tomorrow, next week or next year. In fact, there is an infinite number of factors in the way the world is right now that we don't and can't know. The potential complexity of the interactions between these unknowns is so great that planning based upon a fixed view of the world one week, one month or one year on is almost certain to be erroneous. What should be avoided is that view of plans that says "once it's down on paper it's fixed and any departure from it constitutes a failure". Traditional planning seeks to capture all the things that have to be done and fix them in time. What I think of as "soft planning", on the other hand, is full of qualifications, exceptions and open-ended possibilities. It is, in fact, mainly contingency planning: preparing to take account of the range of possibilities within the "bounded chaos" of the project's environment.[40]

The emergent approach cautions against looking too far ahead, or planning on too grand a scale, because new demands and opportunities can arise close at hand and may be missed because all eyes are on the distant horizon of project completion. This is the principle behind the concept of "organizational health". A healthy organization, just like a healthy living organism, is alert, fit, and prepared to deal with the unexpected, responding to dangers and opportunities as they arise, able to change its mind instantly and abandon or modify its previous intentions in order to deal with the emergent situation. The phrase "*change* its mind" is crucial here; it isn't healthy to have nothing in its mind at all. Rather, it is adaptability that is the key indicator of health in this context.

So, an approach to change that acknowledges the complexity and unpredictability of organizational behaviour doesn't have to be incompatible with a project-oriented approach. It's just that extreme positions at either end of that particular spectrum – like extreme or fundamentalist views in most areas of life – are dangerous because the real world tends not to cooperate with rigid theoretical perspectives.

just a phase

In Chapter 3 I suggested that projects have a natural life cycle, consisting of four basic phases: Definition, Planning, Implementation and Closure, although further sub-divisions may sometimes be necessary or useful. Without losing sight of the weaknesses and risks attached to a planned or project-based approach, we can use this four-phase model as a framework to examine the practical considerations in achieving successful organizational change.

The *Definition* phase is where the project's purpose should be defined. In other words, we begin with a vision of how we would like things to be. This necessarily involves an assessment of how things are now, and these two, presumably very different, images define the start and end-points of the journey we are about to undertake. How great the difference between these two points is determines the magnitude of the task. These two activities of assessing where we are now and determining where we would like to be aren't really separate and distinct from each other. In practice they need to be integrated and to go through several iterations, refining broad concepts until we have something that is sufficiently concrete and detailed to be implemented.[41]

There are many ways of carrying out this kind of analysis, some of which will be specific to certain industries, sectors, and kinds of organization. Also, identification of the need for change can come from anywhere, and any level, in the organization. As Warren Bennis argues, the idea that all successful change must originate at the top is not only "wrong, unrealistic and maladaptive but also, given the report of history, dangerous".[42] It might also be considered extremely arrogant.

In Chapter 6 we explored the concept of work processes and looked at a quite rigorous form of analysis called *process mapping*. For many organizations, re-examining the way(s) they do things is perhaps the most productive analysis they can undertake. It almost always produces ideas for improving efficiency and effectiveness and the exercise itself often results in improved communications between individuals and between departments. I attach a health warning to this, though; usually it's wholly positive, but sometimes it can highlight disagreements and incompatible practices that can lead to conflict. I recommend it, but take people's sensibilities seriously.

One of the most widely used templates for analysis uses the acronym SWOT, standing for

Strengths,

Weaknesses,

Opportunities, and

Threats.

The idea is that, if you identify all the key factors as they appertain to your organization under each of these four headings, you will have a fairly comprehensive analysis of your situation as it is now, and from this you can pick factors to work on: maximizing strengths, buttressing weaknesses, actively exploiting opportunities and building defences against threats. This is quite a useful and robust model if applied rigorously and objectively. These two adverbs are the key to the failure of many SWOT analyses to make any appreciable difference "on the ground". There often seems to be very little connection between the findings of SWOT analyses and the change plans which eventually emerge, suggesting that maybe people feel so much better after the catharsis of a SWOT exercise that they no longer feel the need to deal with the issues it has raised.

Tom Lambert[43] has come up with some variations on SWOT that he suggests will be more useful. At the least, his additional models can reinforce the traditional version and increase the rigour of its application. First, he suggests changing the order of SWOT to WOST, so that the exercise begins by searching out Weaknesses, then looks for Opportunities. After that he recommends a kind of celebration of all the Strengths that can be identified. Threats must be dealt with, but with a positive mindset, planning from the start how to overcome them. If there's a way to avoid a threat, make definite plans to do so. If it can't be avoided, plan to spot it as early as possible and take action to minimise the potential damage.

COST benefit Even better, Lambert suggests, would be a new acronym that changes the sequence to something "psychologically and practically" better. In this version Concerns are dealt with first, rather than weaknesses. Opportunities are dealt with next and Strengths completed third, with Threats completed last, "looking only at things that really might go wrong" and forming the basis for "realistic contingency planning". Lambert may well be right in saying that this order is psychologically preferable, but the greatest resonance for me is in the idea of considering the COST of the status quo as a precursor to making decisions about change.

Another widely used acronym-based model is PEST, which stands for Political, Economic, Socio-cultural and Technical factors. In this model, as elaborated by John Hayes,[44] "Political factors include new legislation, regulation and fiscal policies. Economic factors include exchange rates, cost of borrowing, change in levels of disposable income, cost of raw materials, and the trade cycle. Socio-cultural factors include demographic trends, shifting attitudes towards education, training, work and leisure which can have knock-on effects on the availability of trained labour, consumption patterns and so on. Cultural factors can also affect business ethics and the way business is done in different parts of the world. Technological factors include issues such as the levels of investment competitors are making in research and development and the outcomes of this investment; the availability of new materials, products, production processes; means of distribution, the rate of obsolescence and the need to reinvest in plant and people".

These models can be extremely useful in identifying where attention should be focused, and they can be used on a regular (although not excessively frequent) basis to maintain and develop understanding of where the organization is, and prompt discussion of where it ought to be.

A more change-focused approach to analysis was developed by Peter Checkland and colleagues at Lancaster University in the 1980s.[45–47] Called Soft Systems Methodology (SSM), it uses systems thinking to make comparisons between current "real world" practice and idealized "systems thinking" models. The full application of SSM is very rigorous and can be time-consuming. It can also be challenging, though certainly not impossible, without training or extensive reading. However, the basic concept can be applied by anyone.

The first step is to describe, as fully as possible, the situation in which there is perceived to be some kind of problem. Next, we put the "real world" to one side for a while and describe the features of a system that would be likely to work successfully in, or be relevant to, the problem situation. Essentially, the methodology is asking, "if we were devising a system from scratch to achieve our objectives, what would that system be like?" Because there will certainly be a number of stakeholders in the situation, and they may have differing perceptions of what the system should be trying to achieve, different priorities, concerns and motives, SSM tells us to describe several ideal models, each based on the perspective of one of the stakeholders.

The third step is to compare the "systems thinking" model(s) with what actually exists in the "real world". It's likely that there will be differences. Do these highlight reasons why the current situation isn't wholly satisfactory? Do they suggest "desirable and feasible" changes which should be implemented? These can form the basis of a change project.

from here to there So far we've been concerned with the *definition* phase of a change project: all the activity in SWOT (and its variants), and PEST has been aimed at determining *what* changes are required: how we would like things to be. The point of applying analysis techniques is to arrive at some specific, "visualizable" changes that could actually become viable project objectives. The next phase is concerned with *planning how* to make those changes happen: how to convert visions into reality.

Most models of planned change are based to a greater or lesser extent on the work of Kurt Lewin, a brilliant psychologist who arrived in the USA as a refugee from Nazi Germany and worked at various universities and institutions until his early death in 1947. It seems invidious to reduce Lewin's wide-ranging contributions to social science to two simple models, but these provide a basis of underlying principle for planning a change project which has so far survived through the intervening decades and which can hardly be left out of this discussion.

The first of Lewin's models describes a three-phase process of organizational change:[48, 49]

unfreezing → moving → refreezing

Most social groups, Lewin says, normally operate in a state of "stable quasi-stationary equilibrium". Before they can be changed something has to happen to destabilise this equilibrium, otherwise they will just carry on as they are. Once the equilibrium has been upset, *movement* (i.e. change) to a different state becomes possible, but the new state will be unstable, so a third step is required in which the new state is consolidated and a new, different equilibrium is established.

Proponents of emergent change approaches have been known to scoff at this model as being naïve and simplistic. Organizations, they say, are never frozen, and if there are stages in the change process those stages overlap and merge into each other.[50] This, of course, is true, but it seems to me to misrepresent Lewin's proposition. Had he lived to read this criticism Lewin might have regretted using the term "freezing" because, of course, he never imagined that organizations were as inert as this term implies. Lewin uses the analogy of a river to illustrate his concept of "stable quasi-stationary equilibrium". Clearly, a river is not stationary and from another perspective could be seen as a prime example of continual motion; as the Greek philosopher Heraclitus famously said, "you can't step twice into the same river". But a river, although highly dynamic, can also be a fairly dependable model of constancy. Similarly, according to Lewin, organizations can be active but still be stable.

The pre-change, or no-change, state in Lewin's model refers to a dynamic status that is held in place by a balance of forces, some of which are "pushing" for things to be different – i.e. are tending to promote change – whilst others are acting to prevent or restrain change. This is the essence of the second of Lewin's models which I want to cite here, known as *force field analysis*, illustrated in Figure 9.3.

Lewin suggests that change agents, or anyone wanting to plan and manage change in organizations or other social groups, should under-

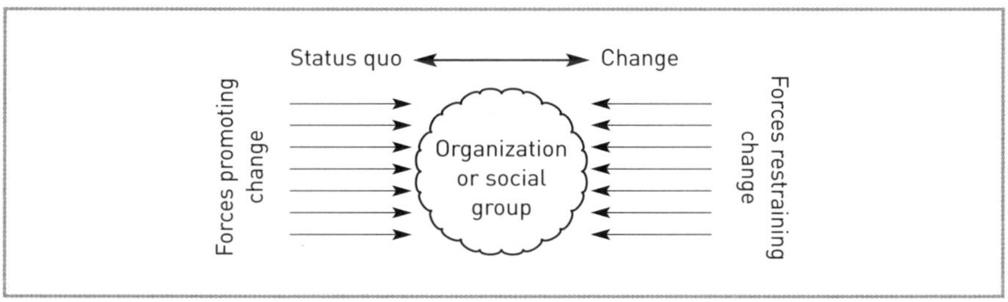

FIG 9.3 ● Force field analysis

take a detailed analysis to identify the various forces on both sides of this balancing act and assess their strengths. This is closely related to the ideas of systems and complexity/chaos theory, and also to the notion of process structures, referred to in Chapter 8.

creating a thaw If you want to bring about change, there are two ways in which you can help to *unfreeze* or destabilize the current situation: you can try either to strengthen the forces for change, or to weaken the forces opposing change. In social situations, it's usually preferable to concentrate on weakening the forces opposing change, because increasing the forces for change has more unpleasant and unwanted side-effects, such as heightened levels of stress, tension and anxiety, and increased resistance.

Earlier in this chapter I drew attention to some of the problems that individuals may have when faced with proposed or impending change. These problems can be many and varied but tend to cluster around two main issues: first, that people may expect or fear that they will lose something as a result of the change, and secondly that people may feel that events are outside their control, which is a primary cause of stress regardless of how good or bad the change may be, objectively.

It makes good sense, then, to address these issues explicitly at the planning stage, to investigate what losses the change will or may cause for individuals, acknowledge these and as far as possible plan to ameliorate or compensate for them. To be blunt, though, it may be that some changes will be detrimental to the well-being of individuals. This isn't a treatise on ethics, but I suggest that anyone in a position of power or influence in an organization has some responsibility towards his or her colleagues and, if it becomes unavoidable that action must be taken that will cause some kind of harm to any of them, there's a duty of care that requires that that harm should be minimized.

In order to keep the cynical or cold-hearted on board with this argument, I would cite research[51–54] that has shown that those who come through changes otherwise unscathed are often adversely affected by bad things that happen to other people. They may feel "I was lucky that time" but their trust and commitment are damaged. People who lose their jobs typically experience a range of emotions beginning with shock and developing into anger, but this same emotional cycle can be experienced by the people who are left behind, and they will inevitably be concerned about the future. They need to know what is planned for the future "and feel they have a say in shaping it".[55]

The importance of involving people in changes which are likely to affect them can hardly be overstated. For a start, it will mean that their local knowledge and expertise can be brought to bear on the project. It will also tend to reduce the perception of loss of control and help to develop a sense of ownership of the project, which is vital in overcoming the inevitable snags, and will help in the *refreezing* process when the project is completed. John Hayes[56] draws attention to this aspect of managing change and lists some of the people issues that any strategy for managing change must address, including "power, leadership and stakeholder management; communication; training and development; motivating others to change and support for others to help them manage their personal transitions".

A review of 40 organizational change programmes by Jennifer LaClair & Ravi Lao[57] found that the most successful involved people at all levels in the organization; "senior and middle managers and frontline employees". Everyone was clear about their own responsibilities, and the reasons for the change were understood throughout the organization. It seemed possible to get away with problems on one or two levels of the organization and still realize most of the benefits of the change initiative; in fact, if *any* of these organizational levels met the criteria the chances of success were improved. This is quite reassuring because it implies that perfection isn't essential; you can still get by if you manage to get most things more or less right.

taking steps John Kotter[58] builds these people factors into his recipe for successful change:

Step 1 – Increase urgency

Step 2 – Build the guiding team

Step 3 – Get the vision right

Step 4 – Communicate for buy-in

Step 5 – Empower action

Step 6 – Create short-term wins

Step 7 – Don't let up

Step 8 – Make change stick

Whether or not Kotter would want this programme to be mapped on to Lewin's three-phase model, the temptation to do so is quite strong. Step 1 looks very much like unfreezing, Steps 2 to 7 are to do with movement, and Step 8 looks like refreezing. Similarly, Rosabeth Moss Kanter, who has been a fierce critic of Lewin's planned model of change, offers "ten commandments for executing change"[59] which, although clearly not intended to be read as sequential steps, do nonetheless seem quite compatible with the three-phase model. They are:

1. Analyze the organization and its need for change.
2. Create a shared vision and a common direction.
3. Separate from the past.

These seem to fit quite well with unfreezing. Then

4. Create a sense of urgency.
5. Support a strong leader role.
6. Line up political sponsorship.
7. Craft an implementation plan.
8. Develop enabling structures.
9. Communicate, involve people and be honest.

These seem to be concerned with the process of movement. And finally

10. Reinforce and institutionalise change.

This last one seems to me to be another way of saying *refreeze*, however much Kanter might want to distance herself from Lewin's sequential model.

previously frozen, *do* refreeze The importance of the refreezing or consolidation phase is that it's all too easy for things to slip back to the way they were before, once the attention and energy of the change process has subsided. Just getting to the new situation isn't enough; the new state needs to be turned into the norm. This doesn't imply that it's going to be permanent, but it will become the new "base line" from which further changes will begin. This involves continual reinforcement of behaviours that are consistent with the new state, and prompt correction of anything that looks like regression.

Translating all this advice into specific elements of "concrete" plans will, of course, depend on the nature of the change that needs to be made, but in general terms planning a change project needs to obey the "natural laws" of project management just like any other project. The basic idea needs to be evaluated and assessed on how well it contributes to corporate objectives and, vitally, on how practical it will be to carry it out; the most exciting project idea is worthless if it can't be successfully implemented. A key factor in this will be the amount of high-level political support the proposal enjoys. It may sound defeatist to advise that unless senior people are genuinely enthusiastic about the proposal – which means they are prepared to spend significant amounts of their own time monitoring and supporting it – it's probably not worth doing, but this will almost inevitably turn out to be the case. On an individual and personal basis my unequivocal advice is: don't get involved unless you are sure that the top brass are committed. If you decide to go ahead anyway, expect frustration, disappointment and grief, and a failed project on your record.

Once plans have been made the next phase of the project, *implementation*, is where they are put into effect. This is where time spent on managing the political aspects of the project will begin to pay off. Change always threatens the existing balance of power in an organization[60] and this has to be recognized and used in the implementation process.

It's also usually wise to work *with* the prevailing culture rather than trying to achieve change by changing the culture, contrary, perhaps, to the "preconception that many managers have about the unwritten rules;

that you can force through a change regardless of them, providing that you push hard enough".[61]

A reporter for a major company's house magazine quite recently asked the newly appointed managing director "will you change the culture?" This is a very naïve question indeed. At one level the answer must be "yes, I'm bound to, but I've no idea in what way and I'll have almost no control over the process". What the reporter should have asked was whether the new MD saw aspects of the current culture that he would *like* to change, and whether he would try to steer the culture's development in a particular direction. More to the point, were there particular *behaviours* that he would like to change.

In the earlier discussion of organizational culture I compared it to an individual's personality, formed by continual interactions between the "hard wiring" that was there at the very beginning and all the experiences that life has brought subsequently. Personality is therefore cumulative: "we can add to our experience, but we cannot subtract from it".[62] The same principle applies to organizational culture, which means that some of the experiences an organization goes through may be amenable to manipulation, which will help to steer its culture's development in a certain direction, but many experiences won't be manipulable. Also, the complexity of interactions between all the factors that may influence cultural development means that you can never be sure what effects your attempts at manipulation may have. It may be possible to nudge the culture a little, but controlling its development is a pipe dream. To continue the analogy, it's also worth considering that a sudden change in personality is almost always the result of trauma of some kind, and is rarely good news.

it may be possible to nudge the culture a little, but controlling its development is a pipe dream

change what people do However, when managers say they want culture change what they usually mean is that they want people to *do* things differently.[63] This means that asking for culture change may actually be something of a red herring. It may be much more effective to help employees to learn new behaviours within the existing corporate culture background.[64] This starts at the top. If senior people themselves demonstrate the behaviours they want everyone else to adopt there's a chance that the new behaviour patterns will cascade down through the organization. Research shows that this does seem to work; change initiatives that concentrate on behaviour have been far more successful than "initiatives concerned with inculcating shared values".[65]

The prevailing view, then, is that managers can't hope to control or change the culture of their organization directly, but it may well be possible to influence overt behaviours, and, because culture is the product of experiences, it may be possible to exercise some control over some of those experiences and thus to influence the way culture develops. It's likely to be an unpredictable process, though. Edgar Schein seems to go at least part of the way with the chaos theorists when he says that "in social systems (as opposed to biological units), there is no such thing as spontaneous change or mutation. There are no cosmic rays hitting the social genes to produce unpredictable changes. There is always someone inside or outside the system who has a motive to make something happen. The actual outcome may be a complex interaction of the forces unleashed by the different intentions of different actors, but the outcome will never be random and unpredictable. The only difficulty may be that the events and interactions are so complex that it is not practical to try to unravel them".[66] I would argue, though, that the impracticality of unravelling these interactions does effectively make them unpredictable, even if they are not, strictly speaking, random.

It's also likely to be a very slow process. Some management writers seem to suggest that following their advice will result in some kind of "cataclysmic shift".[67] In practice, it can take years for any noticeable culture change to emerge, and even this won't happen at all without continual reinforcement. This is hard, time-consuming graft for managers at every level. Every example of desired behaviour has to be noticed and reinforced, and contrary behaviours must never – really, *never* – be reinforced, or the messages will be mixed and you might as well give up.

All this suggests culture change isn't likely to be an attractive mechanism for organizational change projects with finite objectives and timescales. As Tony Manning puts it: "after countless research studies there's precious little evidence that culture can be manipulated, no clear guidelines showing how to do it, and no real proof that a new culture leads to better business results".[68]

celebrate success (however small) The implementation phase, then, should probably concentrate on small, specific changes of processes, procedures and behaviours. It should aim for visible successes, even if they are quite small-scale, so that the progress towards the project objective receives continual reinforcement. Achieving regular, small-scale but visible successes helps to keep the momentum up and weakens opposition.

It should take into account the political factors and personal gains and losses of the people affected and, wherever possible, try to keep people on board. This may not always be possible, in which case the blocking power that individuals may be able to exercise will have to be handled. Don't expect those people to be friendly afterwards, though. It's always better in the long term to persuade rather than coerce.

It's a moot point, and probably a fairly academic one, whether consolidation or *refreezing* takes place during the implementation phase or if it more properly belongs in the final project phase, *closure*. Strictly speaking, closure is concerned with reviewing project performance against schedule, budget, specification and user satisfaction and ensuring a smooth handover of the project's deliverables to the ongoing users. In an organizational change project, however, these factors aren't always easily distinguishable from the general need for "fixing" the changes back into business as usual. What is important is that people with influence don't walk away from the change process but rather continue to show their commitment to the new state by continually reinforcing behaviours that are consistent with the change and never reinforcing any behaviour that shows signs of reverting to the old set-up. This is hard, time-consuming and often tedious, but without it change is unlikely to be effective.

In this chapter I've addressed the mechanisms of continuous improvement: learning and making changes, all at the organizational level. I've tried to make the point that none of these things will "just happen"; they need, first of all, the *will* for them to happen. This is perhaps the most important factor.

If the will exists, then – and only then – the next step becomes possible, which is to put in place the *means* by which they can happen. Learning and change are natural processes which are going on all the time; the issue for organizations is to try to exercise some control over them so that what is learned is positive and useful, and the direction of change is towards something "better" than what we have now. Neither of these desirable goals is by any means assured. The models, theory and advice from practitioners that I have cited in these chapters provide some useful tools that can help managers and other organization members to recognize and understand these processes as they unfold in their own organizational contexts, and so to exercise a greater degree of positive control over what happens to them.

"I can do it better next time" checklist

How do senior people in your organization find out what's going on?

How likely is it that the observations or concerns of very junior employees will ever be discussed in the boardroom?

How is risk-taking and failure regarded in your organization?

What would be the overall effect if, now and then, someone was publicly praised and rewarded for an action that failed (but which seemed like an acceptable risk at the time)?

What would you say was your organization's characteristic "learning style"?

What are the implications of this?

How would your organization need to change before it shows the characteristics of a "learning organization"?

If you think of a change at work that you found positive, what was the defining characteristic that made it seem this way to you?

What about a change that you found negative?

If you think of a situation at work that you would like to see changed in some way, what are the "restraining forces" acting to discourage, block or prevent change?

What are the "driving forces" that might tend to promote, facilitate or encourage change?

What could you do to weaken the restraining forces?

If you think of a change in your organization that failed to "take" – can you say why things went wrong?

What could be done to ensure that the same mistakes aren't made next time?

notes and references

1 Revans, RW (1998) *The ABC of Action Learning,* London, Lemos & Crane

2 Lynch, R (1997) *Corporate Strategy,* London, Pitman Publishing

3 Easterby-Smith, M, Burgoyne, J & Araujo, L (1999) *Organizational Learning and the Learning Organization,* London, Sage

4 Garvin, DA (2000) *Learning in Action,* Boston, MA, Harvard Business School Press

5 Senge, PM (1990) *The Fifth Discipline,* London, Century Business

6 Easterby-Smith *et al., Organizational Learning,* op. cit.

7 Foy, N (1986) "The sad tale of STC", *Management Today,* February, 70–71

8 Senge, *The Fifth Discipline*, op. cit.

9 Douglass, ME & Douglass, DN (1980) *Manage Your Time, Manage Your Work, Manage Yourself,* New York, AMACOM. I've subsequently come across this model in several places, not always attributed to an original source. If the Douglasses didn't invent it I apologize and will gladly correct the attribution in later editions.

10 Argyris, C (1976) *Increasing Leadership Effectiveness,* New York, Wiley

11 Senge, *The Fifth Discipline*, op. cit.

12 ibid.

13 Miles, MM & Huberman, AM (1994) *Qualitative Data Analysis,* London, Sage

14 Oppenheim, AN (1992) *Questionnaire Design, Interviewing and Attitude Measurement,* London, Pinter

15 Easterby-Smith, M (1990) "Creating a learning organization", *Personnel Review,* **19** (5), 24–8

16 Garvin, *Learning in Action*, op. cit.

17 Pedler, MJ, Burgoyne, JG & Boydell, TH (1997) *The Learning Company: A Strategy for Sustainable Development,* 2nd edn, Maidenhead, McGraw-Hill

18 Pedler, M & Aspinwall, K (1998) *A Concise Guide to the Learning Organization,* London, Lemos & Crane

19 Honey, P (1991) "The learning organization simplified", *Training And Development,* July, 30–3

20 Garrat, R (1987) *The Learning Organization,* London, Fontana

21 Kriegel, RJ & Patler, L (1992), *If It Ain't Broke, Break It: And Other Unconventional Wisdom for a Changing Business World,* New York, Warner Books

22 Toffler, A (1970) *Future Shock,* New York, Random House

23 Cox, T (1993) *Stress Research and Stress Management: Putting Theory to Work,* Sudbury, Health and Safety Executive

24 Gray, RJ (2000) "Organizational climate and the competitive edge", in L Lloyd-Reason & S Wall (eds) *Dimensions of Competitiveness: Issues and Policies,* Cheltenham, Edward Elgar Publishing

25 Ayling, D (1995) *Enter The Hippo,* Buckingham, Key Publishing Office

26 Sauser, WI & Sauser, LD (2002) "Changing the way we manage change", *SAM Advanced Management Journal*, Autumn, 34–9

27 Burnes, B (2000) *Managing Change,* 3rd edn, London, Financial Times/Prentice Hall

28 Giles, K (2003) "Changing rules", *People Management*, 6 February, 57

29 Grint, K (1997) *Fuzzy Management,* Oxford, Oxford University Press

30 Giles, "Changing rules", op. cit.

31 Grint, *Fuzzy Management*, op. cit.

32 Cole, A (1996) "Realizing the Benefits of Change", *Project Manager Today,* October, 14–15

33 Caulkin, S (1996) "How late the project was, how late", *Observer,* August, 8, Business Section, 18

34 ibid.

35 Morris, PWG (1994) *The Management of Projects,* London, Thomas Telford

36 Avots, I (1984) "Information systems for matrix organizations", in D Cleland (ed.), *Matrix Management Systems Handbook,* New York, Van Nostrand Reinhold

37 Lientz, BP & Rea, KP (1995) *Project Management for the 21st Century,* London, Academic Press

38 Obeng, E (1994) *All Change! The Project Leader's Secret Handbook,* London, Financial Times/Pitman

39 Burnes, *Managing Change*, op. cit.

40 Gray, RJ (1996) "Gang aft agley", *Project Manager Today,* April, 16–17

41 Hayes, J (2002) *The Theory and Practice of Change Management,* Basingstoke, Palgrave

42 Bennis, W (2000) "Leadership of Change", in M Beer & N Noria (eds) *Breaking the Code of Change,* Boston, MA, Harvard Business School Press

43 Lambert, T (1993) *High Income Consulting,* London, Nicholas Brealey Publishing

44 Hayes, *The Theory and Practice of Change Management*, op. cit.

45 Checkland, P (1984) *Systems Thinking, Systems Practice,* Chichester, Wiley

46 Wilson, B (1984) *Systems: Concepts, Methodologies and Applications,* Chichester, John Wiley

47 Checkland, P & Scholes, J (1990) *Soft Systems Methodology in Action*, Chichester, John Wiley

48 Lewin, K (1952) *Field Theory in Social Science*, New York, Harper & Row

49 Lewin, K (1969) "Quasi-stationary social equilibria and the problem of permanent change", in WG Bennie, KD Benn & R Chin (eds) *The Planning of Change*, New York, Holt Rinehart & Winston

50 Kanter, RM, Stein, BA & Jick, TD (1992) *The Challenge of Organizational Change*, New York, Free Press

51 Kates, N, Greiff, BS & Hagen, DQ (1993) "Job loss and employment uncertainty", in JP Kahn (ed.) *Mental Health in the Workplace*, New York, Van Nostrand Reinhold

52 Cohen, N (1996) "Britain's workers reluctantly at the cutting edge", *Independent on Sunday*, 12 May, 3

53 Heller, R (1996) "Downsizing's other down side", *Management Today*, March, 23

54 Hallier, J & Lyon, P (1996) "Managing to look after number one", *People Management*, 2 May, 38–9

55 Chiumento, R (2003) "How to support survivors of redundancy", *People Management*, 6 February, 48–49

56 Hayes, *The Theory and Practice of Change Management*, op. cit.

57 LaClair, JA & Rao, RP (2002) "Helping employees embrace change", *McKinsey Quarterly*, Issue 2, 17

58 Kotter, JP (2002) in FJ Quinn: "Making change happen – an interview with John Kotter", *Supply Chain Management Review*, November/December, 24–29

59 Kanter *et al.*, *The Challenge of Organizational Change*, op. cit.

60 Clement, RW (1994) "The changing face of organization development", *Business Horizons*, May–June, 6–12

61 Scott-Morgan, P (1999) "Hidden depths", *People Management*, 8 April, 38–44

62 Hope, V & Hendry, J (1995) "Corporate culture change – is it relevant for the organizations of the 1990s?", *Human Resource Management Journal*, **5** (4), 61–73

63 Hassard, J & Sharifi, S (1989) "Corporate culture and strategic change", *Journal of General Management*, **15** (2), 4–19

64 Wilhelm, W (1992) "Changing corporate culture – or corporate behavior? How to change your company", *Academy of Management Executive,* **6** (4), 72–7

65 Hope & Hendry, "Corporate culture change", op. cit.

66 Schein, EH (1985) *Organizational Culture and Leadership,* Oxford, Jossey-Bass

67 Baron, A & Walters, M (1994) *The Culture Factor,* London, IPD

68 Manning, T (1990) "Beyond corporate culture", *IPM Journal* (South Africa), February, 23–5

10 ten

putting it together

At the beginning of this book I said that the catechism of excellence is better represented as a jigsaw than as a flowchart because all the checkpoints need to be addressed concurrently if excellent performance is to be achieved. Each chapter of the book examines one of the "pieces" in detail to show how it fits into the overall design: excellence isn't likely to be achieved while there are pieces missing. But I have also asserted that organizations are *systems*. Hopefully, the meaning and implications of that term are clearer now, and it will be evident that the jigsaw metaphor isn't entirely adequate to convey the complexity of what I have called the "psychological landscape" of the organization.

This complexity is daunting. The nine pieces of the excellence jigsaw cover at least twenty major topics. Some of the topics could be further sub-divided, for example, power, influence and trust. Unlike the pieces of a jigsaw, each of which only has direct connections with the pieces adjacent to it, every topic covered here has links of mutual influence and dependency with every other topic, which adds up to at least 380 relationship links, and probably many more. Each of these relationships

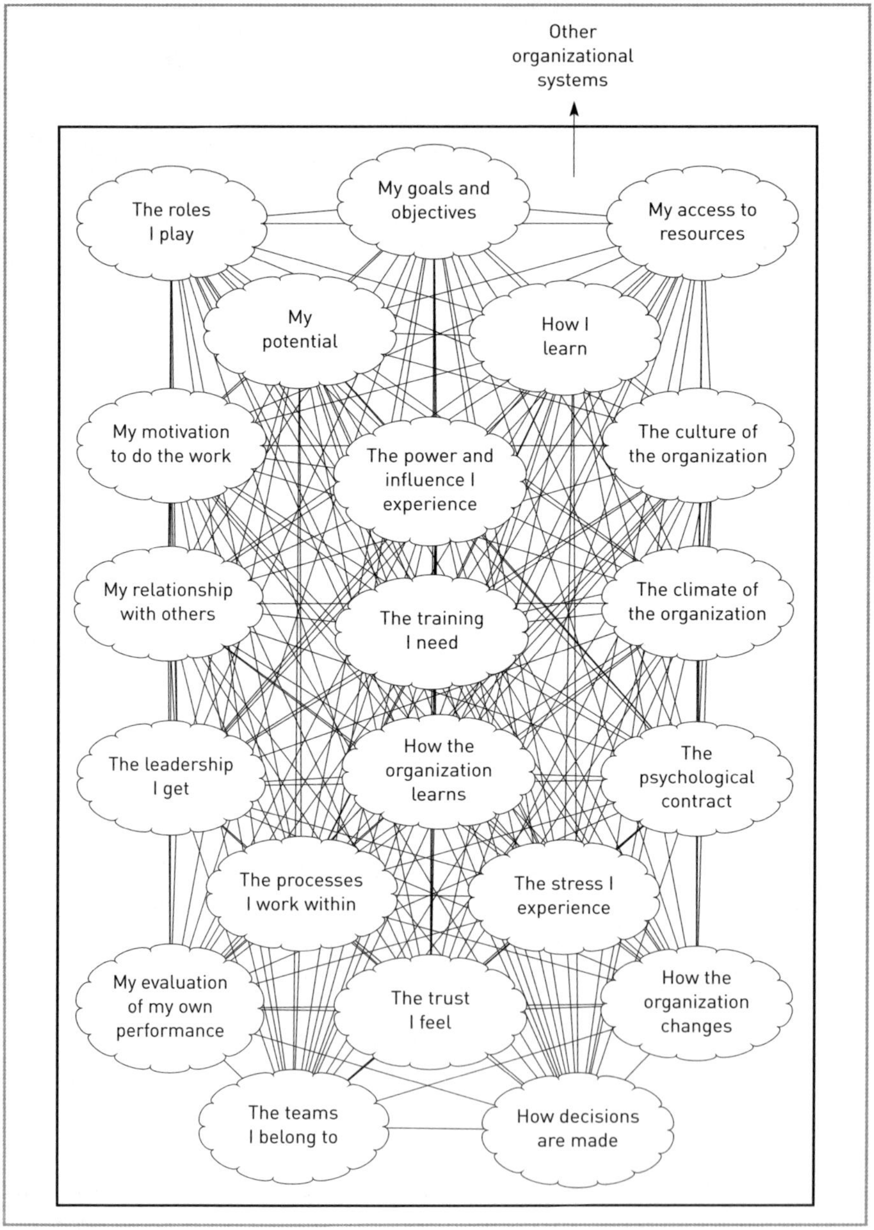

FIG 10.1 ● The excellence system

is bi-directional and/or reciprocal: A exerts influence on or affects B to some extent, but B also exerts influence on or affects A, either simultaneously or asynchronously. This is the nature of systemic structures.

The various topics addressed in this book can be represented as the elements of an organizational system, the purpose of which is to facilitate excellent individual performance as a vital factor in achieving excellent organizational performance. The system map in Figure 10.1 shows these elements together with their *connectivity*, or network of relationships:

Clearly, to explore all the relationships between all these elements here would be impractical, as well as very tedious, but we can look briefly at a few of them as examples of how such connectivity may work in practice.

role play My motivation to do the work is likely to be very susceptible to the influence of the many roles I perceive myself as playing. Briefly, if I am committed to a role I will feel more inclined to want to do the work that is associated with that role, and to do it in ways that I perceive as compatible with and supportive of the best exemplars of that role. Thus, if my role is as some kind of professional it is likely that I will be motivated to keep up to date with current thinking and practice in my profession, as well as perform the tasks that other organization members steer my way because they are appropriate to someone with my professional background. In fact, I may feel indignant if such tasks aren't directed to me, because I may perceive that my professional prerogatives are being infringed.

My membership of a profession may even take priority, for me, over my membership of the organization, so that organizational objectives may seem an irrelevant distraction if they don't support what I perceive to be my professional role. Examples of this are frequently found in the medical or academic spheres, where the professionals may regard the organization as no more than a supportive environment in which they can carry on their professional practice. Endless misunderstandings, frustration and conflict can arise between the professionals and organizational managers from this source.

It may be that, whatever the organization understands to be my job description, I have adopted the role of a sympathetic, empathetic counsellor in my dealings with people who report to me. If so, I may well feel motivated to perform work that is outside my designated organizational role in order to foster the development or wellbeing of a member of staff.

On the other hand, it may be that my motivation to do the work affects the role(s) I play. If I am keen to see the job completed in an exemplary way I may extend my role to include quality checks on related work, or to offer guidance to team members or suppliers.

stressed out The stress I experience will certainly be influenced by the climate of the organization: if bullying, coercion and routine punishment of mistakes feature in the organizational climate my vulnerability to stress will very probably be increased. But, of course, my perception of the organizational climate may well be coloured by the levels of stress I'm currently experiencing; if I'm finding it hard to cope it's quite likely that I will interpret simple queries as criticism, or gentle guidance as a reprimand.

My evaluation of my own performance can't escape the influence of my potential, my capacity to learn, the training I need and/or receive, and my relationships with others. In the same way some of my relationships with others will be influenced by my own evaluation of how well I'm doing: if their assessments are broadly in line with my own, the relationships are likely to be more positive; if not, then they may be less so.

My experiences of the way power and influence are exercised in the organization will certainly affect my willingness to work for the organization's goals; if I perceive that power is exercised arbitrarily or unfairly, or is held by people who don't deserve it, my motivation is likely to be diminished. Such a situation will have inputs into my perception of the terms of the psychological contract, which will also affect my motivation. But if I perceive that power and influence are used wisely and benignly it's more likely that I will feel confidence in the leadership I'm getting, will want to do a good job, and will attach greater importance to my "obligations" under the psychological contract.

These are just a few examples of the two-way relationships between the system elements that go to make up the "Excellence System".

finding gold

The complexity that this model represents is an indication of the difficulty of managing organizational behaviour. There are no short-cuts, no simple triggers that can be pulled that will put any manager in "control". But if complexity can be intimidating it can also be exhilarating. Complexity is a synonym for richness. In the discussion of workplace stress I said that human beings need to feel some level of control over what happens to them, but this shouldn't be interpreted as a need for managers to have rigid control over everything that happens in their organizations. This is a hopeless ambition anyway, but even if it were achievable it would be a recipe for an appallingly predictable, dull and stagnant working life, which many of us might find almost intolerable. Instead, managers should seek to exercise influence and provide guidance, to facilitate performance and reinforce positive behaviours, to boost confidence and develop potential, and capitalize on the endless possibilities that are constantly being created at the *edge of chaos*.

The qualities that this demands of managers are, as Reinhold Neibuhr puts it:

Serenity to accept the things that can't be changed;

Courage to change the things that can;

and the *Wisdom* to know the difference.

index